PROGRAMMING MICROSOFT INFOPATH™

A DEVELOPER'S GUIDE

SECOND EDITION

PROGRAMMING MICROSOFT INFOPATH™

A DEVELOPER'S GUIDE

SECOND EDITION

THOM ROBBINS

CHARLES RIVER MEDIA, INC.
Hingham, Massachusetts

Cover Design: Tyler Creative

CHARLES RIVER MEDIA, INC.
10 Downer Avenue
Hingham, Massachusetts 02043
781-740-0400
781-740-8816 (FAX)
crminfo@thomson.com
www.charlesriver.com

This book is printed on acid-free paper.

Thom Robbins. *Programming Microsoft InfoPath™: A Developer's Guide, Second Edition.*
ISBN: 1-58450-453-6

Library of Congress Cataloging-in-Publication Data

Robbins, Thomas, 1965-
  Programming Microsoft InfoPath : a developer's guide / Thom Robbins.--2nd ed.
     p. cm.
  Includes index.
  ISBN 1-58450-453-6 (pbk. with cd : alk. paper)
  1. Microsoft InfoPath. 2. Business--Forms--Computer programs. I.
Title.
  HF5371.R6 2006
  005.36--dc22
                          2005031787

Printed in the United States of America
06 7 6 5 4 3 2 First Edition

CHARLES RIVER MEDIA titles are available for site license or bulk purchase by institutions, user groups, corporations, etc. For additional information, please contact the Special Sales Department at 781-740-0400.

Requests for replacement of a defective CD-ROM must be accompanied by the original disc, your mailing address, telephone number, date of purchase and purchase price. Please state the nature of the problem, and send the information to CHARLES RIVER MEDIA, INC., 10 Downer Avenue, Hingham, Massachusetts 02043. CRM's sole obligation to the purchaser is to replace the disc, based on defective materials or faulty workmanship, but not on the operation or functionality of the product.

Contents

Acknowledgments

The most important person to thank is my wife and best friend, Denise. Without her patience, understanding, and cooperation, this book would never have been completed. I am always amazed at how she is able to help me focus and succeed at all the challenges that we have met in our life together. I can only hope that she can say the same about me.

Preface

The goal of this book is to provide a developer's reference for application development for Microsoft InfoPath 2003 SP 1, along with the underlying standards and various associated technologies that help to complete an InfoPath-based solution. This book shows how these different technologies work together and describes some of the practical patterns and practices that can be used to develop applications.

HOW TO USE THIS BOOK

This book builds on itself as you move forward. If you have a good understanding of Office 2003, .NET Framework, and InfoPath, you may want to skip Chapters 1 and 2; you can refer back to these introductory chapters as needed.

Many of the topics covered in the text are fairly self-contained so that if you are looking for a quick reference on a specific topic, you should be able to find it quickly. Each chapter of the book examines a specific topic area in order to create an easy-to-find cross-reference of specific samples or how-to information.

This book is designed for the application developer and not the end user. If you are looking for specific end-user features, then this is not the text for you. If you're looking for information on end-user features, I recommend that you take a look at *Special Edition Using Microsoft Office 2003* by Ed Bott. If you are a hard-core enterprise developer who is interested in creating distributed applications that use InfoPath, you are reading the right book.

WHAT YOU NEED TO USE THIS BOOK

This book requires that you have a PC running Windows Server 2003 or Windows XP Professional running at least Microsoft InfoPath 2003. Many of the samples require the use of Microsoft's Internet Information Server (IIS) for the Web-enabled samples. Additionally, you will need Visual Studio.NET 2003, Visual Studio 2005 or the .NET Framework 1.1 and .NET Framework 2.0 to compile and run many of the samples. If you want to take advantage of all the samples mentioned, you will also need to have available the Microsoft Office System 2003 and all the associated products included.

ASSUMED KNOWLEDGE

This book assumes that you have experience developing applications within a distributed environment and that you understand Web-based programming. The examples used in the book are designed to illustrate the various concepts explained throughout, so that you can focus on the various concepts that we will cover. However, the assumption is that you understand basic programming and enterprise architecture concepts.

1 Anatomy of the Microsoft Office System 2003

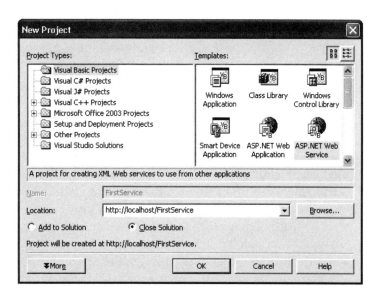

INTRODUCTION

It's been almost five years since Microsoft® announced the .NET strategy. This strategy was centered on a new and innovative platform that would change the way applications and systems were designed and developed. At the announcement, one of the most interesting pieces of the .NET strategy was an almost total reliance on a set of emerging industry-driven standards. At the time, these standards were becoming increasingly important based on the growing integration needs and platform interoperability issues that businesses were facing. Today, these Extensible Markup Language (XML)–based standards are enterprise proven and the .NET platform is a reality. Both .NET and XML have had a substantial impact on the way applications are designed and implemented. The addition of the Microsoft Office System 2003 Service Pack 1 changes the landscape and architecture even more.

This chapter provides a basic overview of the .NET Framework, Microsoft Office 2003 Service Pack 1, and the various technologies used throughout this book. This is an important starting point as we look more deeply at the newest product in the Office family, Microsoft InfoPath 2003. Even if you are an experienced developer, this chapter provides the baseline architectural overview used throughout the rest of the book. It is important to review the concepts here so that you really understand the rest of the book and can explore the full potential of InfoPath 2003 Service Pack 1.

What Is .NET?

It is impossible to say anything about .NET without first explaining the core components.

.NET is a product vision and platform roadmap for Microsoft products. This includes a broad spectrum of products, architectural patterns, and solutions. The confusing part of .NET is the effect this strategy has on your role within the organization. For example, developers have new tools and architectural patterns that are used to develop applications. Business users have new tools and technology that offer them additional productivity enhancement. The .NET platform is really a broad range of solution offerings that are built around three fundamental building blocks. Each of these represents a set of .NET core components.

The first building block is a set of industry-accepted standards that guarantee an application's ability to easily interact and communicate through a message-based architecture. There are a variety of these standards, but the main ones that we will focus on throughout this book are XML, Hypertext Transfer Protocol (HTTP), Universal Description, Discovery, and Integration (UDDI), and Web Services. These standards provide the core building blocks of application enablement across the other two components.

The second building block is a set of client- and server-based application solutions built on top of these standards and designed to solve a business problem. For example, Exchange 2003 Server delivers an email and calendaring solution that uses XML and HTTP. Another example is BizTalk Server 2004, which provides workflow and data transformation services. Also included in this is Microsoft Office System 2003, which delivers both client- and server-based integration and productivity solutions.

The last building block is the development environment of Visual Studio 2005. This component is designed to hide the semantics of the standards and enable developers to create and deploy solutions on top of the .NET Framework that solve problems in addition to interacting with the various products. Basically, the goal is to enhance productivity by enabling developers to solve business problems without having to code for each specific standard. Each of these three core components is an essential piece of the .NET architecture, and all are interrelated in delivering an integrated solutions platform.

.NET Framework

Within each of these core building blocks is the technology stack that makes up the various components of .NET. Figure 1.1 provides a diagram. The most important of these is the .NET Framework, which is the Windows® component that provides the compile and runtime services for applications and Web Services. Consider it the core plumbing that provides the standards-based implementation that allows developers to focus on writing the business logic.

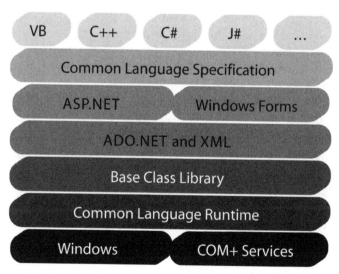

FIGURE 1.1 The .NET Framework consists of various layers.

The .NET Framework contains several different abstraction layers. At the bottom is the Common Language Runtime (CLR). The CLR contains a set of components that implement language integration, garbage collection, security, and memory management. The output of application code compiled within the CLR is Microsoft

Intermediate Language (MIL). MIL is a language-neutral byte code that operates within the managed environment of the CLR. For developers, the CLR provides lifetime management services and structured exception handling. An object's lifetime within the .NET Framework is determined by the Garbage Collector (GC), which is responsible for checking every object to evaluate and determine its status.

The GC traverses the memory tree, and any objects that the GC encounters are marked as alive. During a second pass, any object not marked is destroyed and the associated resources are freed. Finally, to prevent memory fragmentation and increase application performance, the entire memory heap is compacted. This automatically prevents memory leaks and ensures that developers don't have to deal with low-level system resources.

On top of the CLR is a layer of class libraries that contain the interface and classes that are used within the framework abstraction layers. This Base Class Library (BCL) is a set of interfaces that defines things like data types, data access, and I/O methods. The BCL is then inherited into the upper layers to provide services for Windows, Web Forms, and Web Services. All the base controls that are used to design forms are inherited from classes that are defined within the BCL. At the core of the BCL are the XML enablement classes that are inherited and used within the entire framework and provide a variety of additional services including data access.

Data access is one of the most important enhancements within .NET. The pre-.NET data access infrastructure of ActiveX Data Objects (ADO) and OLE DB was a tightly coupled connected environment. The Microsoft Data Access Component (MDAC) stack of services evolved primarily to keep up with the emergence of the Internet. Portions of ADO like Remote Data Services (RDS) were introduced to provide a disconnected data access model that was similar to the traditional ADO model for Web developers. One additional feature of ADO was that it allowed you to load and save disconnected recordsets in and out of XML. Developers found it hard to reconcile the ADO data model, which was primarily relational, with the new world of XML, where data was becoming heterogeneous and hierarchical. In addition, XML came with its own unique object model (Document Object Model [DOM]) and a different set of services—XSL Transformations (XSLT), XML Path Language (XPATH), and Extensible Schema Definition (XSD) schemas. Therefore, developers had to make an architectural choice of whether to use a relational design pattern or a more hierarchical or heterogeneous approach based on the type of application they were writing.

Fundamentally, in being forced to make the design choice, application architecture was inherently limited. In reality, what architects wanted was to use the best of both design patterns. One of the fundamental strengths of the .NET Framework was the uniformity of the model. All components were designed to share a common type system, design pattern, and naming conventions. It just didn't make any sense to re-design the existing model within the context of the Framework. The result was a new design approach—called ADO.NET—which added core classes to the native Framework. For existing applications, a set of Component classes was added; that provided interoperability to the traditional ADO object model.

Among the key design decisions for ADO.NET was that XML and data access are intimately tied together. ADO.NET doesn't just use the XML standards; it is *built* on them. XML support is tied to ADO.NET at every fundamental level. The result was a data access method that didn't require developers to make a choice in their application design.

ADO.NET is divided into two levels. The first is the managed provider. This enables high-speed managed access to the native database. The second level is the dataset, which is the local buffer of tables, or a collection of disconnected XML data collections. Most code that we will cover in this book uses the dataset and the managed provider as the connection and transport for database data.

Layered on top of the data access and XML layers and inheriting all their features is the visual presentation layer of Windows Forms and Web Forms. The data access layer inherits all the features of the bottom level and adds additional objects and classes that enable application developers to present and design a visual interface.

Residing at the top level is the Common Language Specification (CLS), which provides the basic set of language features. The CLS is responsible for defining a subset of the common type system that provides a set of rules that define how language types are declared, managed, and used in the runtime environment. This ensures language interoperability by defining a set of feature requirements that are common in all languages. Because of this, any language that exposes CLS interfaces is guaranteed to be accessible from any other language that supports the CLS. This layer is responsible for guaranteeing that the Framework is language agnostic for any CLS-compliant language. For example, both VB.NET and C# are CLS compliant and therefore interoperable. All the examples within this book are written in VB.NET, but they could have easily been written in any CLS-compliant language.

DEFINING THE SOLUTIONS ARCHITECTURE

Traditional application architecture is distributed across machine and operating system boundaries to improve performance, scalability, and availability. This application design pattern often leads to applications and systems becoming islands of data, each with their own geographic and physical boundaries. Developers are then forced to duplicate concepts and functionalities across systems as a way of compensating for these borders. Also, traditional system architecture didn't account for integration during its design. As a result, additional restrictions and layers that made applications difficult to maintain and, especially, change were created. Tightly coupled systems led to hard connected application layers that often dramatically increased the complexity of integration.

The adoption of Web Services and XML has caused a shift in the way applications are designed. Today, we want to design applications as a collection of interacting services. Each service provides access to a well-defined collection of unique functionality. Exposing functionality as a service gives additional flexibility to applications that allows them to make use of other services in a natural way regardless of their physical location.

A system should be designed to evolve through the addition of new services. This is called a Service Oriented Architecture (SOA). SOA defines the services that are used to compose a system and then maps these into a physical implementation. As a design pattern, SOA provides services to application consumers through standards-based, published, and discoverable interfaces. From a developer's perspective, this elevates code reuse because it allows applications that can bind to services that evolve over time. Also, this provides a clear integration model between systems, both inside the enterprise and across organization boundaries.

THE BENEFITS OF A SERVICE ORIENTED ARCHITECTURE

As we begin to design and develop applications, it's important for us to understand the benefits of an SOA:

Focused Developer Roles: The SOA design pattern forces applications into tiers or application layers. Each layer provides a set of specific developer roles. For example, a database layer needs developers with Structured Query Language (SQL) experience. The presentation layer needs client-side programmers. SOA allows developers to specialize and organizations to rely on these specialists to develop their applications.

Better Return on Investment: The isolation of services into distinct business domains allows the service layer to exist beyond the lifetime of any of the composed systems. For example, if an application needs a credit card authorization routine, developers have two choices. They can create a component that services just a single application, or they can create a component that services all applications. If the credit card authorization is developed as a separate business component and used as a service throughout the enterprise, then most likely it will outlive the original application.

Location Independent: Location transparency is an essential element of the SOA design pattern. The lookup and dynamic binding to services means that the client application doesn't care where the service is located. The natural extension is that services become mobile from one machine to another.

Tighter Security: The separation of an application into services naturally allows a multilevel authentication scheme. Each service can implement a security scheme that makes sense for the sensitivity of the data it presents and then provide additional security layers based on the services they use.

Better Quality: The independent and isolated nature of SOA provides easily testable software units. Services can be tested independently of any application that uses the service. This allows developers and Quality Assurance (QA) to provide a more focused testing suite that will result in better software quality.

Multiple Client Support: SOA makes it easier to implement multiple clients and types. The splitting of software into layers means clients can access services using whatever protocol or methods make sense for the client. For example, a Pocket PC can use the Compact Framework and an ASP.NET Web page can both directly call the same Web Service.

Natural Code Reuse: Traditionally, code reuse has failed because of general language and platform inconsistency. The standardized architecture of a service naturally creates a catalog of evolving and reusable components. The language and platform adherence to a known set of standards ensures an application is able to automatically understand and implement components within this catalog. At the same time, this catalog creates a flexible and secure environment that allows new uses of existing components and is secure enough to ensure data safety. The result is that developers no longer have to worry about compiler versions, platforms, and other incompatibilities that made code reuse difficult.

Lower Maintenance: The business service layer provides a central location for all application logic. This enables developers to locate and correct isolated areas quickly and easily. The loosely coupled interfaces enable individual components to be independently compiled, automatically alleviating the problem of fragile component interfaces.

Faster Development Time: Multiple software layers means multiple developers can work independently of each other. The creation of interfaces guarantees that the individual parts are able to communicate.

Scalable Architecture: The use of location transparency guarantees better scale and availability. Multiple servers may have multiple service instances spread across multiple locations. Fail-over and redundancy can be built on the service end so that clients don't have to worry about implementing specific network features.

WHAT IS A SERVICE?

By definition, a service is really nothing but discrete units of application logic that expose message-based interfaces suitable for access across a network. Typically, services provide both the business logic and state management relevant to the problem they are designed for. When a developer or application architect is designing services, the main goal is to effectively encapsulate the logic and data associated with the real-world process. *Decomposition*, or the process of what to implement within the same or a separate service, is an important design consideration. These types of design patterns evolve as services are implemented and tied together to solve more complex business problems.

State manipulation of a service is governed by Business Rules. These rules are relatively stable algorithms, such as the method in which an invoice is totaled from an item list, and are typically governed by application logic. On the other hand, policies are less static than business rules and may be governed by regional or customer-specific information. For example, a policy may be driven by a lookup table at runtime.

Always remember that services are network-capable units of software that implement logic, manage state, and communicate via messages and that are governed by policy. When defining a service, make sure to identify its specific responsibility within the system architecture. This guarantees that the service acts independently within a multitiered application. The service definition specifies that boundaries are explicit, services are autonomous, services can share schema and contract, but not class, and service compatibility is based on policy.

Logically, a service is similar to a component or an object. The big difference is that a service doesn't have an instancing model. It basically sends a message to a destination and hopes that it will both arrive and be responded to by a return message. Service interfaces are designed to expose functionality. A component or an object interface defines what the method calls should look like. Also, the service interface defines what the message and its sequencing should look like.

Messages are the units of information transmitted from one service to another. These must be highly structured with both sides being either aware or able to discover the format of the message and the exposed types. Typically, this is communicated through the use of schemas. These structures must be clear enough to contain or reference all the information necessary to understand the message. This basic concept allows communication between different technologies and allows you to choose an appropriate technology for every new service. This is the base concept of *loose coupling* that we will discuss throughout this book.

Always remember that a message is not just a function call. It's the loose coupling of components that enables messages to pass easily through both system and process boundaries. Often, messages are processed asynchronously and in any order; it's not guaranteed that they will be delivered multiple times or that an immediate response will be received.

WEB SERVICES

Web Services are one of the core components for the development of a services-based architecture. Technology alone doesn't make the services. It is important that components be designed with a loose coupling—as we will see throughout this book. This ideal scenario enables Office 2003 to take advantage of and provide the greatest application flexibility. Most of the applications developed within this book are based on the SOA design pattern and focus on the use of Web Services.

Web Services Architecture

The .NET Framework supports a variety of managed application types. These include the traditional Windows Forms, ASP.NET, mobile applications, and Web Services. Web Services are important because they provide self-contained business functions that operate over the Internet or an intranet. They are written to a strict set of standards that ensure they are interoperable and callable from other Web Services or front-end applications like Windows Forms or Microsoft Office®.

Web Services are important to a business because they quickly enable interaction between different systems or processes. Web Services allow companies to provide data electronically through a message based infrastructure using a set of reusable and discoverable interfaces. Many of the applications that we will build throughout this book use Web Services to provide back-end data access or integration.

The architecture of a Web Service, as shown in Figure 1.2, is similar to a Remote Procedure Call (RPC) over HTTP using XML as the message payload. The RPC portion of the Web Service implements the Simple Object Access Protocol (SOAP) to manage the underlying communication architecture. SOAP defines structured XML messages that ride over any type of network transport, although HTTP is generally preferred. These messages contain addressing and routing information that determines the delivery of their XML payload. The use of XML guarantees that these messages are firewall friendly and system independent.

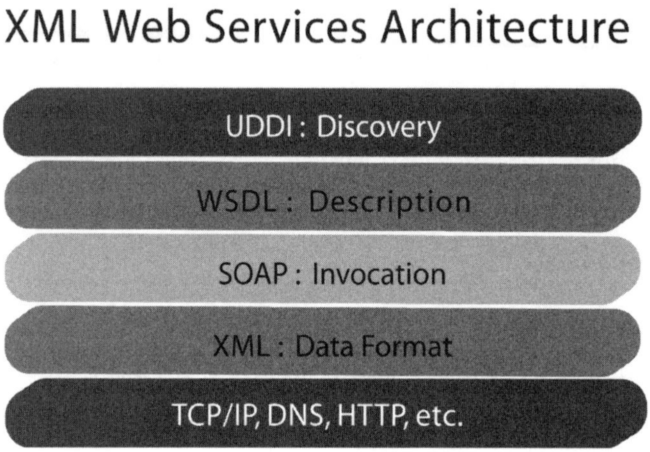

XML Web Services Architecture

UDDI : Discovery

WSDL : Description

SOAP : Invocation

XML : Data Format

TCP/IP, DNS, HTTP, etc.

FIGURE 1.2   Web Services are a stack of technology that enables the creation of a service.

While SOAP provides the intersystem messaging structure, the Web Service Description Language (WSDL) describes the set of operations within each service that the server supports. WSDL is an XML-based file that acts as a service contract between the server (producer) and client (consumer) of a Web Service. As part of this contract, the server agrees to provide a set of services as long as the client provides a properly formatted SOAP request.

As Web Services are created, UDDI enables the lookup and discovery for Web Services. UDDI provides the yellow pages lookup that allows clients to dynamically discover and consume Web Services. There is a public version of the UDDI registry as well as a private one. For the purposes of this book, all code examples use the private version included as part of the Windows Server 2003 operating system.

Creating a Simple Web Service

ON THE CD

To illustrate what we have talked about, let's walk through a simple Web Service that returns the current server time (this is covered on the CD-ROM in the Chapter 1 samples directory—\Code\Chapter 1\FirstServiceSetup\Setup.exe).

Open Visual Studio 2005 and create a new ASP.NET Web Service project named FirstService, as shown in Figure 1.3.

Once you have selected the project, you are brought into the design palette. To write code, we need to switch to the code window, as shown in Figure 1.4.

An XML Web Services consist of an entry point and the code that implements the XML Web Service functionality, as shown in Figure 1.5. In ASP.NET, the .ASMX file serves as the addressable entry point. It references code in pre-compiled

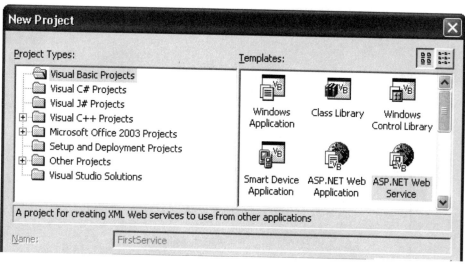

FIGURE 1.3   Within Visual Studio, select the type of project that you want to create.

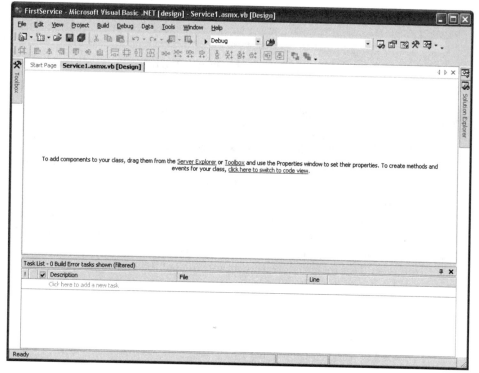

FIGURE 1.4   Visual Studio provides both a design palette and code window.

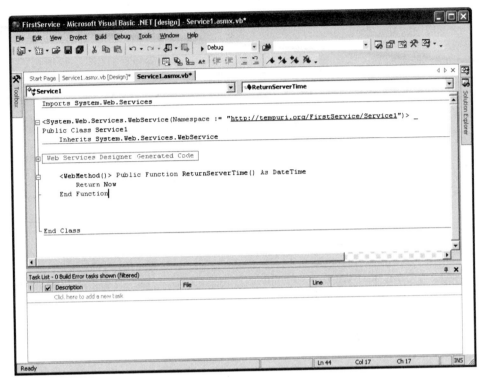

FIGURE 1.5 The code window within Visual Studio 2005.

assemblies, a code behind file, or code contained within the .ASMX file. The *Web Service* processing directive at the top of the .ASMX file determines where to find the implementation of the XML Web Service. When you build an XML Web Service in managed code, ASP.NET automatically provides the infrastructure and handles the necessary processing of XML Web Service requests and responses, including the parsing and creation of SOAP messages.

To expose a method as part of the Web Service, place a WebMethod attribute before the declaration of each public method. This attribute tells the ASP.NET runtime to provide all the implementation required to expose a method of a class on the Web. This includes creating an instance of the WSDL necessary to advertise the service on the Web.

Once the Web Service is compiled and run, it can be accessed from a Web browser and passed a valid query string. The .ASMX file returns an auto-generated Web page, as shown in Figure 1.6. This service help page provides a list of the advertised methods available for this service.

In addition, this page contains a link to the XML Web Services description document. The service description page provides the formal XML WSDL definition

FIGURE 1.6   The compiled Web Service running in a browser.

for the Web Service, as shown in Figure 1.7. This XML document conforms to the WSDL grammar and defines the contract for the message format that clients need to follow when exchanging messages.

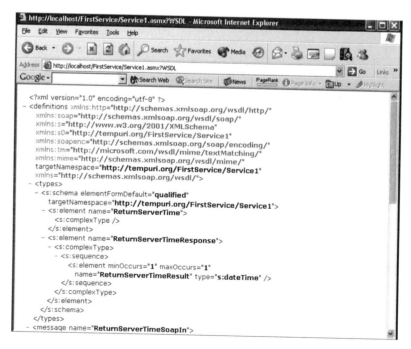

FIGURE 1.7   The auto-generated WSDL for the Web Service.

The service method page provides additional information that relates to a particular XML Web Service method. The page provides the ability to invoke the method using the HTTP-POST protocol, as shown in Figure 1.8. At the bottom of the Web page, the service method help page provides sample request and response messages for the protocol that the XML Web Service method supports.

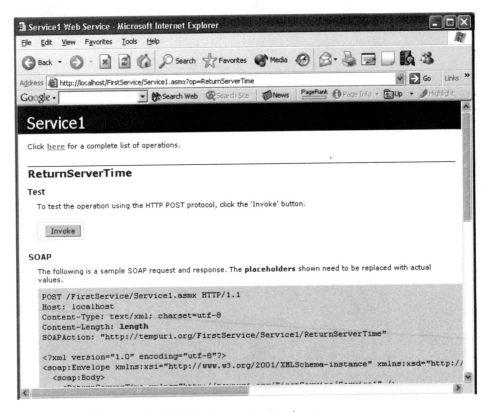

FIGURE 1.8 The compiled Web Service running in a browser.

Once the service is invoked, a new browser window is open and the returned XML message is displayed, as shown in Figure 1.9.

Congratulations! We have just walked through the creation of our first Web Service. Throughout this book we will build many more, but it is important to understand the steps necessary to build and then use a simple Web Service. Now let's move on to how we can use these services.

FIGURE 1.9   The returned XML message from the Web Service.

MICROSOFT OFFICE SYSTEM 2003

Microsoft Office 2003 allows you to create intelligent business solutions that address a variety of requirements while providing an easy-to-use interface. It is a big mistake to think of Office as just a word processor or spreadsheet. The Office System goes beyond that simple definition and combines a series of products and services that enables end users and developers to write managed code, understand XML, and consume Web Services. Combining these features with the familiar Office interface allows Office to become a universal front-end for any application regardless of the system or platform the data is located on.

A few of the traditional Office-based products may be the familiar Microsoft Word, Excel, and Access, but several new ones have been added to the mix. It is important to look at a few of these new products and features because we will be using them throughout the rest of the book to develop customer solutions.

Microsoft Word 2003:   One of the key features of Word 2003 is the native file support of XML, as shown in Figure 1.10. Word 2003 templates can also include an underlying XML schema that allows users to create documents containing XML markup. Developers can create templates based on custom XML schemas and then build intelligent applications around these documents. Word 2003 also provides direct support for Extensible Stylesheet Language (XSL) and XPATH. The native support of these features enables developers to build solutions that capture and reuse document content across applications, processes, devices, and platforms. XML support enables Word to function as a smart client for Web Services and a host for these intelligent XML-based documents.

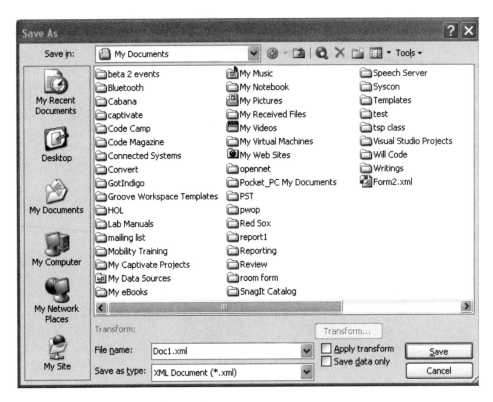

FIGURE 1.10   Saving a Word 2003 document to XML.

Microsoft Excel 2003:   Spreadsheets within Excel 2003 can be designed with an underlying custom XML structure. In defining schemas, businesses can implement a flexible data connection between client and server to describe specific business objects. Excel also provides a new tool for mapping these custom XML elements to spreadsheet cells, as shown in Figure 1.11. As with Word 2003, the native XML support enables Excel to act as a smart client for Web Services and host intelligent XML-based documents.

Microsoft Access 2003:   Access 2003 offers extended capabilities to import, export, and work with XML data files, as shown in Figure 1.12. Many of the new features provide a common error interface that makes it easier to find and correct XML issues.

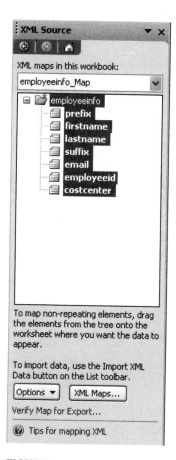

FIGURE 1.11 Importing an XML document into Excel 2003.

Microsoft Office OneNote 2003:   OneNote 2003 is a new application that is designed for note taking and information management, as shown in Figure 1.13. Using OneNote, users can capture, organize, and reuse notes on a laptop or desktop. OneNote 2003 gives you one place to capture multiple forms of information, including typed and handwritten notes, hand-drawn diagrams, audio recordings, photos and pictures from the Web, and information from other programs.

FIGURE 1.12   Importing an XML document into Excel 2003.

FIGURE 1.13   Note taking within OneNote 2003.

Microsoft InfoPath 2003:   InfoPath 2003 is a new application designed to streamline the process of gathering information for teams and individuals. The structure of InfoPath allows these groups to work with a rich, dynamic forms interface that allows the collection and distribution of structured XML data.

The native support of customer-defined XML, Web Services, SQL, or Access databases allows the collected information to integrate easily with a broad range of business processes and systems. This integration allows InfoPath to connect seamlessly and directly to organizational information and SOA.

WHAT YOU NEED TO KNOW ABOUT INFOPATH

For the average end user, InfoPath provides a general-purpose viewer of structured business data. Using this information, business users can collect and distribute forms with no programming. This automatically guarantees data accuracy and adherence to business requirements.

For developers, InfoPath is the power tool for building applications that view, transform, and edit XML-based data. The native XML interface allows developers to easily develop and implement solutions that address organization process and workgroup collaboration scenarios, such as what we see in Figure 1.14.

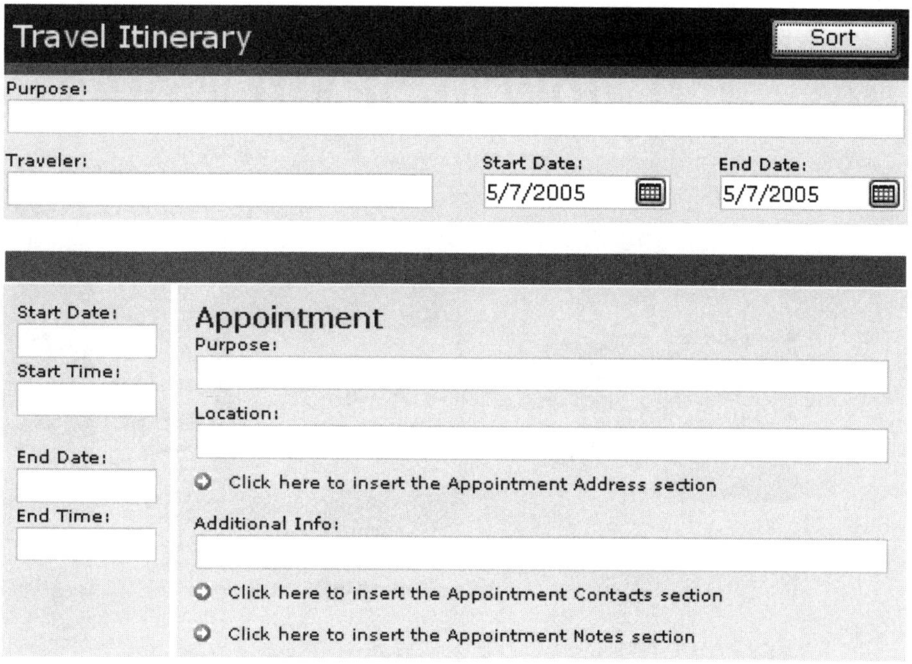

FIGURE 1.14   An XML–based InfoPath 2003 form.

The organization process of gathering information is typically inefficient and often leads to incorrect data with very little reusability. Paper-based forms are the best example of a hard-to-use collection mechanism that provides very little flexibility and integration. Many times, custom applications developed for information gathering are expensive and difficult to maintain. The combination of these two factors often makes data and code reuse impossible with organizations of any size.

The solution to this problem is a SOA that solves the back-end integration issues but not the front-end data collection. InfoPath is designed to become a key piece of this solution. The result is that InfoPath provides reduced IT costs by allowing end users and developers to maintain form-based solutions, and XML provides the direct integration without additional overhead or development work.

Unlike the other Office 2003 applications, XSLT is the only option for data transformation. The structured XML data created by InfoPath is presented through a series of XSLT transforms and based on an object model that expresses documents using Extensible Hypertext Markup Language (XHTML) through a series of Cascading Style Sheets (CSS). The InfoPath object model is actually derived from the Internet Explorer model, and this provides a direct link to SOA, WSDL, and HTTP, as shown in Figure 1.15.

How InfoPath Works

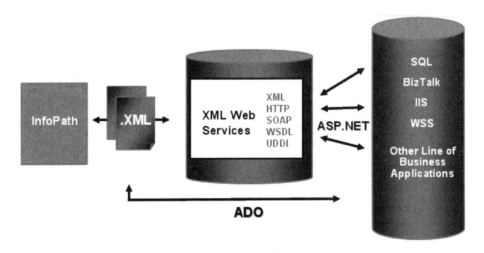

FIGURE 1.15   An overview of how InfoPath works.

OFFICE 2003 AND WHAT'S NEW FOR DEVELOPERS

As we begin to develop applications using Visual Studio and SOA, we need to learn about the variety of components that Office 2003 provides. Many of these are covered in later chapters as part of complete solution examples. At this time, though, it is important to cover the basics. In later chapters, we will extend these types of solutions to use InfoPath as the front end for data collection and aggregation.

Smart Documents

Office 2003 introduces a new technology that enables Word and Excel documents to become more than static repositories of user data. Called *Smart Documents*, this technology enables a new type of automation that can automatically enter data into appropriate Word or Excel fields, access external information, and even combine documents, as shown in Figure 1.16. One of the most important features of Smart Documents is the contextual help that is available to guide users through the preparation of complicated documents.

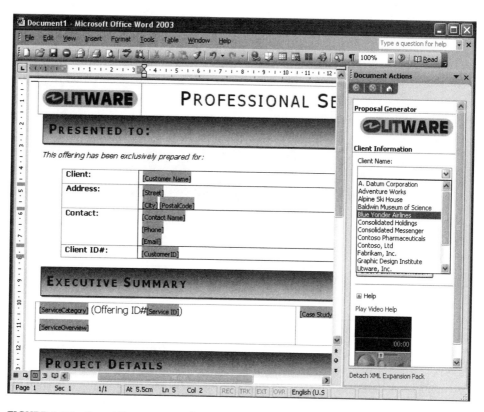

FIGURE 1.16 Smart Document collecting proposal data.

The underlying technology of Smart Documents is an XML structure that is programmed to include the steps a user needs to complete and then to provide help along the way. As a user moves through a Smart Document, the current insertion point determines what is displayed in the task pane. Developers can provide everything from context-sensitive help to external data calculations for a specific section of documents. Smart Documents offers an ideal way to pull and aggregate data into a Word or Excel document.

InfoPath and Smart Documents are really designed to address different issues, although there is definitely some overlap. The purpose of InfoPath is to allow the collection of information from a user and to easily reuse that data in other business processes. Fundamentally, InfoPath provides data validation to ensure that the data collected is validated, rules are included to process a document, and conditional formatting to respond to user input is accessible. Smart Documents are specifically targeted at automating parts of the process of creating a Word or Excel document. Using the Smart Documents task pane, users can make choices to construct documents quickly. Because the Smart Document is aware of changes being made to the document, the task pane can be customized easily to provide appropriate choices to the user at the appropriate times.

Although a document created using Smart Document can be saved as XML, this is not Smart Document's primary purpose. When trying to decide whether to use InfoPath or Smart Documents, you need to determine whether you want to collect structured data from the user that can then be easily reused without requiring retyping, or whether you want to assist the user in constructing free-form documents.

Developing a Smart Document

Take the following steps to develop a Smart Document:

1. Attach an XML schema to Word 2003 or Excel 2003 and annotate the portions of the document that will have Smart Document actions or help topics associated with the XML.
2. Save the document as a template so that others can create an instance of the template from the New Document task pane.
3. Using Visual Studio, implement the ISSmartDocument interface or an XML schema that conforms to the Smart Document XML schema. This is needed to display the contents in the Document Actions task pane and to handle the specific defined actions.
4. Develop an XML-based solutions manifest that references the files used within the Smart Document. You should then save the manifest in a location referred to by the Smart Document custom document properties.
5. Place the solution's file in the locations referred to in the solutions manifest.

Users who want to instantiate and use a Smart Document should open the Word or Excel template and start interacting with the document. The use of templates within Smart Documents allows for a no-touch deployment. Smart Documents also offer enhanced security restrictions that allow them to become a trusted solution.

Smart Document Security Restrictions

The enhanced security restrictions offered by Smart Documents are the following:

- Management by security policy.
- Solution manifests must come from trusted sites. The solution manifest themselves must be code signed or otherwise trusted.
- Code that runs as part of the Smart Document solution is subject to the user's Office security settings.
- Users are prompted whether to initiate an install of a Smart Document solution.

Smart Tags Version 2

Smart Tags as shown in Figure 1.17 provide another way to visualize and integrate with XML based content. Smart Tags were first introduced as part of Office XP and have been substantially enhanced within Office 2003. This includes the addition of

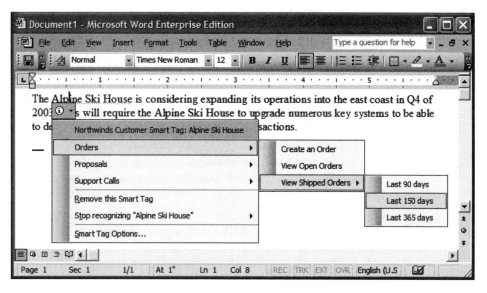

FIGURE 1.17 Smart Tags recognize key words.

Smart Tags to PowerPoint 2003 and Access 2003 as well as additional enhancements for Word 2003, Excel 2003, and Outlook 2003 when you're reading HTML email and writing email with Word as your default email editor. Also, there are a variety of enhancements to the Smart Tag recognizer and the Microsoft Office Smart Tag List (MOSTL) that provide support for regular expressions and context-free grammar based recognition, as well as advanced support for property settings on items in a list of terms.

Smart Tag functionality has also been improved to include the capability to execute actions immediately on recognition without requiring any user intervention. For example, a Smart Tag could recognize a product name and automatically start an action that opens the browser or links to a related page. Also added was the ability to modify the current document, which allows developers to automatically format a recognized term. For example, a product ID could automatically be turned into a product name.

This also allows developers to add required content such as a product description or to update a reference to a product catalog. Smart Tags provide a great way to connect to a variety of different data sources that exist within an organization and serve contextually valid or recognized terms. For example, within an Excel spreadsheet, you can connect a list of general ledger accounts to specific types of assets. Although, these are not directly supported with InfoPath, they are important to understand. For example, in later chapters, we will convert an InfoPath document to a Word document that can then leverage Smart Tags.

Windows SharePoint Services and SharePoint Portal Server

Windows SharePoint Services (WSS) is a collaboration platform that is a core component of Windows Server 2003. WSS is an ASP.NET-based page and platform container for componentized user interfaces called Web Parts. WSS provides an out-of-the-box solution for team-based collaboration that includes a portal interface and document management system.

The portal interface is built on ASP.NET and SQL Server 2000 and offers personalization, state management, and load balancing. WSS offers self-service capabilities that allow users to create, maintain, and customize their own portal pages. Document management allows you to manage and maintain the revision history of not only traditional documents types like Word, Excel, and PowerPoint, but also InfoPath forms through a special forms library function, as shown in Figure 1.18. This provides the ideal repository and versioning mechanism for the distribution and location of enterprise forms.

WSS provides sites for team-based collaboration and increased productivity through the creation of a team portal site. SharePoint Portal Server (SPS) 2003

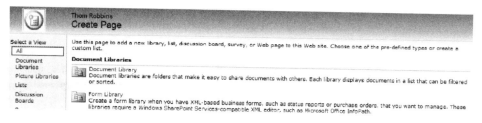

FIGURE 1.18 Create Page allows document and form libraries.

connects site, people, and information together for the enterprise. Built on top of WSS and the .NET Framework, SPS inherited all the features of WSS and provides the core features of portal sites for people and documents within an enterprise.

Sites created within SPS are specific to the SPS framework, but they use the base WSS technologies of Web parts and document libraries. The direct integration between the two helps to lower the amount of code associated with the development, training, and support of an enterprise portal site.

SPS extends the capabilities of WSS by providing a site registry and search mechanism. The *site registry* is a centralized repository of Web site and portal pages, as shown in Figure 1.19. It provides an easy-to-use Web site locator and structure mechanism for defining the overall site navigation. The search within SPS is another important feature, which is an intelligent crawling service that can index and search Web sites, public folders, file shares, documents, and XML files.

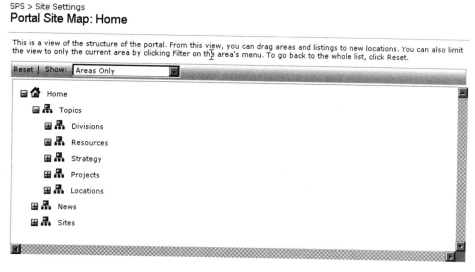

FIGURE 1.19 Managing the portal structure within SharePoint Portal Server.

VISUAL STUDIO TOOLS FOR OFFICE

The Visual Studio Tools for Office (VSTO) enables developers to build managed application solutions for Word 2003, Excel 2003, and InfoPath 2003 using Visual Studio 2005. The managed code executes behind documents and spreadsheets enables Office 2003 to take advantage of the .NET Framework. This includes no-touch deployment, Web Service Integration, and security. When a user opens a Word 2003, Excel 2003, or InfoPath 2003 file associated with a custom solution, the application will query the server and download the new Dynamic-Link Libraries (DLL) to the user's machine. Developers won't need to touch every desktop, and users won't have to download files.

No-touch deployment provides a mechanism to hook Internet Explorer 5.01 and later versions to listen for .NET assemblies that are requested by an application. During the request, the executable is downloaded to an area on the local hard drive called the assembly download cache. The application is then launched by a process named IEEcex into a constrained security environment.

Office 2003 is still a primary unmanaged application. The result of this is that, typically, development has been done using things like Visual Basic for Applications (VBA). VSTO provides a set of Component Object Model (COM) interoperable assemblies that enable the direct integration into the .NET Framework 2.0 and Visual Studio 2005. The key is the primary interop assembly. This unique assembly contains type definitions of COM implemented type. By default, there can be only one Primary Interop Assembly (PIA), which must be signed with a strong name for security reasons. However, this assembly can wrap more than one version of the same library. The traditional COM type library that is imported as an assembly is signed by someone other than the original publisher and for security reasons is not able to function as a primary interop assembly. PIAs are important because they provide a unique type identity.

The release of Visual Studio 2005 and the .NET Framework 2.0 introduced a new set of PIAs that is available for Office 2003. The sample solution provided on

the CD-ROM (\Code\Chapter 1\ReportingService\Setup.exe) demonstrates an easy sample method for publishing analytical data from a Web Service into a Word or Excel document where it can be further analyzed. As an example, let's create a reporting Web Service that pulls sales data from the local Northwinds database. The code in Listing 1.1 is provided on the CD-ROM and is available after you install the program.

LISTING 1.1   Creating a Web Service-Based Dataset That Returns SQL Server Data

```
<WebMethod()> Public Function GetUpdatedTotals() As DataSet
Dim sqlConn As SqlConnection
Dim sqlCmd As SqlCommand
Dim strConstring As String
Dim intUserID As Integer
strConstring = ConfigurationSettings.AppSettings("constring")
sqlConn = New SqlConnection(strConstring)
sqlConn.Open()
sqlCmd = New SqlCommand

  With sqlCmd
    .Connection = sqlConn
    .CommandTimeout = 30
    .CommandType = CommandType.Text
    Dim sqlInfo As String

    sqlInfo = "SELECT Employees.Country, Employees.LastName,
              _Orders.ShippedDate, Orders.OrderID, " & """" & _
              "Order Subtotals" &"""" & ".Subtotal AS SaleAmount "
    sqlInfo = sqlInfo & "FROM Employees INNER JOIN " _"(Orders INNER
              JOIN" & """" & "Order Subtotals" & """" _ &
              " ON Orders.OrderID = " & """" & "Order Subtotals" _
              & """" &".OrderID) "
    sqlInfo = sqlInfo & "ON Employees.EmployeeID = Orders.EmployeeID"

    CommandText = SqlInfo
  End With

  Dim DataDA As SqlDataAdapter = New SqlDataAdapter
  DataDA.SelectCommand = sqlCmd
  Dim DataDS As DataSet = New DataSet
  DataDA.Fill(DataDS, "SalesData")

  Return DataDS
  sqlConn.Close()
End Function
```

Once the Web Service is published, you are ready to create an Excel application that consumes this service. Once installed, VSTO provides a new type of project in Visual Studio 2005, as shown in Figure 1.20.

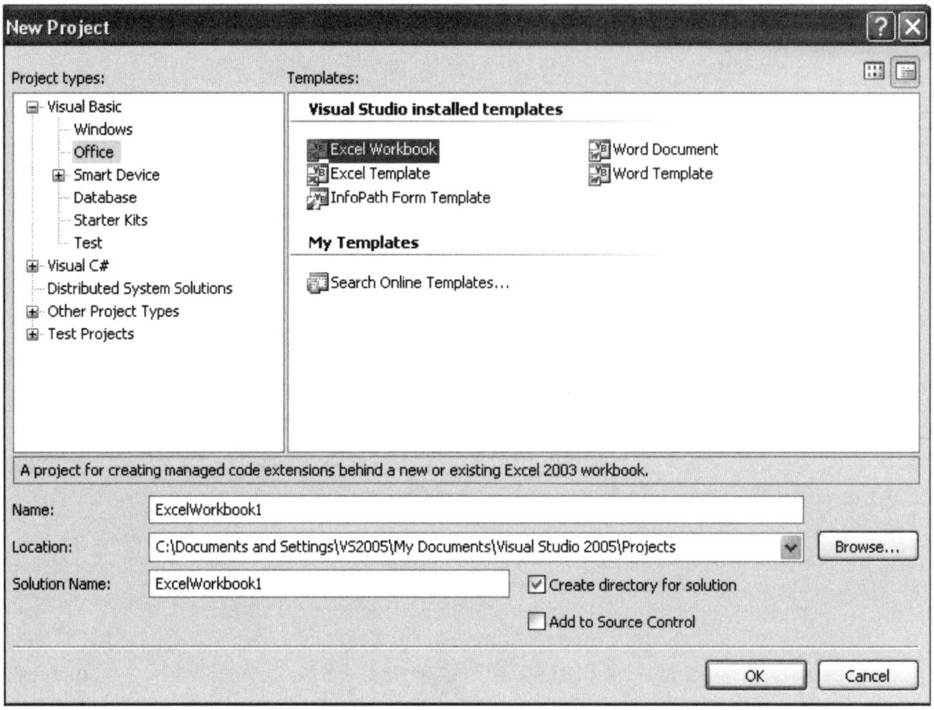

FIGURE 1.20 The VSTO project as it appears in Visual Studio 2005.

Using Visual Studio, you create a new Office 2003 project. This creates an Excel-based project that provides managed code behind pages. For our code, we want to create an application that when opened would instantiate and call the reporting Web Service and then create a Pivot Table that the user could analyze and drill into the received data. Do this by entering the code in Listing 1.2 into the This-Workbook Open handle. This code is activated on the *open* of the spreadsheet and will publish the data within an Excel Pivot Table.

LISTING 1.2 Generating the Pivot Table from the Dataset Returned by a Web Service

```
Private Sub ThisWorkbook_Open() Handles ThisWorkbook.Open
Dim ReportingInfo As New ReportingServices.ReportingService
Dim ds As New DataSet
Dim XMLFile As String
XMLFile = ("C:\employee.xml")
```

```
' call the web service and write the XML file to local disk
ds = ReportingInfo.GetUpdatedTotals()
ds.WriteXml(XMLFile)

' load the XML file into Excel
ThisApplication.Workbooks.OpenXML("C:\employee.xml")
' set the pivot table up
ThisApplication.ActiveWorkbook.PivotCaches.Add(SourceType:=
Excel.XlPivotTableSourceType.xlDatabase,
SourceData:=
"employee!R2C1:R832C7").CreatePivotTable(TableDestination:="",
TableName:= "PivotTable1",   DefaultVersion:=
Microsoft.Office.Interop.Excel._
XlPivotTableVersionList.xlPivotTableVersion10)
ThisApplication.ActiveSheet.PivotTableWizard(
TableDestination:=ThisApplication.ActiveSheet.Cells(3, 1))
ThisWorkbook.ActiveSheet.Cells(3, 1).Select()
With ThisWorkbook.ActiveSheet.PivotTables("PivotTable1")._
    PivotFields("/SalesData/Country")
    .Orientation = Microsoft.Office.Interop.Excel._
    XlPivotFieldOrientation.xlPageField
    .Position = 1
End With

' clean up the XML file
Kill(xmlfile)
    End Sub
```

At this point, we are ready to distribute the application to end users who can open the spreadsheet and further analyze their sales numbers without having to be concerned with actually gathering or publishing the data.

SUMMARY

In this chapter, we covered the basic architecture and technology concepts we will use throughout the rest of the book, including how .NET and Office 2003 fit together. Within that, we have introduced InfoPath 2003 as the power tool that developers can use to create XML-based solutions.

In the next chapter, we will take a more detailed look at the InfoPath application and how the integrated environment takes advantage of XML, as well as provides additional capabilities that you can use to develop forms-based solutions. In subsequent chapters, we will start to build on the concepts started here to create services-oriented solutions using InfoPath 2003.

2 Understanding the InfoPath IDE

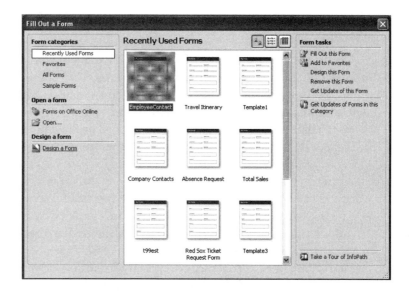

INTRODUCTION

Microsoft InfoPath 2003 (Service Pack 1) is a new application that is an integrated part of the Microsoft Office System. The goal of InfoPath is to streamline the process of gathering, sharing, and using information across teams and enterprises. InfoPath enables this by allowing form designers and users to interact and build rich dynamic forms. The use of XML as the native file format allows the collected data to be easily reusable across both the organization and traditional process boundaries.

Unlike the traditional binary formats of Word or Excel, the native use of XML makes it inherently easier for information to be reused across different documents or systems. One of the clear strengths of InfoPath is that its integrated environment enables easy form design and rapid data entry. This chapter is focused on the WYSIWYG design environment and how it can be used to develop InfoPath solutions. We will also cover how InfoPath uses XML to generate its own internal schema structure. Much of the information we will cover in this chapter serves as the basis that we will use later as we start to dive deeper into developing InfoPath solutions.

THE INFOPATH INTERFACE

InfoPath provides two modes of operation: form fill in and form design mode. Regardless of the mode that InfoPath is in, the user interface is divided into two sections, as shown in Figure 2.1. The first is the form area, a large open area on the lefthand side of the workspace. When an InfoPath solution is open, this area contains the data form that is being either designed or filled in. As a form is filled in or designed, this area provides the results of the actions performed from the menu, toolbar, or task pane; this area is also where InfoPath users tend to spend most of their time. During runtime (form fill-in mode), this area acts as the data entry surface and provides immediate feedback for any type of data entry validation errors.

The second area is the task pane. The task pane is, by default, located on the righthand side of the form, but can be repositioned, resized, and even closed according to the user's Office preferences. The task pane is designed to contain InfoPath commands such as spell check, text formatting, or design tasks. In addition, developers can extend the task pane to include form- or context-specific commands or tasks.

The combination of these two areas, being open simultaneously, allows InfoPath users and designers to complete a set of tasks with the entire window in full view. Therefore, there is no need to either tab or toggle between multiple windows for either screens or dialog boxes.

Form Area

Visually, an InfoPath form contains spaces reserved for entering information; this form is very similar to a Web page or other types of structured document-editing tools. As we will see later, the pattern for developing InfoPath forms is similar to the design of table-driven Web pages. The InfoPath solution template includes things

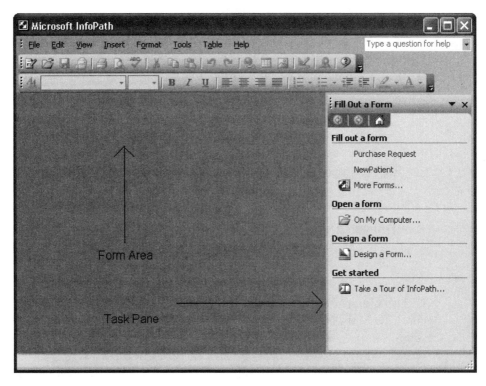

FIGURE 2.1 The InfoPath interface is divided into two sections.

such as the XML schema that determines the structure of the completed data and it is packaged as a single compressed cabinet file. At runtime, all InfoPath forms are based on the definitions stored in the solution file and all saved data is contained in a single XML file. This solution template is usually created by a single person and is then distributed or published to a shared location such as a Web site, file share, or a WSS Forms Library.

Both stored data forms and solutions files can be identified and stored within a Uniform Resource Locator (URL) or a Uniform Resource Name (URN). InfoPath forms that are based on URL identifiers are stored in a shared network storage location. Forms that contain a URN are installed on the local computer or digitally signed with a trusted certificate. These forms are considered part of a trusted solution and are automatically given greater security access and file permissions on the user's local computer. We will cover these topics more in Chapter 9, when we discuss developing trusted forms, and in Chapter 10, when we discuss deployment strategies.

The InfoPath client displays either the URN or URL address at the bottom left of the InfoPath workspace, as seen in Figure 2.2. All form modifications are maintained by a form designer, and InfoPath provides an automated mechanism to maintain version information within the existing form template. This ensures existing XML document compatibility and provides a deployment guarantee for changed solutions.

FIGURE 2.2   A template trust level based on location, as seen in InfoPath.

A user can create a runtime version of a form by clicking on either the URN or URL that points to the solution file and opens the form solution in the InfoPath client. Once the form is open, the user fills in the blanks, fixes any errors, and then submits a separate completed XML document for processing. One of the important features of the InfoPath solution file is that it guarantees a separation of the presentation and data. Depending on the design and business rules, users may add additional or repeating sections, or change business rules within the solution file. When completed during runtime, this results in a completely separate well-formed XML document that points back to the solution file that created it. Also, unlike a Web page, which requires a server post to notify the user of data entry errors, InfoPath actually validates the data during data entry.

Data entry, validation, processing, and formatting rules are built and stored into the form template during the design process. This centralized structure is used to specify things such as data types, values, and data validation that are applied to the InfoPath form data. The form template is responsible for maintaining these rules for both the solution and editable fields. If any data item fails the validation rules, InfoPath immediately adds a red border around the editable region, as shown in Figure 2.3. This notification provides immediate visual feedback of the error and provides a field- and form-level validation mechanism. End users by default are able to save the form locally to complete later with errors but are unable to submit the form for approval or processing until all errors are fixed.

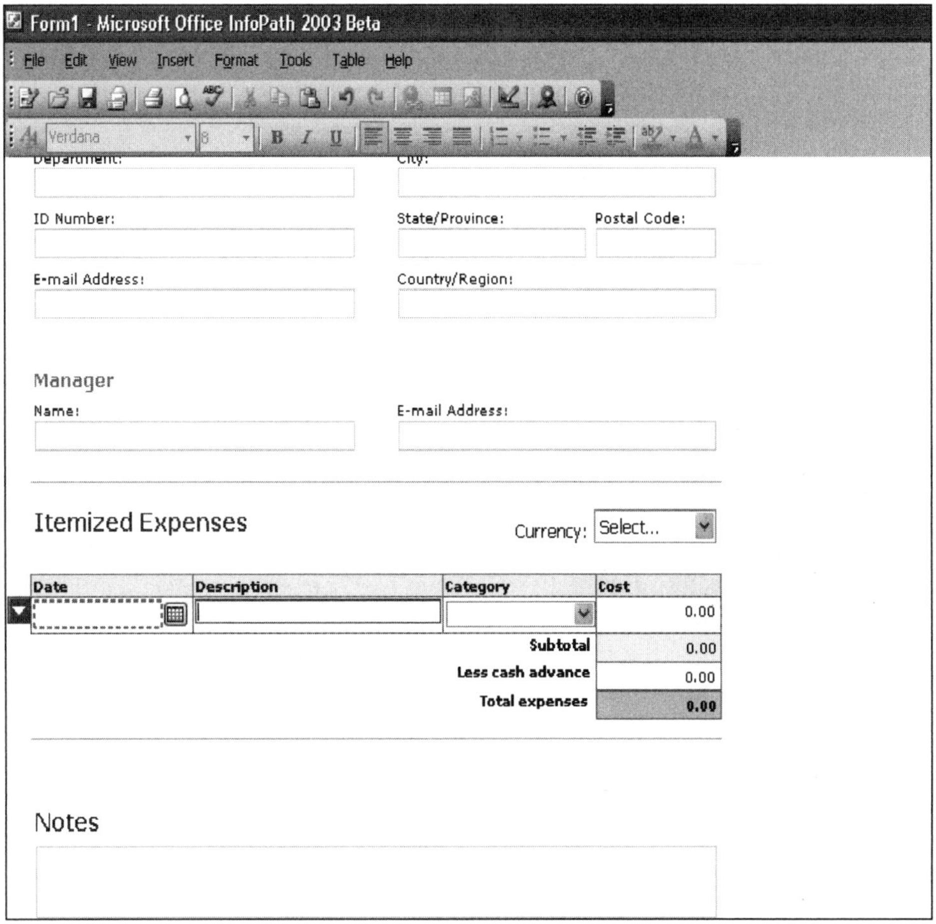

FIGURE 2.3 A field that has failed data validation.

Solution templates control both the schema and layout of forms, and this combination is used to determine the runtime experience. However, the end user isn't able to edit every aspect of an InfoPath form during runtime. For example, only form designers can edit text labels. InfoPath provides additional visual cues to allow users and designers to see when and where they can make changes. For example, when a user filling in a form hovers over a region, the field becomes highlighted with a gray border indicating that the section can be updated. As another example,

Figure 2.4 shows an editable region in a table with the drop-down indicator that appears when the user enters the area by pressing the Tab key or a mouse click.

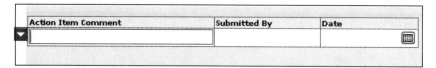

FIGURE 2.4 A drop-down indicator within a form.

Repeating and Optional Sections

An InfoPath form may contain a wide variety of controls. One of the most important is the Repeating and Optional control types, as shown in Figure 2.5. This set of controls includes lists, tables, optional control sections, and a master-detail section. This makes forms more flexible when users are entering data. For example, rather than designing an expense report with a set number of lines, users or business rules can determine the number of expenses that they need to add. The following repeating and optional controls are available:

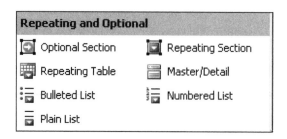

FIGURE 2.5 Repeating and Optional control section.

Lists: Each item in a list represents a single field. For example, an employee contact form could have a list of departments. Lists can be formatted for data entry as plain lists, numbered lists, or bulleted lists, as shown in Figure 2.6.

Company Departments|

- •

■ Bulleted List

FIGURE 2.6 A bulleted list used to collect department data.

Repeating Sections: A derivation of the lists is shown in Figure 2.7, in which each item of the list can contain more than one field. For example, a single item within a form that contains name, address, and phone number for each employee. A repeating section can also include a table, list, or sections.

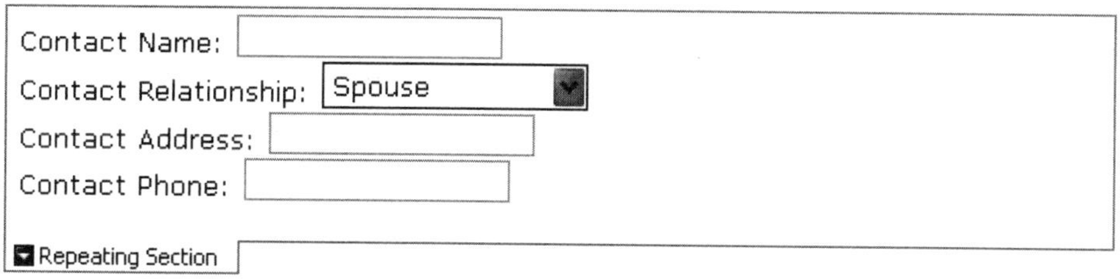

Contact Name:

Contact Relationship: Spouse

Contact Address:

Contact Phone:

■ Repeating Section

FIGURE 2.7 Repeating section used to collect contact information.

Repeating Tables: In a table, each column represents a field and each row represents an additional occurrence of the group of fields. For example, repeating sections and repeating tables, as shown in Figure 2.8, are used to create an entire record, such as a list of contacts.

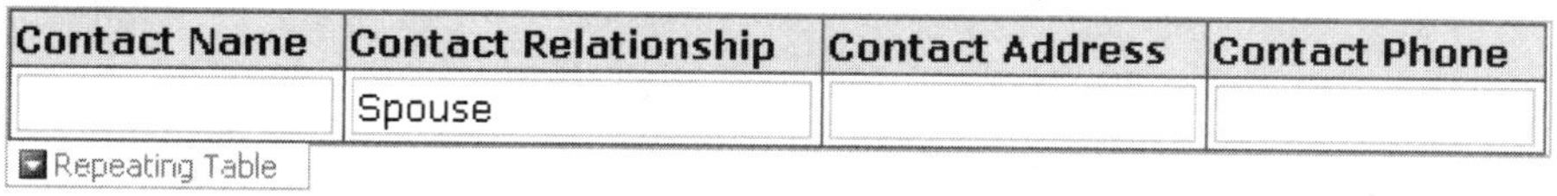

Contact Name	Contact Relationship	Contact Address	Contact Phone
	Spouse		

■ Repeating Table

FIGURE 2.8 A repeating table used to contact information.

Optional Sections: These sections are inserted or removed by users while they are filling out the form (see Figure 2.9). The form designer specifies whether these sections should appear in a blank form, or during runtime if a user decides to insert them. For example, a notes field could appear on a contact form only when a user inserts it. If the user decides not to insert a note, he can delete the entire section instead of deleting the field data. A repeating section or repeating table, such as a list of account numbers or expense items, can appear if users decide they want to insert it. Also, any sections can be made optional when they are placed within an optional section.

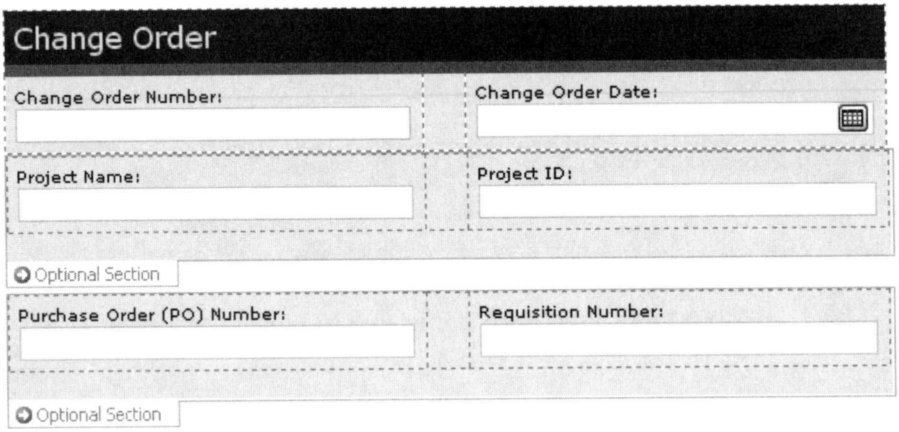

FIGURE 2.9   An optional section to collect data.

Master/Detail Sections: A master/detail control is actually a set of two related controls (see Figure 2.10). One of these controls is the designated master control; the other is the designated detail control. The master control is always a repeating table. The detail control can be either a repeating table or a repeating section. When inserted onto a form, a one-to-one relationship between the master control and the detail control is automatically established. This means that for each selected row in the master control, there is only a single matching

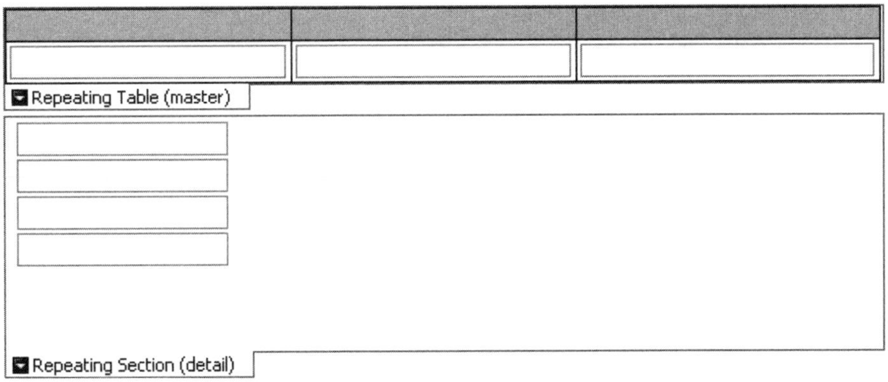

FIGURE 2.10   A master/detail section to collect data.

result in the detail control. By default, this one-to-one relationship will bind both the master and detail controls to the same repeating group.

Task Panes

Task panes are a major part of the Office 2003 environment. They are used throughout the entire system for various management and administrative tasks. Form designers can add custom task panes to their form templates. The content of these HTML files is displayed in a window next to a form. Custom task panes can provide form-specific command and help content. Essentially, they are designed to provide form-specific content, such as command buttons and data dialogs. Task panes provide an easy way for users to complete tasks with their forms in full view. Depending on the form and whether it is being filled out or designed, different task panes may be available at different times.

Figure 2.11 shows the title bar at the top of the task pane that contains the name of the active pane. On the right of the title bar is a drop-down indicator that allows quick navigation to other task panes that are enabled globally or within the current form. Within each task pane to the right of the title bar are the navigation panes, as shown in Figure 2.12. These navigation panes consist of a set of buttons and selectors that are similar to Internet Explorer. They are designed to enable navigation easily between the task panes that are currently available within the form.

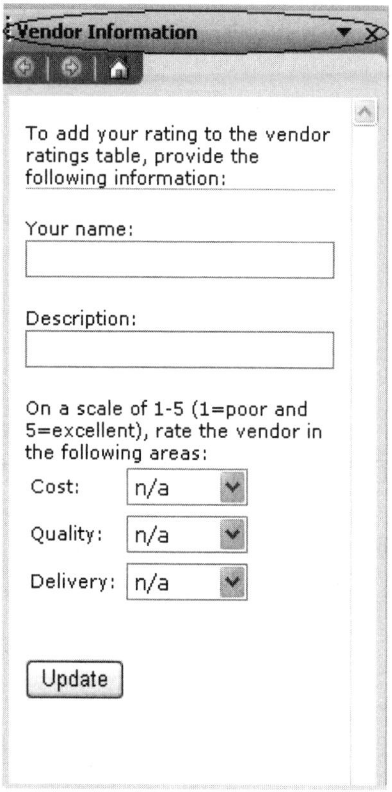

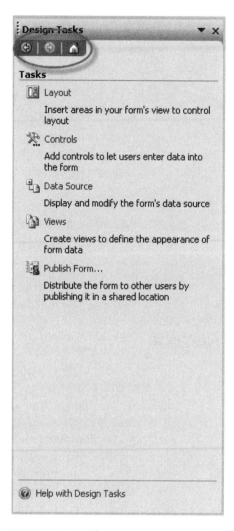

FIGURE 2.11   The task pane title area.

FIGURE 2.12   The task pane navigation options.

THE BASICS OF FORM DESIGN

The acceptance and usage of XML has substantially influenced the industry and software development. One of the most important effects has been the creation of additional supporting standards and meta-languages that are derived from the original XML standard. Each of these supporting standards has evolved to meet a specific business need or requirement that has arisen from the broader industry use of XML. InfoPath was designed to leverage many of these standards, so it is important to understand how InfoPath uses these, as shown in Table 2.1. Each of the files types and additional source code files are combined to form a single solution file.

TABLE 2.1 An Overview of InfoPath Using XML

Name	Description
XML	This is the output format produced by InfoPath solutions. XML is also used to contain default data that is used to preload form fields.
XSLT	This is the format of the view files produced when a form is designed.
XML Schema	This is the primary means of data validation within a form and defines the underlying structure of XML within a form. XML schemas are also used to define the structure of the form definition file. This file provides the entry point and definition for an InfoPath solution and is generated when a form is designed or edited.
XHTML	This data format is well-formed HTML and is used primarily when you are developing rich text areas.
XPATH	XPATH is an XML expression language that is used to bind controls to a form and store conditional formatting expressions.
Document Object Model (DOM)	Within InfoPath, the DOM is used to programmatically access the contents of a form as well as the various portions of the form definition file.
XML Signature	This is used to digitally sign InfoPath forms. One of the important features of this is the ability to have multiple signatures within a single InfoPath form. This allows multiple users to work on the same XML document, with each user providing a new digital signature on top of signatures that are added by other users.
XML Processor	This is used to load the source XML of a document into memory, validate the XML schema, and produce XSLT document views. The InfoPath base processor relies on the Microsoft XML Core Server 5.0.

InfoPath 2003 does not provide support for XML-Formatting Object (XSL-FO), arbitrary, or dynamic XSL files within the InfoPath client, XML Data Reduced (XDR) or document type definitions (DTDs). If support is required for these formats, they can be applied directly to the external XML file.

When you're looking around for your first InfoPath application, many times the easiest place to start is with the paper forms that are being used today. These are generally pretty easy to convert into an InfoPath solution, and the resulting XML makes them highly portable.

Included on the companion CD-ROM (\Code\Chapter 2\Contact Form\ EmployeeContact.xsn) is an example of an employee contact form. We have included the original form as a separate Word document. This initial Word-based form was the standard data collection method until it was converted to InfoPath. Based on the feedback that was received when it was initially deployed, the administration department was looking to add additional emergency contacts, add doctors' names, and include a current picture of the employee. During the rest of the chapter, we will cover how this form is built.

Use the following steps to create a blank design form:

1. Start the InfoPath client from the start menu, as shown in Figure 2.13.

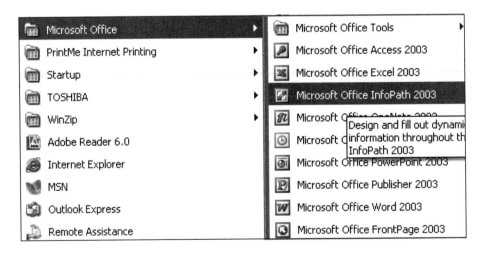

FIGURE 2.13 Starting the InfoPath client.

2. From the Fill Out a Form dialog, select Design a Form, as shown in Figure 2.14.

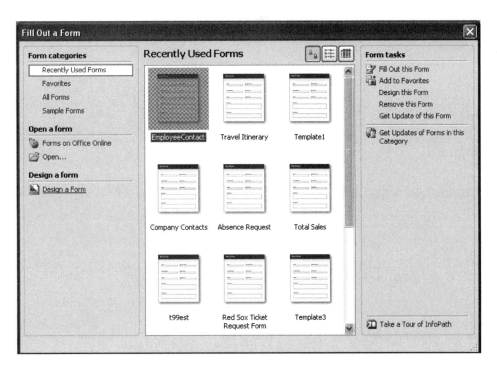

FIGURE 2.14   Selecting the Design a Form.

3. From the Design a Form task pane, select New Blank Form, as shown in Figure 2.15.

Creating Data Sources

The main data source, which stores all data entered into a form and produces the saved XML file, is made up of field groups. Similar to the way file cabinets contain and organize individual files, form fields contain data, and groups contain and organize the fields. For example, company name, address, city, and state can be

FIGURE 2.15 Selecting the New Blank Form.

contained in a "company" group. Here are the simple definitions for field and groups:

> **Field:** An element or attribute in the data source that contains data. If the field is an element, it can contain attribute fields. Fields store the data that is entered into controls.

> **Group:** An element in the data source that can contain fields and other groups. Controls that contain other controls, such as a repeating table and sections, are bound to groups.

You work with fields and groups through the task pane, as shown in Figure 2.16. Controls that are placed on the form are bound to the fields and groups in the data source. In turn, when a field or group is placed on a form, the control is then bound to the data source. This binding allows you to save the data entered into a control. As information is entered into a bound control, the data is saved to the field associated with it.

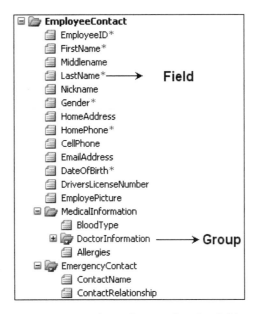

FIGURE 2.16   The task pane showing fields and groups.

Often, the structure of the data source doesn't exactly match the layout of the form, but there are similarities, particularly for groups and fields that are associated with repeating tables, sections, and optional sections. In these cases, a table or section is bound to a group in the data sources, and all the controls in the table or section are bound to fields that are part of the group.

XML Schema

InfoPath makes a very clear distinction between data format and structure. When an end user fills out a form, this data is stored in an external XML document. This output format is initially defined as part of the form definition through the data source for a form template that defines an XML schema structure. Each group in the data source is an XML element that can contain other elements and attributes, but not data. Each field in the data source is an XML element that can contain data. When designing a data source, additional schema details are viewed by using the Details tab of the field's or group's properties, as shown in Figure 2.17.

FIGURE 2.17   Viewing details for the current data source object.

When a form is designed based on an existing XML schema, InfoPath creates a data source that is based entirely on the structure and field names expressed within that document. By default, existing XML schemas are more restrictive than are new blank forms, so that existing fields or groups in that data source can't be modified. In addition, depending on the design of the schema, one may be restricted from adding additional fields or groups to all or part of the data source. By default, when a form is designed based on an existing XML document, InfoPath creates the main data source based on the information contained in that XML document. Essentially, InfoPath treats the XML document as a combination schema and default data. The more detailed the XML document is, the more detailed the resulting data source will be.

As we will see in later chapters, when you're designing a new form that is connected to a database or Web Service, InfoPath builds the data source for the form based on the database or the exposed operations of the Web Service or the database table structure. You can use the resulting InfoPath form to submit and query data to the database or Web Service. The data source must match the database or Web

Service, so existing fields or groups in the data source cannot be modified. In addition, with this limited extensibility, you can only add fields or groups to the root group in the main data source.

Creating Schema Objects

The data source task pane allows you to add, move, reference, and delete fields or groups. Using this task pane, you can add new elements to the schema structure, as shown in Figure 2.18. This dialog box enables you to add a field or group to the document structure using the required parameters given in Table 2.2.

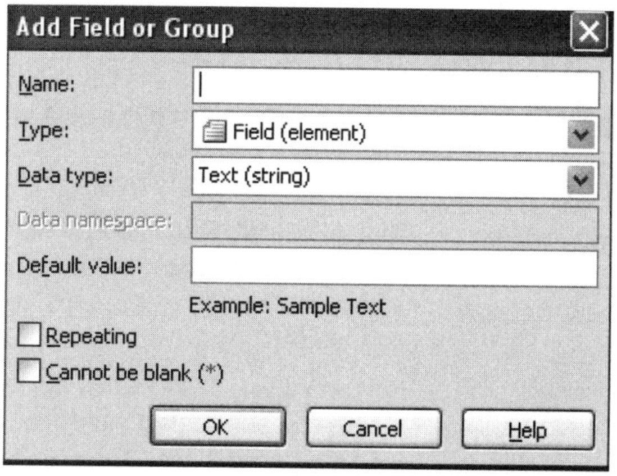

FIGURE 2.18   Adding a new schema object to the data source.

TABLE 2.2   Parameters Available When Adding a New Field or Group to a Data Source

Parameter	Description
Name	The unique name of the field or group. Names cannot contain spaces and must begin with an alphabetic character or an underscore. The only allowable characters within a name are alphanumeric characters, underscores, hyphens, and periods.

$\rightarrow$

Parameter	Description
Type	The type of specific data element. These are element fields (default), attribute fields, groups, and external XML documents and schemas. Fields are used to store data entered into controls. Groups contain fields and are unable to store data.
Data Namespace	Used to define the namespace for groups that are associated with custom Microsoft ActiveX controls.
Data Type	Defines the type of data that a field can store. Data types include text, rich text, whole number, decimal, true/false, hyperlink, date, time, time and date, and picture. Fields are the only element types that can have data types.
Default Value	The initial value that a field will use when the user first opens the form. Fields are the only element types that can contain default values.
Repeating	Determines if a field or group can occur more than once in a form. List controls, repeating sections, repeating tables, and controls that are part of a repeating section or table can be added to repeating field and groups.
Cannot Be Blank	Requires a value entered for a field. Once the checkbox is selected, any control bound to this field will cause a validation error if it is left blank.

As you start to create and change schemas, remember that under the following conditions, the versioning of an InfoPath document can cause data loss:

- If you move, delete, or rename a field or group
- If you change a rich text field to a different data type

As you design schema, you can create matching or referencing fields and groups when you need to store the same type of data in more than one form location. An example is if you need to create a home and work address for an employee. Referencing a field within InfoPath creates a new field whose name and data type are linked and matched to the properties of the original. Both fields are then considered reference fields and a change to one field updates the other automatically.

Reference groups, like reference fields, share the same properties. In addition, they contain the same fields and groups.

For example, Figure 2.19 shows the InfoPath schema when you use the paper employee contact form and add the additional user requirements.

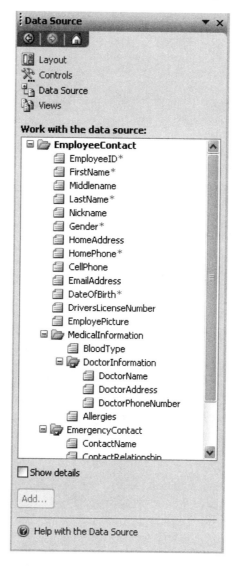

FIGURE 2.19 Viewing the employee contact schema.

As shown in Table 2.3, InfoPath supports a wide variety of XML data types.

TABLE 2.3   XML Types Supported by InfoPath

InfoPath Type	Description
Text	String
Rich Text	XHTML that can include formatting
Whole Number	Integer
Decimal	Double
True/False	Boolean
Hyperlink	Any Uniform Resource Indicator (URI)
Date	Date
Time	Time
Date and Time	Date/Time
Picture or File Attachment	Base 64 Binary
Custom (Complex Type)	An external XML namespace

Laying Out a Form

As with Web page design, InfoPath is based on the idea of layout tables are a way of organizing and designing forms. *Layout tables* define the boundaries of your page grid and help line things up on the page. These are used like normal tables within a Web page, except for two main differences. First, a layout table is designed to support a document layout; it's not for data presentation. Second, by default, a layout table doesn't have a visible border. When in design mode, the borders are visible as a set of dashed lines that provide a visual border. When a user is filling in a form, these borders become invisible. The goal is to provide a better user experience during form entry.

Once the visual structure or layout is created, the designer can add text, fields, controls, sections, and tables that the end user uses to fill in the form. In addition to layout tables, both repeating and optional sections can be added and can act as containers for controls and text.

The layout task pane, as shown in Figure 2.20, provides a collection of drag-and-drop layout tables and sections that can be placed on a blank form. If none of the predefined tables and sections meets the designer's needs, a custom table can be used. This allows the designer to format the exact rows and columns that are needed. Layout tables can be edited like any other Office application, either through selecting either the table menu or a right-click on the table properties.

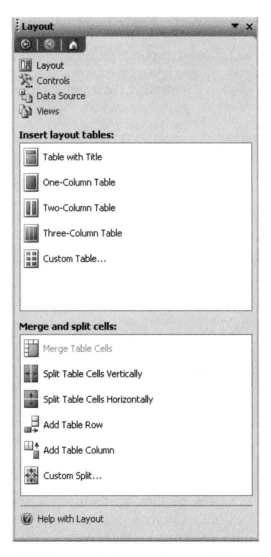

FIGURE 2.20 The layout task pane within InfoPath.

To keep your formatting simple, it's typically a good idea to break your form into sections with a separate layout table for each of the main sections. This allows the designer to reposition the individual layout tables more easily and will automatically align them to the desired layout. This method allows designers to create complex forms, while remaining free from the restrictions of cell resizing, splitting, and merging adjacent table rows and columns.

Placing Controls

Once the table layout is completed, the designer can start to build the data entry portion of the form. This is done by dragging the schema fields or groups onto the InfoPath workspace. During this process, InfoPath attempts to match the specific data type to a control type that makes sense for the data entry needs. Once the field is dropped on the form, the control and the form are bound together. For example, dropping a string field will result in a text box field. You can verify that your schema is properly bound by hovering over the control and seeing the green light, as shown in Figure 2.21.

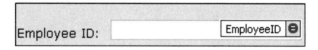

FIGURE 2.21 Validating that a field is bound correctly.

Often, the default rendered field will provide the appropriate control for the specific schema type. However, you can change the specific type of control if the rendered control is not appropriate. For example, you might have a text box that needs to contain a list of choices, so it will make better sense to create a drop-down list. This can be done by right-clicking on the control and selecting the Change To option, as shown in Figure 2.22.

Creating Views

Within InfoPath, a *view* is defined as a form-specific display setting that is saved with the form template. Views are applied to the form data when the form is being filled out. During the initial rendering process, InfoPath applies XSLT to the underlying data source to transform and present the structured form data. By default, each InfoPath form has a default view called View 1 that is created during the initial design process.

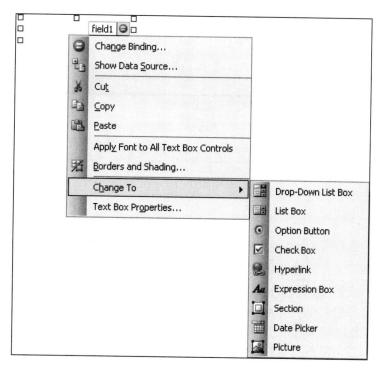

FIGURE 2.22   Changing one control to another.

During the design process, form designers can create multiple custom views for their forms. Creating custom views provides several benefits. For example, if a form is too long or complex for everyone in the company, you can move various parts of the form into different custom views. Also, you can present important sections of information within certain views. Finally, views can be combined with user Roles to define a security boundary to protect data.

To create custom views, use the Views task pane during design mode, as shown in Figure 2.23. Users completing a form can access the form's View menu. When a user switches views, the form's underlying data is not changed in any way; only the presentation of the form and the amount of data displayed changes.

In addition to custom views, you can create print views for forms. By default, if a user selects the Print command when filling out a form, the current view is printed. Form designers can also designate any existing view as a print view and specify custom printing options that include headers, footers, and page orientation

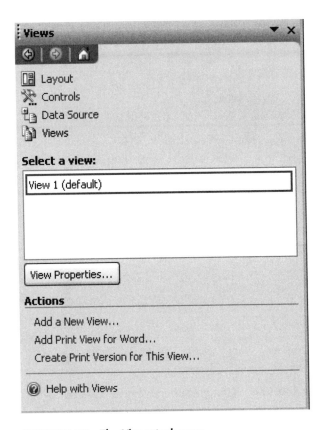

FIGURE 2.23   The Views task pane.

using the dialog box, as shown in Figure 2.24. When users fill out and print out a form that contains a designated print view, InfoPath will use the alternate print view instead of the current view to print the form.

Publishing Forms

After finalizing the form's data structure, design, and view, you can then deploy it. We will cover each of the possible options in more depth during Chapter 10, but for now, we'll introduce the InfoPath Publishing Wizard, as shown in Figure 2.25. This wizard allows you to either save or publish the completed form to a shared location where it becomes available to end users to complete and submit.

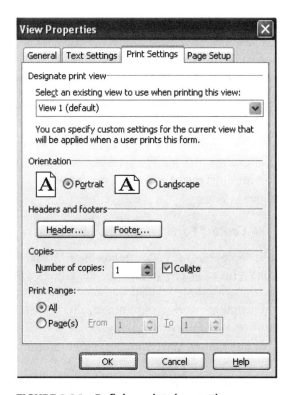

FIGURE 2.24 Defining print view settings.

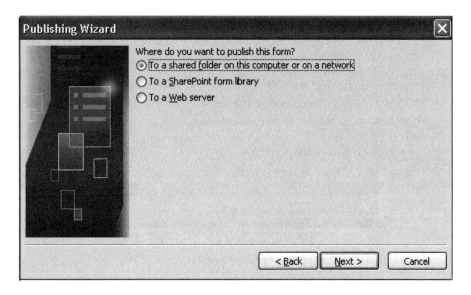

FIGURE 2.25 The Publishing Wizard for distributing InfoPath forms.

The Publishing Wizard allows form distribution to:

- **Create a form template library based on WSS.**   A form library is a specialized SharePoint library that can store, distribute, and collect a group of InfoPath forms. When users select Fill-Out this Form, a blank InfoPath form is rendered and opened. This form is based on the template associated with the form library.
- **Save the form template to a Web server or network file share.**   These shared network locations provide file level access to the InfoPath solution file, but don't provide any type of collection mechanism.

Testing the Employee Contact Form

Once a form is deployed, InfoPath extends the end-user experience to include a variety of options. These options are designed to enhance the experience and provide features that are commonly needed by business users. In later chapters, we will cover how these options work programmatically; however, it is important to review how these features work within the IDE.

Export to Excel

When users are filling out a form, the Export to Excel feature on the File menu allows them to save either their current InfoPath view or several related form views into an Excel spreadsheet. This export wizard (shown in Figure 2.26) allows users to analyze and work with the collected data using the aggregation and analysis features of Excel. Excel provides the ideal solution for analyzing and aggregating data.

InfoPath fully supports digital signatures. If any of the documents that you want to export to Excel contain a digital signature, you must remove the signature before you can complete the export. Digital signatures are considered an authentication that the document or data has not been altered from its original state. The minute that you export the document, this invalidates the signature on the specific documents. However, once the export is complete, you can guarantee authenticity by reapplying the InfoPath signatures in addition to signing the Excel document.

InfoPath uses XML signatures to enable a form to be digitally signed. The certificate used to create the signature confirms that the form originated from the signer and that the signature has not been altered.

FIGURE 2.26   The Export to Excel Wizard.

Export to Web Page

When users are filling out a form, the Export to Web feature on the File menu (shown in Figure 2.27) allows them to save their current form view as a single file Web page in Mail Enabled HTML (MHTML) format. This is an HTML document formatted for Multipurpose Internet Mail Extensions (MIME). This content type allows the message to contain an HTML page and other resources such as documents, pictures, and applets directly in the MIME hierarchy of the message. The data is referenced through links from the HTML content and used to complete the document rendering. The main benefit of MHTML is that all links within the document are rendered locally, and this means that there is no network traffic and that documents can be used offline. The ability to export to a Web page is an important feature for interacting with users that don't have InfoPath installed.

FIGURE 2.27   Exporting to a single file Web page.

If you review the sample file found in the Chapter 2 sample directory (\Code\ Chapter 2\Contact Form\EmployeeContact_View 1.MHTML) on the CD-ROM, you can see that MHTML defines the naming of objects that are normally referred to by URLs as a means of aggregating these resources together. Two MIME headers, Content-Base and Content-Location, are defined to resolve the references to the additional content stored locally or in related body parts. Content-Base provides that absolute URLs which appear in other MIME headers and in HTML documents don't contain any base HTML elements. Content-Location specifies the URL corresponds to the content of the body part that contains the header. This format easily compresses the data into a single file structure that is viewable from a Web browser. It is important to remember that this is a read-only version of the form and that this type of form-editing requires the InfoPath client.

Send to Mail Recipient

Often, users who are completing an InfoPath form need to send a copy of the form to another user. One way of doing this is to use the Send to Mail Recipient option on the File menu. This allows end users to share forms with other users by sending InfoPath forms in a body of an email message or as an attachment, as shown in Figure 2.28. If users don't have the InfoPath client application, they will receive the form in a read-only mode.

File → Save

When you save a form that you have filled out, you are saving it in an external .xml file. This file contains the data saved into the schema structure designed for the data source and a pointer to the form template to view and edit the file. The XML file contains only the data representation and defined structure. For example, when the employee contact form is completed and saved, the XML file contains the data shown in Listing 2.1.

LISTING 2.1   Employee Contact Form

```
<?xml version="1.0" encoding="utf-8"?>
<?mso-infoPathSolution solutionVersion="1.0.0.3"
productVersion="11.0.4920" PIVersion="0.9.0.0"
href="file:///D:\Programming%20Microsoft%20InfoPath%20A%20Developers%20
Guide\Chapter%202\Samples\Contact%20Form\EmployeeContact.xsn" ?>
```

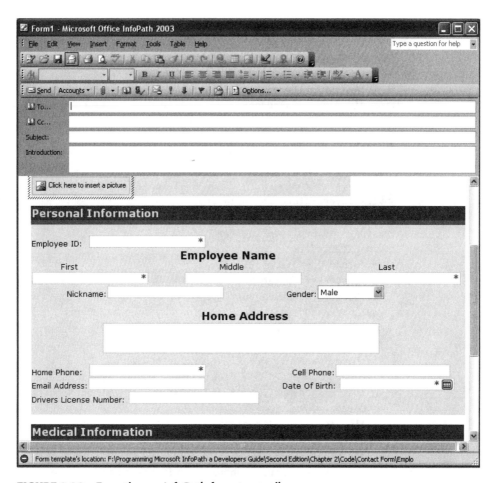

FIGURE 2.28 Exporting an InfoPath form to email.

```
<?mso-application progid="InfoPath.Document"?><my:EmployeeContact
xmlns:my="http://schemas.microsoft.com/office/infopath/2003/myXSD/2003-
05-17T01:23:36" xml:lang="en-us">
  <my:EmployeeID>1234</my:EmployeeID>
  <my:FirstName>Thomas</my:FirstName>
  <my:Middlename>Jared</my:Middlename>
  <my:LastName>Robbins</my:LastName>
```

```
  <my:Nickname>Tommy</my:Nickname>
  <my:Gender>Male</my:Gender>
  <my:HomeAddress><div xmlns="http://www.w3.org/1999/xhtml">123
Anywhere Street</div>
<div xmlns="http://www.w3.org/1999/xhtml">Bedford NH
03110</div></my:HomeAddress>
  <my:HomePhone>603-456-7891</my:HomePhone>
  <my:CellPhone>603-478-9612</my:CellPhone>
  <my:EmailAddress>trobbins@microsoft.com</my:EmailAddress>
  <my:DateOfBirth>1965-01-31</my:DateOfBirth>
  <my:DriversLicenseNumber>123-98-6541-985</my:DriversLicenseNumber>
  <my:EmployeePicture xsi:nil="true"
xmlns:xsi="http://www.w3.org/2001/XMLSchema-
instance"></my:EmployeePicture>
  <my:MedicalInformation>
    <my:BloodType>O+</my:BloodType>
    <my:DoctorInformation>
    <my:DoctorName>Sally Sue</my:DoctorName>
    <my:DoctorAddress>NE Medical Bldg</my:DoctorAddress>
    <my:DoctorPhoneNumber>603-421-8465</my:DoctorPhoneNumber>
  </my:DoctorInformation><my:DoctorInformation>
    <my:DoctorName>Joe Franklin</my:DoctorName>
    <my:DoctorAddress>123 MedicalCenter</my:DoctorAddress>
    <my:DoctorPhoneNumber>603-412-7123</my:DoctorPhoneNumber>
  </my:DoctorInformation>
  <my:Allergies></my:Allergies>
</my:MedicalInformation>
  <my:EmergencyContact>
    <my:ContactName>Denise Robbins</my:ContactName>
    <my:ContactRelationship>Spouse</my:ContactRelationship>
    <my:ContactAddress>123 Anywhere St</my:ContactAddress>
    <my:ContactPhone>603-456-7891</my:ContactPhone>
  </my:EmergencyContact><my:EmergencyContact>
    <my:ContactName>Marvin Robbins</my:ContactName>
    <my:ContactRelationship>Parent</my:ContactRelationship>
    <my:ContactAddress>2910 Huntingdon Ave</my:ContactAddress>
    <my:ContactPhone>410-987-4561</my:ContactPhone>
  </my:EmergencyContact>
</my:employeecontact>
```

Form Submission

One of the things we will cover in Chapters 4 and 5 is how InfoPath can submit directly to a Web Services, SQL, or Access database. This can be done through a direct connection or through a scripted execution model that provides additional validation and enhancement scenarios around an XML structure.

FORM TEMPLATE ARCHITECTURE

Each InfoPath solution is saved and distributed through a solution file. An InfoPath solution file is saved in the file system with an .xsn extension. This template file is actually several files compressed and stored in a cabinet (.cab) file format. This set of known files is combined to provide the necessary semantic information for the InfoPath client to render within a form. When starting, InfoPath interrogates the .xsn solution to retrieve information about views, menu options, data structure, and forms. The files stored in the template file are designed in a hub and spoke relationship, with the form definition file providing the single entry point. The form definition file stored in the cabinet file uses an .xsf extension and is, by default, named manifest.xsf. This file consists of XML documents that use the namespace and associated schema of http://schemas.microsoft.com/office/infopath/2003/SolutionDefinition. Table 2.4 lists the types of files contained within the solution file and their extensions.

To run an InfoPath form, you first load the XML instance associated with it. The information in the form definition file, as shown in Listing 2.2, allows InfoPath to display XML data and to define the associated user interface and interactivity. During the loading procedure, the XML data instance has an XML processing instruction (PI) that determines the type of application and points to the location of the InfoPath solution to use when loading the instance data.

LISTING 2.2   InfoPath XML processing instructions

```
<?xml version="1.0" encoding="utf-8"?>
<?mso-infoPathSolution solutionVersion="1.0.0.3"
productVersion="11.0.4920" PIVersion="0.9.0.0"
href="file:///D:\Programming%20Microsoft%20InfoPath%20A%20Developers%20
Guide\Chapter%202\Samples\Contact%20Form\EmployeeContact.xsn" ?>
<?mso-application progid="InfoPath.Document"?>
<my:employeecontact
xmlns:my="http://schemas.microsoft.com/office/infopath/2003/myxsd/2003-
05-17t01:23:36" xml:lang="en-us">
```

TABLE 2.4   The Information Contained in an InfoPath Solution File

File Type	Extension	Description
Template Definition	.xsf	This is an InfoPath-generated XML file that serves as the entry point. It contains all the information about all the other files and components within a form template. This files acts as the packing list or manifest for the solution.
Schema	.xsd	The XML schema file that is used to determine the types, names, and constraints of a valid document.
View	.xsl	The presentation logic files that are used to present, view, and transform the data contained in the XML document files.
XML Sample File	.xml	An XML file that contains the default data for fields when a new file is created based on the document class described in the form template.
Presentation	.htm, .gif, .xml	Files that are combined with the view files to create the custom user interface. This also includes the default XML sample file that is used to populate default values.
Business Logic	.js, .vbs	The script files (either JavaScript or VB Script) that contain the programming code. This code implements specific editing restrictions, data validation, event handlers, and data flow.
Template	.xml	The editing controls that are used in design mode when users are creating and filling out a form.
Binary	.dll, .exe	Custom Component Object Model (COM) components or managed assemblies that provide additional business logic.
Packaging	.xsn	A compressed file format that packages all the form templates into one file with an .xsn extension.

THE TEMPLATE DEFINITION FILE (MANIFEST.XSF)

The template definition file, as shown in Listing 2.3, is the main entry point for all InfoPath solutions. This file contains the pointers and references that are needed to both run and manage solutions. This structured XML document contains a variety of elements that define the behavior and functionality of the InfoPath document.

LISTING 2.3 The Structured XML Format of the Template Definition File

```
<xsf:xdocumentclass name= '...'   ...global metadata for the InfoPath
form...>
  <xsf:taskpane .../>
  <xsf:views default="...">
    <xsf:view name="..." ...    >
      view XSLT, toolbar, and menu definitions, etc,
      <xsf:editing>
        define editing services for this view
      </xsf:editing>
    </xsf:view>
    ... other views
  </xsf:views>
  <xsf:applicationParameters ...>
    properties specific to design mode
  </xsf:applicationParameters>
  <xsf:dataObjects>
    auxiliary DOMs used for binding to view controls, etc.
  </xsf:dataObjects>
  <xsf: documentSchemas>
    Schema declarations and locations for offline usage
  </xsf: documentSchemas>
  <xsf:scripts>
    script blocks, command definitions, accelerator bindings, event
bindings, etc.
  </xsf:scripts>

  <xsf:validationConstraints>
    declarative validation constraints for XMLDOM changes
  </xsf:validationConstraints>
  <xsf:errorMessages>
    declaratively override validation error messages returned by
Microsoft XML Core Services (MSXML)
  </xsf:errorMessages>
```

```
<xsf:domEventHandlers>
  script-based event handlers for XMLDOM changes and validation, etc.
</xsf:domEventHandlers>
<xsf:importParameters>
  aggregation parameters for merging multiple forms of this class
</xsf:importParameters>
<xsf:listProperties>
  <xsf:fields>
    list of properties to be promoted when form is saved in a
Microsoft® Windows® SharePoint™   Services form library
  </xsf:fields>
</xsf:listProperties>
<xsf:submit>
  routing, data transport information for submitting form's data to a
server process
</xsf:submit>

<xsf:query>
  routing, data transport information for loading form's data
dynamically from a server process
</xsf:query>
<xsf:fileNew>
  <xsf:initialXMLDocument caption="..." href="..."   /> XML data to
be used for File/New
</xsf:fileNew>

<xsf:package>
  <xsf:fileList>
    list of all files used by the form
  </xsf:fileList>
</xsf:package>
</xsf:xdocumentclass>
```

Template Customization

There are two ways to alter an InfoPath template file outside of the InfoPath environment. The first way is declaratively. In this method, you are opening and customizing the template files in an editor and changing the elements, attributes, and values of the files manually. The second way to alter templates is programmatically. In this method, you are writing code using a scripting language or managed code using Visual Studio 2003 in conjunction with the InfoPath object model or COM components to extend or enhance the template behavior.

Here is a list of typical declarative customization:

- Modifying the template schema
- Modifying view files in design mode
- Modifying the form definition or manifest file
- Extending built-in toolbars, menu bars, buttons, or a task pane
- Creating the package list
- Using specific event and error handlers
- Connecting to a back-end service such as a SQL database, Web Service, or WSS

Here is a list of typical programmatic customization:

- Enhancing document life-cycle processing
- Enhancing data validation
- Adding custom error processing
- Implementing custom data routing or data submission

InfoPath provides built-in facilities for custom programmability. These facilities include the following:

- Accessing the InfoPath object model
- Modifying the source XML document
- Using custom COM components
- Connecting programmatically to databases, Web Services, or other back-end systems

SUMMARY

ON THE CD

This chapter provided the core plumbing overview of what is in the InfoPath environment. This included the differences between form design and runtime, and how XML is the core component of an InfoPath solution. Review the employee contact form on the CD-ROM (\Code\Chapter 2\Contact Form\SampleData.xml) as an example of some of the capabilities of an InfoPath solution. This sample didn't use any of the advanced customization features that can be done through InfoPath. We will cover those in the next chapter and look at more detailed examples of how you can use InfoPath to generate XML schemas that define services. In later chapters, we will start tying these together with advanced coverage of integration with Web Services, and we'll start to define how more fully how InfoPath fits within the SOA environment.

3 Generating XML Forms

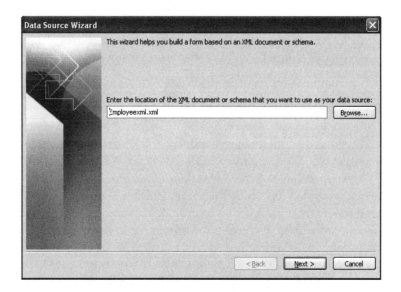

INTRODUCTION

XML has become the industry-standard format for data interchange and is the core-enabling technology of InfoPath. One reason XML was successful in gaining industry acceptance is its self-describing nature. Unlike HTML, XML isn't based on a set of predefined tags and data structures. XML documents can contain any type of structured data elements delimited by a set of descriptive tags that act as both the record boundaries and built-in data documentation. When viewed together, the combination of the hierarchical data elements enclosed by descriptive tags defines a vocabulary of data.

Unfortunately, the lack of any predefined data elements and structure can inherently make an XML file unpredictable. Seeing this as a problem, the industry standards body, the World Wide Web Consortium (W3C), created a new XML-based language for describing these documents. The goal of this specification was to provide a way to describe XML documents and structures, support XML namespaces, promote reusability, enable inheritance, and provide predictability. The result of this was an XML-based vocabulary to describe XML-based vocabularies.

The industry recommendation that describes the structures of this language is broken into three parts: XML Schema Part 0: Primer, XML Schema Part 1: Structures, and XML Schema Part 2: Data Types. Using this standard as the starting point, this chapter covers how you can use InfoPath to develop form-based solutions that provide data validation, formatting, and rules support using XML-based data sources. Also, this chapter starts to look at the InfoPath object model that enables programmatic access and control of solution files.

WHAT IS AN XML SCHEMA?

Schemas describe an object and any of the interrelationships that exist within a data structure. There are many different types of schema definitions. Relational databases such as SQL Server use schemas to contain the table names and column keys, and provide a repository for trigger and stored procedures. Within class definitions, developers define schemas to provide the Object-Oriented (OO) interface to properties, methods, and events. Within an XML data structure, schemas describe both the object definition and the relationship of data elements and attributes. Regardless of the context that schemas are used in, they provide the data representation and serve as an abstracted data layer. Schemas define the object design that establishes the implementation framework for a particular object.

XML is fundamentally a meta-language used to create and describe other languages. Extensible Schema Definitions (XSD) is an example of an XML-based modeling language defined by the W3C for creating XML schemas. Represented in XML, XSD defines and enforces the legal building blocks for formatting and validating an XML file. InfoPath stores completed forms as XML documents based on the XSD defined during form design.

Creating a Data Source

The creation of a new InfoPath solution generates a variety of supporting files. One of these, one probably the most important, is the XSD file. This schema file is stored as part of the InfoPath solution file (*.xsn). Anytime InfoPath accesses this schema, it is done through a data source. The data source is responsible for storing all the data entered into a form. It is structured as fields, attributes, and groups. Within the data source, a group is a set of XML elements that serve as a container for fields and attributes. When an InfoPath solution is opened, the form binds controls to the data source based on the defined data type and uses this to save the field-level data.

Listing 3.1 shows a sample XML file that describes an employee (it is also available on the companion CD-ROM, in \Code\Chapter 3\EmployeeInformation\Employeexml.xml).

LISTING 3.1   An XML File That Describes an Employee

```
<?xml version="1.0" encoding="utf-8"?>
<employeeinfo>
<prefix>Mr</prefix>
<firstname>Thomas</firstname>
<lastname>Robbins</lastname>
<suffix></suffix>
<email>trobbins@microsoft.com</email>
<employeeid>191912</employeeid>
<costcenter>1200</costcenter>
<employeeurl>http://www.company.com/trobbins</employeeurl>
</employeeinfo>
```

Using InfoPath, we can create a data source based on this XML that is defined within the form template file. Within InfoPath, select the Design a new form option, as shown in Figure 3.1, from the Design a Form task pane.

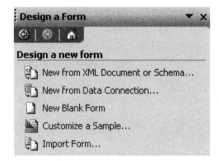

FIGURE 3.1   Selecting the data source for a new XML-based form.

Using this wizard, we can specify the location of the XML file that we will use to create a form, as shown in Figure 3.2.

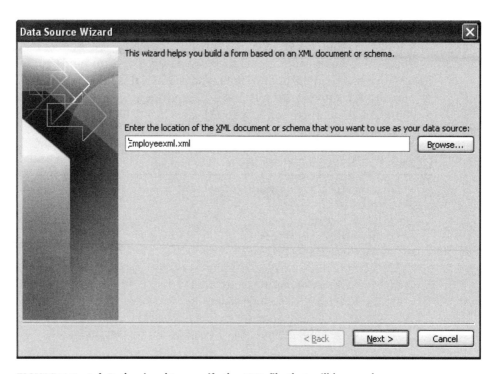

FIGURE 3.2   InfoPath wizard to specify the XML file that will be used.

Using the structure of the employee XML file, InfoPath infers and implements an XSD schema based on the structure of this file. After the creation of the XSD, InfoPath form designers are given an option to assign the XML values as the default global values, as shown in Figure 3.3. These values become built into the form template, and any new forms are automatically assigned these initial values.

FIGURE 3.3   Defining a set of global defaults.

The InfoPath solution file contains a variety of default files. To see these, extract the individual InfoPath files into a file directory from the solution using the "Extract Form Files" function available on the File menu. The extracted file schema.xsd, shown in Listing 3.2 and provided on the companion CD-ROM, contains the default schema. (\Code\Chapter 3\EmployeeInformation\Extracted is a file directory that contains the extracted files.)

ON THE CD

LISTING 3.2 The schema.xsd File Defined Within the InfoPath Solution

```xml
<?xml version="1.0" encoding="UTF-8" standalone="no"?>
<xsd:schema
xmlns:my="http://schemas.microsoft.com/office/infopath/2003/myXSD/2005-
07-04T00:07:01" xmlns:xsd="http://www.w3.org/2001/XMLSchema">
    <xsd:element name="employeeinfo">
        <xsd:complexType>
            <xsd:all>
                <xsd:element ref="prefix" minOccurs="0"/>
                <xsd:element ref="firstname" minOccurs="0"/>
                <xsd:element ref="lastname" minOccurs="0"/>
                <xsd:element ref="suffix" minOccurs="0"/>
                <xsd:element ref="email" minOccurs="0"/>
                <xsd:element ref="employeeid" minOccurs="0"/>
                <xsd:element ref="costcenter" minOccurs="0"/>
                <xsd:element ref="employeeurl" minOccurs="0"/>
            </xsd:all>
            <xsd:anyAttribute processContents="lax" namespace="http:
//www.w3.org/XML/1998/namespace"/>
        </xsd:complexType>
    </xsd:element>
    <xsd:element name="prefix" type="xsd:string"/>
    <xsd:element name="firstname" type="xsd:string"/>
    <xsd:element name="lastname" type="xsd:string"/>
    <xsd:element name="suffix" type="xsd:string"/>
    <xsd:element name="email" type="xsd:string"/>
    <xsd:element name="employeeid" type="xsd:string"/>
    <xsd:element name="costcenter" type="xsd:string"/>
    <xsd:element name="employeeurl" type="xsd:string"/>
</xsd:schema>
```

XSD Schema Definitions

All XSD schemas contain a single top-level element. Underneath this element is the schema element that contains either simple or complex type elements. Simple elements contain text-only information. A complex element is a grouping element that acts as a container for other elements and attributes. There are four types of complex elements: empty elements, elements that contain other elements, elements that contain only text, and elements that contain both other elements and text.

The XML employee file that we created earlier was generated using Notepad and then imported into InfoPath. InfoPath then took the XML output file and created an XSD representation that matched the format and structure defined in the XML file. Let's create the same schema representation manually using XSD. Instead of having InfoPath generate the XSD based on a XML data file, we will provide the exact schema representation that we want InfoPath to use.

ON THE CD

The result, shown in Listing 3.3, is available on the companion CD-ROM (\Code\Chapter 3\ExtendableSchema\defaultemployee.xsd). One thing you will notice, as we will see later in this chapter, is that this schema is not extensible and we will need to change the attributes to allow this.

LISTING 3.3 XSD Representing an Employee

```
<?xml version="1.0"?>
<dis><xsd:schema xmlns:xsd="http://www.w3.org/2001/XMLSchema">
<xsd:element name="prefix" type="xsd:string"/>
<xsd:element name="firstname" type="xsd:string"/>
<xsd:element name="lastname" type="xsd:string"/>
<xsd:element name="suffix" type="xsd:string"/>
<xsd:element name="email" type="xsd:string"/>
<xsd:element name="employeeid" type="xsd:string"/>
<xsd:element name="employeeurl" type="xsd:string"/>
<xsd:element name="costcenter" type="xsd:string"/>

<xsd:element name="employeeinfo">
<xsd:complexType>
  <xsd:sequence>
    <xsd:element ref="prefix"  minOccurs="0"/>
    <xsd:element ref="firstname"/>
    <xsd:element ref="lastname"/>
    <xsd:element ref="suffix" minOccurs="0"/>
    <xsd:element ref="email"/>
    <xsd:element ref="employeeid"/>
    <xsd:element ref="employeeurl"/>
    <xsd:element ref="costcenter"/>
  </xsd:sequence>
</xsd:complexType>
</xsd:element>
</xsd:schema>
```

In reviewing Listing 3.3, you will notice that the simple types contain the individual elements or fields that describe the employee object. These are then grouped into a complex type (employeeinfo) that provides the entire object representation.

Extending Schemas with Validation

XSD enables schemas to include more than just simple object definitions that define structure and context. When you use XSD, a schema can provide validation on both elements and attributes. Table 3.1 shows a number of validations that can be defined within XSD and that can be applied to XML documents.

TABLE 3.1   Types of Validation Supported by XSD

Validation Type	Description
Data Type	Schemas can control the expected data type of an element or attribute.
Constraints	Schemas can limit the allowed values of an element to include length, pattern, or minimum or maximum value.
Cardinality	Schemas can control the number of specific element occurrences. For example, a specific element may be allowed only once, or one or more times within an attribute or element.
Choice	Schemas can limit the available choices within a selection list.
Sequence	Schemas can define the order that elements are used in. For example, a business name may require multiple address types.
Defaults	Schemas can define a default value that is used when no other value is specified. This is the XSD feature that InfoPath uses when defining global default values.

To create validation rules within a schema, you use a simple type element that defines the specific validation type. The following XSD snippet, available on the companion CD-ROM (in \Code\Chapter 3\Timesheet\schema\restriction.xsd), shows how to force a validation rule on the employeeurl that enables inheritance based on a pattern restriction.

ON THE CD

```
<xsd:simpletype name="weburl">
  <xsd:restriction base="xsd:string">
  <xsd:pattern value="http://.*"/>
  </xsd:restriction>
</xsd:simpletype>
```

Once the simple type definition is completed, this then becomes a base data type webURL defined within the document that enforces an HTTP pattern. To apply the constraint on the employeeurl field, change the data type to the newly defined simple type, as shown here:

```
<xsd:element name="employeeurl" type="weburl"/>
```

Often, XML documents contain key required fields necessary to define an object reference. Within the employee file, this includes first name, last name, and employee id. Enforcing cardinality within a data structure is done through the instance element. This element can define either a minimum or maximum amount of times that the specific element must exist, as you can see here:

```
<xsd:simpletype name="requiredstring">
  <xsd:restriction base="xsd:string">
  <xsd:minLength value="1"/>
  </xsd:restriction>
</xsd:simpletype>
```

One of the built-in benefits of XSD is inheritance. This enables any of the base elements that are defined within the employee schema to inherit from a new derived base type of requiredString, as shown here:

```
<xsd:element name="firstname" type="requiredstring"/>
<xsd:element name="lastname" type="requiredString"/>
<xsd:element name="employeeid" type="requiredstring"/>
```

ON THE CD

Using the newly defined XSD, InfoPath can define a data source based on the constrained schema, as shown in Figure 3.4. Contained on the CD-ROM (in \Code\ Chapter 3\Timesheet\schema\restriction.xsd) is the full text of the base XSD schemas that are defined in this example.

FIGURE 3.4   The data source of an InfoPath form using the constrained schema.

What Are Namespaces?

Namespaces are an optional set of declarations at the top of an XSD file. They provide a unique set of identifiers that associate a set of XML elements and attributes together. The original namespace in XML specification was released by the W3C as a URI-based way to differentiate various XML vocabularies. This was then extended under the XML schema specification to include schema components rather than just single elements and attributes. The unique identifier was redefined as a URI that doesn't point to a physical location but, rather, to a security boundary that the schema author owns. The namespace is defined through two declarations: the XML schema namespace and the target namespace. The xmlns attribute uniquely defines a schema namespace and is then divided into three sections:

xmlns Keyword: This is defined first and separated from the target namespace prefix by a colon.

Prefix: This defines the abbreviated unique name of a namespace and is used when you are declaring all elements and attributes. Both xmlns and xml are reserved keywords that can't be used as valid prefixes.

Definition: This unique URI identifies the namespace and contains the security boundary owned by the schema author.

Anytime an xmlns attribute is defined within an XML document, any element or attribute that belongs to that namespace must contain the prefix. In addition to custom defined, a variety of standard namespace definitions are available for use within schema structures, as shown here:

XML Schema Namespace: xmlns:xsd=http://www.w3.org/2001/XMLschema.

XSLT Transform Namespace: xmlns:xsl=http://www.w3.org/1999/XSL/ Transform .

InfoPath namespace: xmlns:my=http://schemas.microsoft.com/office/ infopath/2003

The target namespace attribute identifies the schema components described within the current document. This attribute acts as a shortcut method for describing the elements in the current schema. There are three variations in how the namespace and target namespace attributes can be combined within a valid XSD document. The full text of each approach, including the full XSD that is defined for each approach, is on the CD-ROM.

ON THE CD

Approach 1 is where there is no default namespace. (You can find the full text of this approach on the companion CD-ROM in \Code\Chapter 3\Namespace\ Approach1.xsd.) If there is no default namespace, then the XSD must qualify both the XML schema and the target namespace, as shown in Figure 3.5.

ON THE CD

With no default namespace, all schema components are explicitly qualified, including components in the target namespace. Even though it may look a little cluttered, all elements have a consistent, defined set of references.

Approach 2 is where you define a default XML schema. (You can find the full text of this approach on the companion CD-ROM in \Code\Chapter 3\Namespace\ Approach2.xsd.) Defining a default schema allows you to remove default reference elements within an XSD, as shown in Figure 3.6.

ON THE CD

The default assigned namespace is valid for all XML-defined XML schema definitions. This approach becomes more limited than the other approaches as the complexity of a schema document increases; however, this approach is the easiest of the three both to read and understand within a schema document.

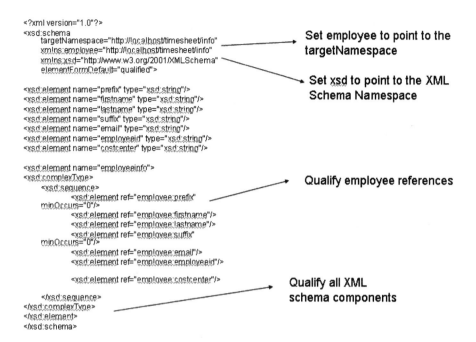

```
<?xml version="1.0"?>
<xsd:schema
    targetNamespace="http://localhost/timesheet/info"
    xmlns:employee="http://localhost/timesheet/info"
    xmlns:xsd="http://www.w3.org/2001/XMLSchema"
    elementFormDefault="qualified">

<xsd:element name="prefix" type="xsd:string"/>
<xsd:element name="firstname" type="xsd:string"/>
<xsd:element name="lastname" type="xsd:string"/>
<xsd:element name="suffix" type="xsd:string"/>
<xsd:element name="email" type="xsd:string"/>
<xsd:element name="employeeid" type="xsd:string"/>
<xsd:element name="costcenter" type="xsd:string"/>

<xsd:element name="employeeinfo">
<xsd:complexType>
    <xsd:sequence>
            <xsd:element ref="employee:prefix"
    minOccurs="0"/>
            <xsd:element ref="employee:firstname"/>
            <xsd:element ref="employee:lastname"/>
            <xsd:element ref="employee:suffix"
    minOccurs="0"/>
            <xsd:element ref="employee:email"/>
            <xsd:element ref="employee:employeeid"/>

            <xsd:element ref="employee:costcenter"/>

    </xsd:sequence>
</xsd:complexType>
</xsd:element>
</xsd:schema>
```

Set employee to point to the targetNamespace

Set xsd to point to the XML Schema Namespace

Qualify employee references

Qualify all XML schema components

FIGURE 3.5 Fully qualifying the XML schema and target namespace.

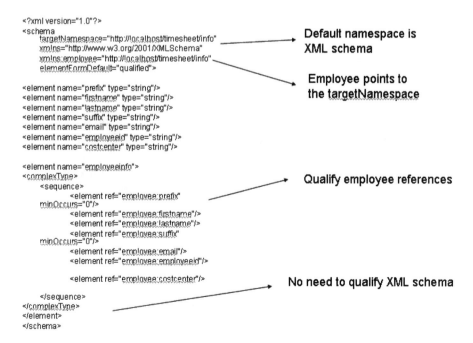

```
<?xml version="1.0"?>
<schema
    targetNamespace="http://localhost/timesheet/info"
    xmlns="http://www.w3.org/2001/XMLSchema"
    xmlns:employee="http://localhost/timesheet/info"
    elementFormDefault="qualified">

<element name="prefix" type="string"/>
<element name="firstname" type="string"/>
<element name="lastname" type="string"/>
<element name="suffix" type="string"/>
<element name="email" type="string"/>
<element name="employeeid" type="string"/>
<element name="costcenter" type="string"/>

<element name="employeeinfo">
<complexType>
    <sequence>
            <element ref="employee:prefix"
    minOccurs="0"/>
            <element ref="employee:firstname"/>
            <element ref="employee:lastname"/>
            <element ref="employee:suffix"
    minOccurs="0"/>
            <element ref="employee:email"/>
            <element ref="employee:employeeid"/>

            <element ref="employee:costcenter"/>

    </sequence>
</complexType>
</element>
</schema>
```

Default namespace is XML schema

Employee points to the targetNamespace

Qualify employee references

No need to qualify XML schema

FIGURE 3.6 Defining a default schema.

Approach 3 is where you qualify the XML schema. (You can find the full text of this approach on the companion CD-ROM in \Code\Chapter 3\Namespace\ Approach3.xsd.) If both the target namespace and default namespace are defined, you don't need to qualify the employee reference, as shown in Figure 3.7.

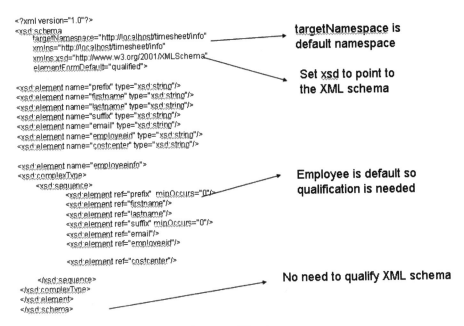

FIGURE 3.7   An XML schema with no qualification.

This scenario is actually the mirror image of Approach 1, where the target namespace is also defined as the default. When you use Approach 3, all portions of the XSD must be fully qualified within a document. This is by far the easiest approach for maintaining readability, but it becomes a bit cluttered as additional namespaces are added, as we will see later in this chapter as we create more complex schema definitions.

Unlocking the InfoPath Schema

Regardless of the design pattern, XML schemas imported into InfoPath are by default read only, as you may remember from our earlier discussion of the employee schema. This is a design feature of InfoPath that preserves the integrity and intent of the original schema definition. Within InfoPath, this prevents the form designer from initializing the automatic data source engine and adding or removing required elements. Within the designer, the schema appears locked, as shown in Figure 3.8. Schema designers can add the XSD <any> attribute to allow authors to extend XML documents with elements not specified by the schema.

FIGURE 3.8   A schema showing as locked.

When the XSD <any> attribute is applied to the original employee schema, this enables the schema to include other namespaces. For example, within the InfoPath designer, this would allow you to include the default InfoPath namespace and allow additions to the schema. This is shown in Listing 3.4, which is also available on the companion CD-ROM (\Code\Chapter 3\ExtendableSchema\Anyelement.xsd).

LISTING 3.4   A Sample XML Schema That Appears as Extensible Within InfoPath

```
<?xml version="1.0"?>
<xsd:schema xmlns:xsd="http://www.w3.org/2001/XMLSchema">
```

```
<xsd:element name="prefix" type="xsd:string"/>
<xsd:element name="firstname" type="xsd:string"/>
<xsd:element name="lastname" type="xsd:string"/>
<xsd:element name="suffix" type="xsd:string"/>
<xsd:element name="email" type="xsd:string"/>
<xsd:element name="employeeid" type="xsd:string"/>
<xsd:element name="costcenter" type="xsd:string"/>

<xsd:element name="employeeinfo">
<xsd:complexType>
<xsd:sequence>
    <xsd:element ref="prefix"  minOccurs="0"/>
    <xsd:element ref="firstname"/>
    <xsd:element ref="lastname"/>
    <xsd:element ref="suffix" minOccurs="0"/>
    <xsd:element ref="email"/>
    <xsd:element ref="employeeid"/>
    <xsd:element ref="costcenter"/>
<xsd:any namespace="##other" processContents="lax" minOccurs="0"
maxOccurs="unbounded"/>
</xsd:sequence>
</xsd:complexType>
</xsd:element>
</xsd:schema>
```

Using another variation, shown in Listing 3.5 and available on the companion CD-ROM (\Code\Chapter 3\ExtensibleSchema\AnyAttribute.xsd), allows you to include other attributes with non-schema namespaces specified in the original definition.

LISTING 3.5 An Extensible Schema That Allows You to Add Non-Schema Namespaces

```
<?xml version="1.0"?>
<xsd:schema xmlns:xsd="http://www.w3.org/2001/XMLSchema">

<xsd:element name="prefix" type="xsd:string"/>
<xsd:element name="firstname" type="xsd:string"/>
<xsd:element name="lastname" type="xsd:string"/>
<xsd:element name="suffix" type="xsd:string"/>
<xsd:element name="email" type="xsd:string"/>
<xsd:element name="employeeid" type="xsd:string"/>
<xsd:element name="costcenter" type="xsd:string"/>
```

```
<xsd:element name="employeeinfo">
<xsd:complexType>
    <xsd:sequence>
            <xsd:element ref="prefix"  minOccurs="0"/>
            <xsd:element ref="firstname"/>
            <xsd:element ref="lastname"/>
            <xsd:element ref="suffix" minOccurs="0"/>
            <xsd:element ref="email"/>
            <xsd:element ref="employeeid"/>
            <xsd:element ref="costcenter"/>
            </xsd:sequence>
        <xsd:anyAttribute/>
</xsd:complexType>
</xsd:element>
</xsd:schema>
```

The <any> attribute is an important part of schema definitions within the enterprise. This enables the creation of a default schema definition that becomes extensible. When you're designing XSDs for use within InfoPath, this attribute enables extensibility within the designer. For example, solutions that leverage external schemas often require extensibility within a solution.

THE EMPLOYEE TIMESHEET APPLICATION

Many organizations already have a variety of schemas defined and being used. The nature of a schema represents a consistent set of values and definitions about an object. The benefit is that this consistent representation is reusable in a variety of solutions and enables a consistent enterprise vocabulary. For example, timesheets are often a combination of various objects and relationships across an organization.

ON THE CD

NOTE

The entire employee timesheet application is included on the companion CD-ROM(\Code\Chapter 3\Timesheet\Timesheet.xsn).

Schema Inheritance

Through their namespaces, individual XSD schemas are provided a level of independence and isolation for the objects they describe. A main objective of the XML schema definition was to promote reusability and enable inheritance. You can do this by creating a composite object, the combination of individual namespaces to form a new inherited object relationship. The timesheet application represents the combining of the company and employee into a new timesheet object with the structure, as shown in Figure 3.9.

Timesheet Schema

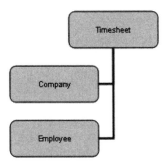

FIGURE 3.9   The structure of the timesheet.xsd.

Enabling schema inheritance is a two-step process:

1. Add each individual namespace into the timesheet.xsd, as shown here:

```
<xsd:schematargetNamespace=
    "http://schemas.mycompany.com/ns/timesheet/ info" xmlns:employee=
    "http://schemas.mycompany.com/ns/employees/info"
xmlns:restriction=
    "http://schemas.mycompany.com/ns/restriction/info"
xmlns:company=
    "http://schemas.mycompany.com/ns/company/info"
xmlns:timesheet=
    "http://schemas.mycompany.com/ns/timesheet/info"
xmlns:xsd=
    "http://www.w3.org/2001/XMLSchema">
```

2. Issue the import statement to enable the XML parser with a physical path to the inherited schemas, as shown here:

```
<xsd:import namespace="http://schemas.mycompany.com/ns/company/info"
schemaLocation="company.xsd"/>
<xsd:import namespace="http://schemas.mycompany.com/ns/employees/info"
schemaLocation="employee.xsd"/>
<xsd:import namespace="http://schemas.mycompany.com/ns/restriction/
info" schemaLocation="restriction.xsd"/>
```

Defining an Enumeration Drop-Down

Value spaces are declared within an XSD as a set of defined enumerations within a data type. Each value is represented by a set of defined literal values using the enumeration element. This forces a data type restriction that allows a value to contain one or more list items. Within the timesheet schema, this is used to enforce cardinality for the work type element, as shown here:

```
<xsd:simpleType name="worktypes">
<xsd:restriction base="xsd:string">
<xsd:enumeration value="Regular"/>
 <xsd:enumeration value="Vacation"/>
 <xsd:enumeration value="Sick"/>
 </xsd:restriction>
</xsd:simpleType>
```

When imported into InfoPath, the data source converts and renders this as a drop-down list box that contains the defined enumerations, as shown in Figure 3.10.

FIGURE 3.10   Field properties showing an enumeration.

Repeating Sections

Within the InfoPath designer, repeating sections are a data source grouping that can occur more than once. Controls within the data source are bound to either sections or tables that allow for multiple field entry. Within the timesheet schema, this allows users to enter their daily work hours. As part of the XSD schema, this is defined using the `<maxoccurs>` attribute and setting the value to unbounded, as shown here:

```
<xsd:element ref="timesheet:weekof" minOccurs="0" maxOccurs="unbounded"/>
```

When the completed timesheet schema is imported into InfoPath, the data source translates and renders this as a repeating section on the Data Source tab, as shown in Figure 3.11.

FIGURE 3.11 An imported schema showing a repeating section.

Setting Default Values

It is the responsibility of both the schema and forms designer to make form entry as simple and quick as possible for end users. One way to accomplish this type of design requirement is to set default values. These values attach either the initial or expected values to element definitions within the schema structure. Ideally, these are fields that always contain the same value. As an example, within the company schema, "name" is a required field that by default contains the same value. Using XSD, you can define a default value using the default property value of the element definition, as shown in the following line:

```
<xsd:element name="name" type="restriction:requiredString"
default="Extra Large Inc."/>
```

The InfoPath data source attaches the default value to the element definition and marks the field required, as shown in Figure 3.12.

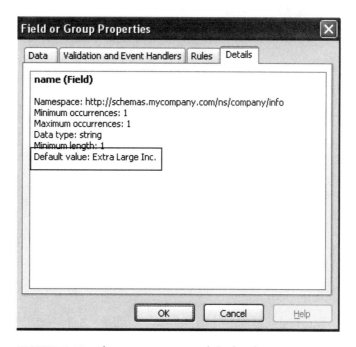

FIGURE 3.12 The company name default value.

Form Design

The timesheet.xsd file represents a completed schema that defines the timesheet object. This object uses both inherited and extended XSD elements and extensions. Once this is imported into InfoPath, the next step to developing the timesheet application is form design. Form development using InfoPath is similar to traditional Web-based development that use tables as container structures for data entry items.

Creating the Form Header

Forms are designed from the top down. The top-level table is considered the form header that contains the form name and any instructions for completing the form. Within the timesheet application, this is a two-column layout table. One column contains a form graphic and the other column contains the form instructions, as shown in Figure 3.13.

FIGURE 3.13 View of a layout table.

The form graphic is defined as an external resource object. These types of resources are maintained as part of the solution (.xsn) file and defined within the form manifest document as shown here:

```
<xsf:file name="2A34A480.gif">
<xsf:fileProperties>
  <xsf:property name="fileType" type="string"   value="viewComponent">
</xsf:property>
</xsf:fileProperties>
</xsf:file>
```

InfoPath applications deployed as part of an intranet solution are required only to provide a file path or URL to the location of the resource. Any other deployment type requires the resource to be stored within the solution file, with the manifest maintaining a reference back to itself. In this scenario, the size of the resource directly impacts the overall size of the solution file. When a form is loaded, the manifest file provides a handle to the data source that binds this to a picture control for display within the form.

Defining the Input Area

Once the form header is complete, the form designer can then move into the design of the data entry area of a form. The timesheet application captures input using a custom table. This type of layout table allows you to visually define the number of columns and rows contained in a table, as shown in Figure 3.14.

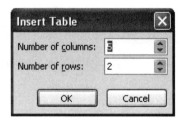

FIGURE 3.14 Defining a custom table.

All InfoPath tables are fixed width during rendering instead of being HTML percentage-width tables. This is mostly to circumvent the performance hit that typically occurs with this type of rendering. During the InfoPath rendering process, the engine always defaults back to the fixed-width table definitions defined during the design process. As fields are dropped onto the design surface, they expand to the width of the current table column.

InfoPath does allow the fields within a table to be adjusted. The control property page within the form allows you to define both the width and height of specific controls through the data source, as shown in Figure 3.15. Using the property pages, you can reduce the sizes of the employee name fields and place them on the same data-entry line. The auto-size function in the height column adjusts column width based on the size of the table. Only the list box and drop-down list box adjust the width based on the amount of fields shown within a table cell.

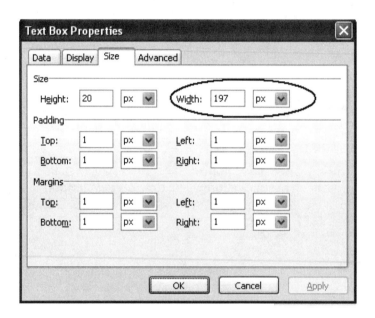

FIGURE 3.15   Setting the width of a field.

Color schemes are another way for designers to customize forms. In design mode, a color scheme can be applied to a form, as shown in Figure 3.16. This scheme is applied to the XSL style sheet that is used to render the form. Depending on the way a form is designed, these schemes can include body and heading styles, table cells, and row borders.

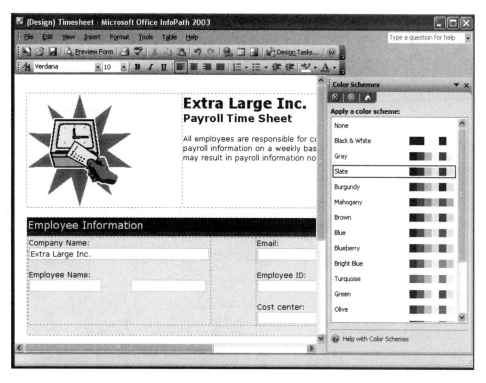

FIGURE 3.16   Changing the color scheme.

EXTENDING FORMS WITH FORMATTING AND VALIDATION

At this point, the form layout and entry are complete. The problem is that the form doesn't contain any specific validation or business logic needed to verify the user-entered data. Typically, this is logic applied outside the default schema and may be specific to the form instance. InfoPath provides form designers with this type of control through conditional formatting and applying data validation to the form.

Conditional Formatting

Conditional formatting enables designers to control the formatting of rich-text boxes, sections, and repeating tables based on a set of predefined conditions. These controls can change their appearance based on a set of values entered during form design. Each control can maintain a set of conditions—such as style, font, color, text background, and visibility—that can be associated with a set of rules. Controls can maintain multiple conditional formatting rules that are stored as part of the XSLT within the solution file as a view. Whenever the defined condition is met, the rule is applied and rendered to the form.

For example, within the timesheet application, one of the business requirements is that the cost center field contains a number less than 4000. Within the designer, you can double-click on the cost center field and from the display window enter the conditional formatting, as shown in Figure 3.17.

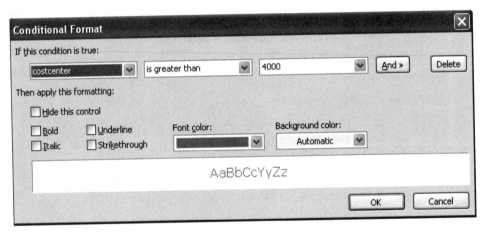

FIGURE 3.17   Adding the conditional formatting.

It is always important for designers doing any type of formatting or validation to preview and test the form. This will ensure that the form is working correctly and that the defined formatting and validation rules are functioning as expected. To do this, select the Preview Form button within the design mode. The word "Preview" appears in the title bar to inform designers they are in a preview window. During a form preview, the form is simulated and certain menu command and toolbar options (such as the Save command) are disabled.

Data Validation

In addition to conditional formatting, another main requirement of data-driven applications is data validation. InfoPath can handle this in a couple of different ways. At the lowest level is schema-based validation. Within the timesheet.xsd, this was done through restrictions applied to the base elements. InfoPath automatically validates the data entered into forms against the data stored in the data source as a way of enforcing XSD-based schema requirements. Data validation is a declarative way of testing the accuracy of data. It enables a set of rules that can be applied to a specific control that specifies the type and range of data that a user can enter. Data validation is used to display immediate error alerts when a user enters incorrect values into a control. Rather than checking for errors after the form is completed, data validation verifies values as the form is being filled out. Both of these methods can also be extended with either script or managed code using the InfoPath object model, as we will see later. Data validation always occurs at the field level, and depending on the complexity of the form, multiple conditional formats or validations may be applied to a field within the data source. Table 3.2 shows the type of data validation that is available within InfoPath.

TABLE 3.2 Types of Validation Supported by InfoPath

Validation Type	Description
Required Controls	Requires that users enter a value into the control.
Data Type Validation	Requires that users enter a particular type of data that matches the type of the control.
Range Checking	Ensures that the value entered into a control is within a specified range.
Dynamic Comparisons	Compares the values in different controls and then validates a condition.
Code-based Validation	Uses a script to perform an advanced validation on a control.

The validation-based engine built into InfoPath allows form designers to display an error alert when incorrect values are entered into a form. InfoPath validates data when a user leaves the control, rather than what Web applications do, which is typically validate only when a form is posted. This provides the end user with immediate feedback on the state of his form. Unlike conditional formatting, any errors defined within data validation prevent the form from being submitted to a database or Web Service. Users can save the form locally or navigate through the form using the tools menu and correct errors.

InfoPath provides inline and dialog box error notification. The inline alert marks the control that reported the error with a dashed red border. The dialog error displays a modal form with a custom error message when invalid data is entered. Users completing the form can right-click and display the full error message for further information.

For example, one of the business requirements for the timesheet application was to enforce a sick day rule for employees. The rule required that any employee who selected the "work type" of "Sick" couldn't report more than eight total hours for the day.

Within the InfoPath properties, we could define the rule shown in Figure 3.18 to enforce this.

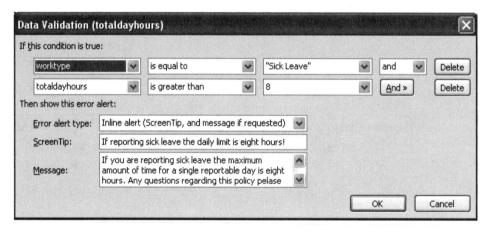

FIGURE 3.18 Defining the employee absence requirement.

Striking a balance between conditional formatting and data validation is an important requirement in making forms that are easy and intuitive for end users to complete.

Conditional Required Fields

Required fields are an important part of any InfoPath form. They are used to ensure that the form contains the necessary data element to adequately describe a complete entity or business processes. Typically, this is done at the field level during the initial design of a form. Often, this may not provide an ideal solution for many types of dynamic forms and business processes.

For example, in these types of scenarios, a field may become required based on other data elements or certain conditions occurring during form completion. This is enabled in InfoPath through the user of conditional required fields. To illustrate how this can be done, we can create a simple contact form, as shown in Figure 3.19. When the form is designed as shown in Figure 3.20, it contains a drop-down list of names and a text box for contact names.

FIGURE 3.19   The contact form data source.

FIGURE 3.20   The company contact form.

Normally, as a user completes the form, the contact name isn't a required field as defined by the InfoPath data source. However, because of a business requirement, any time the company name "Enormous Company" is selected, the contact name becomes a required field. This dynamic setting is accomplished through data validation. The following steps show how this can be enabled within the form:

1. Within the form, select the properties of the contact name, as shown in Figure 3.21.
2. Select the data validation button, as shown in Figure 3.22.

FIGURE 3.21   Contact name properties.

FIGURE 3.22   Defining the data validation

3. Define the data validation rule, as shown in Figure 3.23.

Once the form is run and "Enormous Company" is selected from the drop-down list, the contact name becomes required, as shown in Figure 3.24.

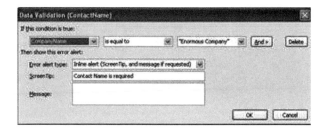

FIGURE 3.23   Building the data validation rule

FIGURE 3.24   Dynamically required field.

Rules-Based Validation

In addition to data validation, InfoPath provides an event-based rules engine. This engine allows form developers to add an unlimited number of data validation expression groups and fields, as shown in Figure 3.25.

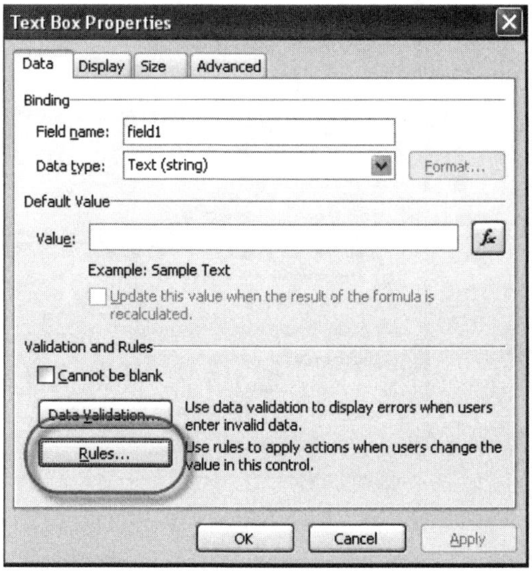

FIGURE 3.25   Adding an event-based rule.

FIGURE 3.26 Event-based rules occur in order.

Event-based rules are applied in sets, as shown in Figure 3.26. They are applied in sequential order. For example, the UpdateCustomer will execute before the NotifyCustomer rule.

Within a specific rule set, each action is condition-based. This means that an action such as that shown in Figure 3.27 is executed based on a condition. Conditions are based on values within the form, as shown in Figure 3.28. For example, this can include whether the value of a field is blank and is within a specified range, equals the value of another field, or starts with or contains certain characters.

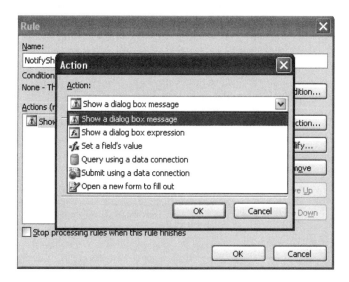

FIGURE 3.27 The type of event-based actions.

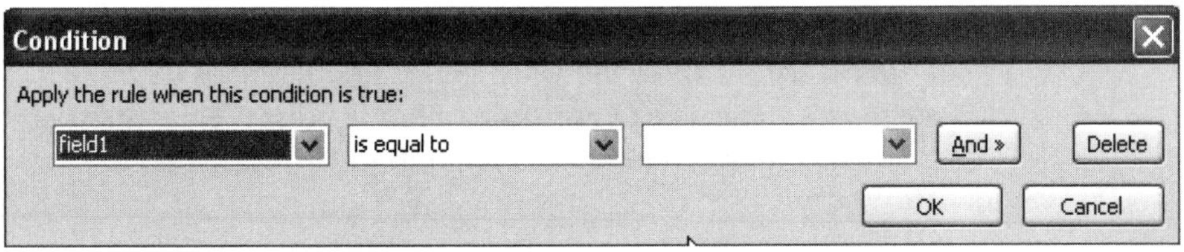

FIGURE 3.28 Setting a condition for an event-based rule.

EXTENDING FORMS WITH SCRIPT

InfoPath enables developers to extend functionality of forms using both script and managed code. Many different areas within InfoPath are programmatically extensible. These include the ability to include custom data validations, form submissions, and error handling. InfoPath is a client application. This means that, by default, all code will execute on the local machine. For unmanaged or COM-based scripts, InfoPath uses the Microsoft Script Editor (MSE) as the integrated development environment. MSE supports either VBScript or JavaScript for writing and debugging components. For managed code extensions, InfoPath uses Visual Studio .NET. For either extension, all programmatic components are stored within the InfoPath solution file (.xsn). For script code, this is a single file (either with a .js or .vbs extension) in the InfoPath solution file. The manifest.xsf file is responsible for providing the entry points that control the firing and execution of script or managed code elements. Within the manifest.xsf, the type and location of code executed is identified by XML elements. A single InfoPath form is capable of supporting both script and managed code executing together. Within the manifest.xsf, each programmatic entry point is identified by a language element. For scripts, this is identified by a script element tag as shown here:

```
<xsf:scripts language="jscript">
        <xsf:script src="script.js"></xsf:script>
</xsf:scripts>
```

NOTE

Within the solution file, script files are stored in a file named script.js or script.vbs.

InfoPath provides a variety of areas that are extensible. The most common extension point is the object model. This is the hierarchical type library composed of collections, object, properties, methods, and events that give template developers programmatic control over the various aspects of the InfoPath editing environment and XML source data. Object model changes are often used to control other portions of the form template and provide integration points for solution extensibility. Table 3.3 provides an overview of the common programmatic integration points within InfoPath.

TABLE 3.3   Common InfoPath Areas for Adding Application Code

Name	Description
Data Validation	The combination of XML schema, expressions, and script code that is used to validate and constrain the data that users are allowed to enter within a form template.
Error Handling	The combination of event handlers, object model calls, and XSF entries that are used to generate errors within an InfoPath form template.
Customizable User Components	These include menus, toolbars, command bars, and task panes.
Security	The set of security levels that are used to restrict access to the InfoPath object model and independent system resources.
Data Submission	The set of predefined functions that are used to implement custom posting and submission functionality for an InfoPath form template.
Business Logic	The set of custom scripting files that contain programming code used to implement specific editing behavior, data validation, event handlers, and control of data flow. This can often include accessing external COM components.
Form Template Integration	The use of other Office applications such as Microsoft Excel or Outlook to integrate with InfoPath 2003.

A complete overview of the InfoPath object model is located in Appendix A.

Declarative versus Programmatic Development

Based on the type of customization, template files are modified using either declarative or programmatic styles. Within the designer, a developer may extract form files into a file folder, manually edit the extracted form files, and then make changes to the elements and attributes using any text editor or Visual Studio.NET. This type of modification is considered *declarative*. Using the InfoPath designer, a developer can also programmatically add script using MSE or Visual Studio. This is usually done in conjunction with the InfoPath object model to extend or enhance the form template behavior. The main difference is that programmatic access is always done within the InfoPath designer, MSE, or Visual Studio, and declarative modification is completed outside the InfoPath environment and then loaded back into the designer.

THE INFOPATH OBJECT MODEL

Using MSE, developers can write script code that is activated in response to events. The InfoPath object model provides a set of events that can occur at both the document and node level. An *event* is just a script function that runs in response to one of the predefined events. These functions are defined by InfoPath as an association to the event name. Both the event names and definitions are referred to in the form definition file (.xsf) and are not extensible. Within the manifest.xsf, these are maintained as part of the document structure, as shown in Listing 3.6.

LISTING 3.6   manifest.xsf Document Structure

```
<xsf:domEventHandlers>
    <xsf:domEventHandler
    handlerObject="msoxd_timesheet_endtime" match="/
    timesheet:payinformation/timesheet:weekof/timesheet:worktime/
    timesheet:endtime">
    </xsf:domEventHandler>
    <xsf:domEventHandler handlerObject="msoxd_timesheet_totaldayhours"
    match="/timesheet:payinformation/timesheet:weekof/
    timesheet:worktime/timesheet:totaldayhours"></xsf:domEventHandler>
</xsf:domEventHandlers>
<xsf:scripts language="jscript">
  <xsf:script src="script.js"></xsf:script>
</xsf:scripts>
```

Do not change the names of your functions because this will cause your code to stop working. Function names are hardcoded and should never be modified except by InfoPath.

Both the function names and parameters are hardcoded within the base InfoPath engine. Once activated, the event functions are given access to the InfoPath object model, which creates an interface to the various nodes and element level data (as shown in the `<xsf:domeventhandler handlerobject>` XML node in Listing 3.6). Document lifecycle and node-level data are two sets of events associated with all documents.

The InfoPath object model is a COM-based object model that is used to interact with InfoPath forms. Even if you use managed code to extend your InfoPath solution, it will execute through a series of interoperability layers as a COM-based application. This is similar to the object models of other Office applications except that it supports a more limited set of automation methods. Table 3.4 shows some of the more important InfoPath objects.

TABLE 3.4 Key InfoPath Objects

Object	Description
Application	Is the top-level object; provides access to lower-level objects and general-purpose functions.
XDocument	Provides a number of properties, methods, and events that are used to programmatically interact with and manipulate the source XML data of a form.
TaskPane	Provides a number of properties that allow programmatic access to working with the custom and built-in task panes.
DataObject	Provides properties and methods that are used to access and interact with data adapter objects. These include the ability to retrieve information and access the data sources they are connected to.
UI	Provides a number of properties and methods for displaying custom and built-in dialog boxes within the user interface. Based on the security model defined within InfoPath, there are security restrictions on the UI object. (More information about the security restrictions defined within the InfoPath object model is provided in Appendix A.)

→

Object	Description
Error	Provides properties that are used to programmatically interact with InfoPath-generated form or submission errors.
MailEnvelope	Provides a number of properties that are used to programmatically create custom email messages using Outlook 2003 and attach the current form to the message.
Window	Provides a number of properties and methods that are used to programmatically interact with InfoPath windows. These include the ability to activate or close a window, and interact with task panes and command bar objects. This object also provides properties for accessing the underlying XML document associated with a window.
Solution	Provides properties for getting information about the form template. This includes version information, URL, and one XML DOM containing the manifest information.
View	Provides properties and methods that are used to programmatically interact with InfoPath views. These include methods for switching views, accessing data contained within the view, and executing form synchronization with the underlying data source
ViewInfo	Exposes properties and methods that are used to get the name of a view and programmatically decide which view is being accessed.
ExternalApplication	Implements a very limited set of methods that are used to automate InfoPath by external COM-based programming languages.

Document Lifecycle

At the document level, a series of events allow global access and control of the entire document. These events are designed for document-level access and fire in the following order:

OnVersionUpgrade: This event occurs when the user opens the document and a new document version is not the same as the one installed on the user's client machine.

OnLoad: This event occurs when the user first opens the document.

OnSwitch: This event occurs when the user changes views.

OnSubmitRequest: This event occurs when the user presses the Submit command.

OnAfterImport: This event occurs when the user imports a form.

Node Change Data

At the node level, additional events fire based on actions within a form. Most scripting within InfoPath is done at the node level in response to data changes. The order of events becomes important when you are determining where to place your code. These events fire in the following order:

OnBeforeChange: This event occurs after the data in a field is modified but before the data in the node bound to the field is changed. This event is typically used to validate information or status before continuing.

OnValidate: This event occurs after the data in a field is modified and after the data is checked against the schema. This event occurs after successful schema validation and is used to further validate the data and error reporting.

OnAfterChange: This event occurs after the data in the field is modified, after the data is checked against the schema, and after the data in the node bound to the field is changed. This is the last event and occurs after schema validation is successful, so it is used often to perform updates on the underlying template.

Extending the Timesheet

Within the timesheet sample, one of the business requirements is to provide a form total based on the hours entered.

Calculate Time Worked

To calculate the time worked, first make the Total Hours field read only using the properties page, as shown in Figure 3.29. This prevents users from having to enter data into this field and also will make entry much faster.

When you use script to accomplish this task, the total calculation is implemented in the OnAfterChange event for the End Time field. You can access this field through the Data Validation property pages, as shown in Figure 3.30. This

FIGURE 3.29   Making a field read only.

event provides access to the DOM values entered within the start time and end time, and can then be used to update the Total Day Hours field.

Within MSE, add the code shown in Listing 3.7 to the OnAfterChange event for the End Time field. This calls the calculation function that updates the fields.

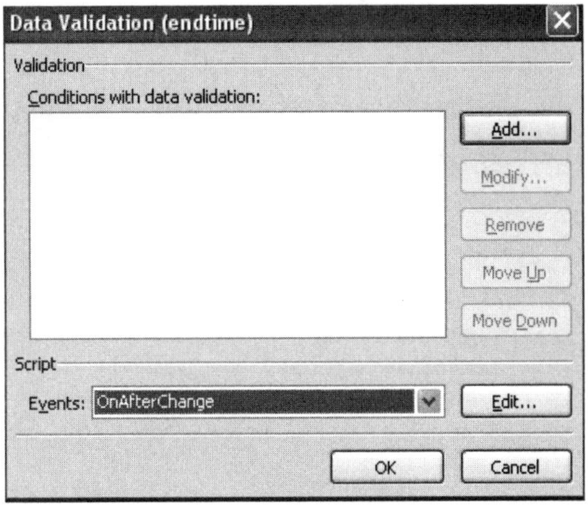

FIGURE 3.30   Accessing the OnAfterChange event using client script.

LISTING 3.7 The `OnAfterChange` Event That Calls the Time Calculation Function

```
function msoxd_timesheet_endtime::OnAfterChange(eventObj)
{
// Write code here to restore the global state.

  if (eventObj.IsUndoRedo)
    {
      // An undo or redo operation has occurred and
      // the DOM is //read-only.
      return;
    }

// A field change has occurred and the DOM is writable.
// Write code here to respond to the changes.
  updatehoursworked(eventObj)
}
```

The eventObj function is a container object that is created by InfoPath and contains all the DOM-level data within the current form. This is passed to the update function, which uses this to calculate the total hours for the day. Once calculated, the TotalHours field is updated with the code shown in Listing 3.8.

LISTING 3.8 Calculating the Time Worked by the Employee

```
function updatehoursworked(xmlitem)
{
var nhours = 0;
varstarttime = 0;
var endtime = 0;

starttime =
parseFloat(xmlitem.Site.previousSibling.previousSibling.text);
endtime = parseFloat(xmlitem.Site.text);

if (starttime==0){return;}

if (starttime > endtime){
  nhours += (24 - starttime) + endtime;
}
else{
 nhours += endtime - starttime;
}
xmlitem.Site.nextSibling.nextSibling.text = nhours;
}
```

The eventObj function contains both a Site and Source object. The Site object provides the DOM data based on a tree structure defined around the control that is currently firing the event. This allows navigation based on the current control within the DOM structure. The Source object provides data from the entire row and isn't fully updated until the current row is complete.

Calculate Total Time Entered

The last step in creating the timesheet application is to calculate the total time worked as reported on this form. This is another calculated field that is a chained event fired from the update of the Total Day Hours field on each row of the table. After making the Total Day Hours read only, add the code in Listing 3.9 to the Total Day Hours within the OnAfterChange event. This ensures that the value we add or subtract includes the current field.

LISTING 3.9   Calculating the Time Worked and Updating the Node Fields

```
var totalhours = 0
var xmlnodes =
XDocument.DOM.selectNodes("/timesheet:payinformation/timesheet:weekof/
timesheet:worktime");

  for (var xmlnode=xmlnodes.nextNode();xmlnode
!=null;xmlnode=xmlnodes.nextNode())
 {

    var totalworked =
xmlnode.selectSingleNode("timesheet:totaldayhours").text;

   if (totalworked >= 0) {
   totalhours = parseFloat(totalworked) + parseFloat(totalhours);
   }
 }

  if (totalhours >= 0){
XDocument.DOM.selectSingleNode("/timesheet:payinformation/timesheet:wee
kof/timesheet:totalhours").text = totalhours;
 }
```

One of the major differences between Listings 3.9 and 3.8 is the navigation of the data nodes. Within Listing 3.9, the navigation was done through an aggregation of all the Total Day Hours within the table.

Once the form is completed, you can then deploy it within the enterprise.

SUMMARY

This chapter covered a lot of information about building and extending XML schemas within the InfoPath environment. We also covered how InfoPath provides an extensible object model for programmatic access. we covered how this can be done using COM-based script. InfoPath, like many other Office applications, provides a rich development environment for customizing and creating forms. Using these components, application developers can build and deploy InfoPath solutions that meet specific business requirements.

These first several chapters have provided the foundation needed to understand the more advanced topics we will be covering. This starts in the next chapter, where we will cover Web Services and how they can be used within InfoPath.

4 Generating Web Service Forms

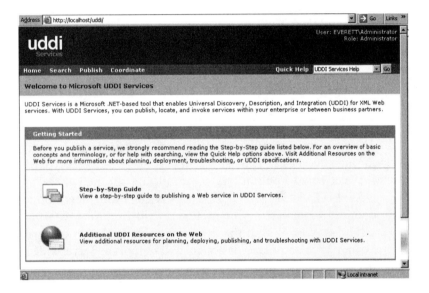

INTRODUCTION

The last chapter covered a lot of information about XML and InfoPath. These are important concepts to understand as we begin to look at InfoPath and how it is used within the Web Services architecture. Web Services are defined within a set of industry standards as self-contained, self-describing modular applications that are published, located, and invoked across a network. They are deployed as a set of software that provides a service to a client application over a network using a standardized XML messaging system that provides encoded communication in and out of the Web Service.

Technically, a Web Services implementation is composed of four layers. First is the transport layer, which enables message communication between applications using standard wire protocols—HTTP, Simple Mail Transfer Protocol (SMTP), and File Transfer Protocol (FTP). Second is the XML-based encoding schema, which defines common message formats—SOAP and XML Remote Procedure Calls (XMLRPC). Third is the XML-based Web Services Description Language (WSDL), which defines the public interfaces. Finally, there's the service discovery mechanism (UDDI), which provides the central repository and registry for the Web Service publish-and-find capabilities. This chapter focuses on each of these technology layers and how they can be extended using Visual Studio.NET 2005 and the .NET Framework. We will also discuss how once deployed, InfoPath can discover and then interface with these services to create a document-centric application. Web Services are an important data source for InfoPath-based solutions and a major part of the Services Oriented Architecture (SOA).

THE HTTP PIPELINE MODEL

The programming model for Web Services defines applications that communicate through messages. This isn't a new concept for Web-based applications. Most Internet-based applications communicate through three basic HTTP message types: PUT, POST, and GET. Web Services are an extension to this model and are designed to enable the Internet to provide not only information but also application services. Within the .NET Framework, the set of types defined within the System. Web namespace is designed to support all server-side HTTP programming using a pipeline model of message processing. This general-purpose framework defines a set of processing types to receive and send HTTP requests through Internet Information Services (IIS).

Each of these processing types is mapped against a set of file extensions stored in the IIS metabase. The metabase is a hierarchical store of configuration information and schema that are used to configure IIS. During the installation of the .NET Framework, a set of known file extensions—including ASP.NET pages (.aspx) and Web Services (.asmx)—is registered with IIS. The metabase is organized into a hierarchy of nodes, keys, and subkeys in a structure that mirrors that of the physical IIS sites. Nodes are the top level and represent a specific Web site or virtual directory within IIS. Underneath a node are one or more keys that contain a specific IIS configuration value for the site defined within the node. As new sites or directories are created, each of these properties inherits its initial values from a similar property stored at a higher level in the hierarchy. Using Windows Server 2000, Windows

Server 2003, or Windows XP, you can configure each of these settings and properties through the Internet Services Manager Snap In for the Microsoft Management Console, as shown in Figure 4.1.

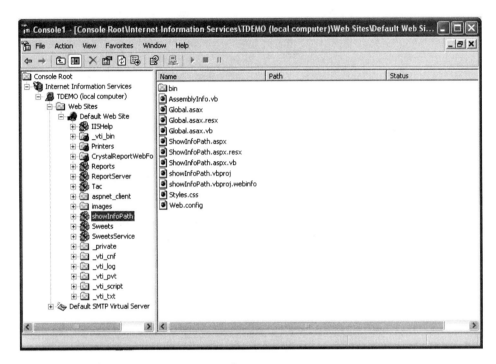

FIGURE 4.1   The IIS management console.

Windows Server 2003 provides a new feature called "edit-while-running", which enables you to export the metabase into an editable XML file that uses an XSD based on IIS. To turn on this feature, select the Enable Direct Metabase Edit checkbox on the Properties tab of the IIS Properties window, as shown in Figure 4.2.

Enabling this feature exports the entire binary metabase structure to an XML file stored in the c:\windows\system\inetsvr directory. By default, this file is named metabase.xml. Any changes to this XML configuration file are automatically applied to IIS. To edit this file, system administrators can use a standard XML editor or notepad. Because of schema restrictions, InfoPath can only read and report from the file, as shown in Figure 4.3, but this can make a handy tool for system administrators. Consult the CD-ROM in the Chapter 4 samples directory for the InfoPath application (\Code\Chapter 4\IISMetaEdit\IISMetaRead.xsn).

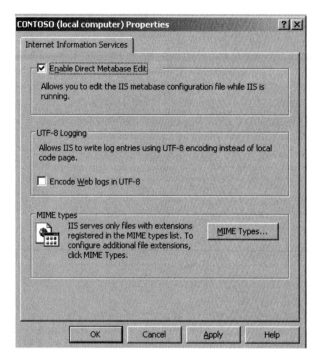

FIGURE 4.2 Enabling "edit-while-running" within IIS 6.

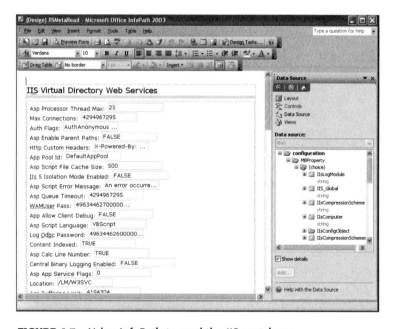

FIGURE 4.3 Using InfoPath to read the IIS metabase.

When IIS receives a processing request, it matches the file extension of the target URL to determine the type of executable to run. The .aspx or .asmx requests are associated with the aspnet_isapi.dll, as shown in the IIS Properties window in Figure 4.4.

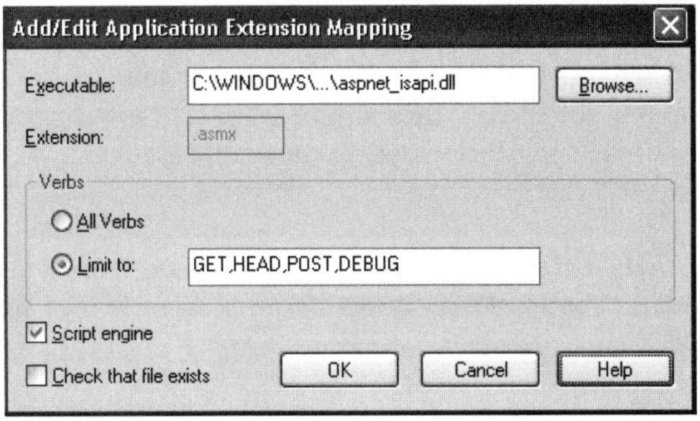

FIGURE 4.4   An executable file association as seen in IIS.

The aspinet_isapi.dll is an Internet Server API (ISAPI) DLL extension that maps to the address space of the inetinfo.exe process. The inetinfo.exe process acts as a forwarding agent that passes the incoming message to the ASP.NET application worker process, aspnet_wp.exe, which performs the actual request processing. This process then instantiates an instance of the HTTP Runtime class as an entry point into the HTTP pipeline. The redesign of the IIS 6.0 kernel mode HTTP listener within Windows Server 2003 enables you to directly pass requests to the worker process without involving the inetinfo.exe. The major advantage is that this offers better performance and security over both IIS 5.0 and Windows Server 2000.

In the pipeline, the HTTP handlers match the request to a compiled assembly. The association of both ASP.NET pages and Web Services is in the <httphandlers> section of the .NET Framework global machine configuration file and by default contains the code in Listing 4.1.

LISTING 4.1   The Association of Page Types by the .NET Framework

```
<httpHandlers>
    <add verb="*" path="*.aspx" type="System.Web.UI.PageHandlerFactory"/>
    <add verb="*" path="*.ashx" type="System.Web.UI.SimpleHandlerFactory"/>
```

```
<add verb="*" path="*.asmx"
type="System.Web.Services.Protocols.WebServiceHandlerFactory,
System.Web.Services, Version=1.0.5000.0, Culture=neutral,
PublicKeyToken=b03f5f7f11d50a3a" validate="false"/>
</httpHandlers>
```

Once the request is in the pipeline, the Framework maps it to the WebService-HandlerFactory, which compiles the associated source code into a class, instantiates it, and then using reflection translates the incoming SOAP messages into a method invocation. The use of reflection allows you to programmatically inspect the assembly or class to determine the proper data types and method calls. This is what enables the direct mapping of a SOAP message to a method invocation.

Reflection is part of the System.Reflection namespace and contains classes and interfaces that provide a managed view of the currently loaded types, methods, and fields that can dynamically create and invoke types.

The .NET Framework provides two ways to develop XML Web Services. The first is using the low-level custom IHTTPHandlers, which plug directly into the HTTP pipeline. This is the more code-intensive approach of the two and requires programmatic control of the system XML APIs to process the SOAP envelopes in the HTTP body and custom WSDL to describe the entire implementation. The second and preferred method of development, and the one used here, is the Web-Methods Framework. When this is installed, the .NET Framework implements a custom IHTTPHandler class for Web Services called the WebServiceHandler. This handler provides a customizable XML, XSD, SOAP, and WSDL template that we used in the first chapter to develop the reporting Web Service.

THE WEBMETHODS FRAMEWORK

Web Services are implemented using classes. Within a class, the developer can control the XML namespaces for the Web Service along with an optional string that describes the class. When the Web Service is deployed within a production environment, it is important to match the namespace to those used with the enterprise. The following is the default namespace used by Visual Studio in a default project:

```
<System.Web.Services.WebService _
(Namespace:="http://tempuri.org/InterviewFeedback/Service1")>
_Public Class Feedback
```

Visual Studio.NET uses a default namespace of http://tempuri.org. It is important to remember to change this name before you move applications into your production environment.

Methods of a class implemented within an XML Web Service project can't automatically communicate over the Web. The WebMethods Framework uses the `<WebMethod()>` attribute to identify and map an incoming SOAP message to a specific .NET class method. This attribute is derived from the System.Web.Services namespace and marks public methods that you can call from a remote Web client. Once the attribute is added to a public method, the component becomes part of the service architecture.

THE INTERVIEW FEEDBACK APPLICATION

The Interview feedback application is designed to collect comments and opinions of people who conducted interviews. The entire application can be installed from the CD-ROM (\Code\Chapter 4\Manager Feedback\RetrieveFeedback.xsn). This application is broken into three tiers with a Web Service acting as the middle tier, as shown in Figure 4.5.

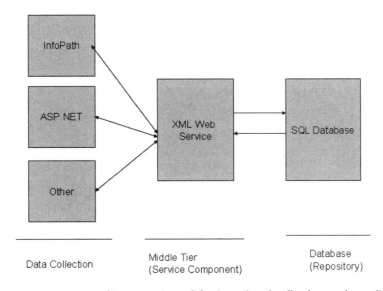

FIGURE 4.5 Architecture view of the interview feedback sample application.

The front end acts as the data collection tier that submits completed data to the middle-tier service component. For this example, an InfoPath form provides the data-collection engine. For other scenarios, this may also include other front-end collection schemes like an ASP.NET application that leverages the same service component. The actual data repository is maintained in an SQL Server 2000 database that contains the schema, as shown in Figure 4.6.

Column Name	Data Type	Length	Allow Nulls
ApplicantID	int	4	
EvaluatorName	varchar	75	
ApplicantName	varchar	75	
PositionAppliedFor	varchar	50	
InterviewDate	datetime	8	
InterviewType	varchar	50	
ExperienceO	bit	1	
ExperienceG	bit	1	
ExperienceI	bit	1	
ExperienceU	bit	1	
ExperienceN	bit	1	
ExperienceComment	varchar	255	
JobKnowledgeO	bit	1	
JobKnowledgeG	bit	1	
JobKnowledgeI	bit	1	
JobKnowledgeU	bit	1	
JobKnowledgeN	bit	1	
JobKnowledgeCommei	varchar	255	
CommunicationSkillsO	bit	1	
CommunicationSkillsG	bit	1	
CommunicationSkillsI	bit	1	
CommunicationSkillsU	bit	1	
CommunicationSkillsN	bit	1	
CommunicationSkillsCc	varchar	255	
EducationO	bit	1	
EducationG	bit	1	
EducationI	bit	1	
EducationU	bit	1	
EducationN	bit	1	
EducationComment	varchar	255	
MotivationO	bit	1	
MotivationG	bit	1	
MotivationI	bit	1	
MotivationU	bit	1	
MotivationN	bit	1	
MotivationComment	varchar	255	

FIGURE 4.6 The database structure of the interview feedback sample application.

The Middle Tier

The middle-tier Web Services component is a public method and contains the following parameters:

```
<WebMethod()> Public Function SendFeedback(ByVal EvaluatorName As
String, ByVal ApplicantName As String, ByVal PositionAppliedFor As
String, ByVal InterviewDate As String, ByVal InterviewType As String,
ByVal ExperienceO As Boolean, ByVal ExperienceG As Boolean, ByVal
ExperienceI As Boolean, ByVal ExperienceU As Boolean, ByVal ExperienceN
As Boolean, ByVal ExperienceComment As String, ByVal JobKnowledgeO As
Boolean, ByVal JobKnowledgeG As Boolean, ByVal JobKnowledgeI As
Boolean, ByVal JobKnowledgeU As Boolean, ByVal JobKnowledgeN As
Boolean, ByVal JobKnowledgeComment As String, ByVal EducationO As
Boolean, ByVal EducationG As Boolean, ByVal EducationI As Boolean,
ByVal EducationU As Boolean, ByVal EducationN As Boolean, ByVal
EducationComment As String, ByVal CommunicationSkillsO As Boolean,
ByVal CommunicationSkillsG As Boolean, ByVal CommunicationSkillsI
As Boolean, ByVal CommunicationSkillsU As Boolean, ByVal
CommunicationSkillsN As Boolean, ByVal CommunicationSkillsComment As
String, ByVal MotivationO As Boolean, ByVal MotivationG As Boolean,
ByVal MotivationI As Boolean, ByVal MotivationU As Boolean, ByVal
MotivationN As Boolean, ByVal MotivationComment As String) As Long
```

The Web Services interface is responsible for collecting a set of parameters from the front-end InfoPath form. Once collected, the data is inserted into the SQL database using a stored procedure. The Web Method contains the code shown in Listing 4.2 that receives the parameters, validates, and then calls the stored procedure.

LISTING 4.2 Performing an Insert into a SQL Server Database Using ADO.NET

```
'creating the DB connection
    Dim sqlConn As SqlConnection
    Dim sqlCmd As SqlCommand
    Dim strConstring As String
    strConstring = ConfigurationManager.AppSettings("Constring")
    sqlConn = New SqlConnection(strConstring)
    sqlConn.Open()
    sqlCmd = New SqlCommand

    With sqlCmd
        .Connection = sqlConn
        .CommandTimeout = 30
        .CommandType = CommandType.StoredProcedure
```

```
            .CommandText = "spInsertFeedback"
            .Parameters.AddWithValue("@EvaluatorName", EvaluatorName)
            .Parameters.AddWithValue("@ApplicantName", ApplicantName)
            .Parameters.AddWithValue("@PositionAppliedFor",
                                PositionAppliedFor)
            .Parameters.AddWithValue("@InterviewDate", InterviewDate)
            .Parameters.AddWithValue("@InterviewType", InterviewType)
            .Parameters.AddWithValue("@ExperienceO", ExperienceO)
            .Parameters.AddWithValue("@ExperienceG", ExperienceG)
            .Parameters.AddWithValue("@ExperienceI", ExperienceI)
            .Parameters.AddWithValue("@ExperienceU", ExperienceU)
            .Parameters.AddWithValue("@ExperienceN", ExperienceN)
            .Parameters.AddWithValue("@ExperienceComment",
                                ExperienceComment)
            .Parameters.AddWithValue("@CommunicationSkillsO", _
CommunicationSkillsO)
            .Parameters.AddWithValue("@CommunicationSkillsG", _
CommunicationSkillsG)
            .Parameters.AddWithValue("@CommunicationSkillsI", _
CommunicationSkillsI)
            .Parameters.AddWithValue("@CommunicationSkillsU", _
CommunicationSkillsU)
            .Parameters.AddWithValue("@CommunicationSkillsN", _
CommunicationSkillsN)
            .Parameters.AddWithValue("@CommunicationSkillsComment", _
CommunicationSkillsComment)
            .Parameters.AddWithValue("@JobknowledgeO", JobKnowledgeO)
            .Parameters.AddWithValue("@JobknowledgeG", JobKnowledgeG)
            .Parameters.AddWithValue("@JobknowledgeI", JobKnowledgeI)
            .Parameters.AddWithValue("@JobknowledgeU", JobKnowledgeU)
            .Parameters.AddWithValue("@JobknowledgeN", JobKnowledgeN)
            .Parameters.AddWithValue("@JobknowledgeComment", _
JobKnowledgeComment)
            .Parameters.AddWithValue("@EducationO", EducationO)
            .Parameters.AddWithValue("@EducationG", EducationG)
            .Parameters.AddWithValue("@EducationI", EducationI)
            .Parameters.AddWithValue("@EducationU", EducationU)
            .Parameters.AddWithValue("@EducationN", EducationN)
            .Parameters.AddWithValue("@EducationComment", _
EducationComment)
            .Parameters.AddWithValue("@MotivationO", MotivationO)
            .Parameters.AddWithValue("@MotivationG", MotivationG)
            .Parameters.AddWithValue("@MotivationI", MotivationI)
            .Parameters.AddWithValue("@MotivationU", MotivationU)
```

```
            .Parameters.AddWithValue("@MotivationN", MotivationN)
            .Parameters.AddWithValue("@MotivationComment", _
    MotivationComment)
            .ExecuteNonQuery()
        End With
        sqlConn.Close()
```

ADO.NET classes are found in the System.Data.dll and are integrated into the base XML classes found in the System.XML.dll. These ADO.NET components are designed to provide all data access and manipulation within the .NET Framework using a common structure. The Connection and Command objects are the two main objects within the hierarchy.

The Connection object is responsible for providing connectivity to the data source. To take advantage of connection pooling within SQL Server, use the same connection string for each connection. The easiest way to ensure this is by adding the connection string to the Web Services Web.Config file. The System.Configuration namespace gives you access to these settings and enables error handling within the configuration files. The System.Configuration.ConfigurationManager object provides the methods and properties that allow applications to open configuration files and retrieve specific sections. In the XML configuration file, the <appSettings> tag is appended to the <System.Web> tag, as shown here:

```
<appSettings>
  <add key="Constring"
value="Server=basexp;Database=applicant;Trusted_Connection=True;"/>
</appSettings>
```

This tag is appended in a key/value combination that allows for an indexed retrieval of the data using the following code from the load event of the Web Service:

```
strConstring = ConfigurationManager.AppSettings("Constring")
```

Database Access

The Command object is responsible for enabling database commands to return, modify, or run stored procedures from an associated Connection object. It is always a best practice within SQL Server to access and manipulate data using stored procedures. A stored procedure is a pre-compiled query that guarantees the fastest data retrieval. Insert statements are used to update the database. SQL statements that don't return data should use the ExecuteNonQuery option, which allows the passing of ADO.NET-based parameters that match the stored procedure input parameters. Within the interview feedback sample, the insert statement shown in Listing 4.3 is used to update the feedback data.

LISTING 4.3 Insert Stored Procedure to Update Feedback Data

```
CREATE PROCEDURE [SpInsertFeedback]
  (@EvaluatorName       [varchar](75),
   @ApplicantName       [varchar](75),
   @PositionAppliedFor  [varchar](50),
   @InterviewDate       [datetime],
   @InterviewType       [varchar](50),
   @ExperienceO [bit],
   @ExperienceG [bit],
   @ExperienceI [bit],
   @ExperienceU [bit],
   @ExperienceN [bit],
   @ExperienceComment [varchar](255),
   @JobKnowledgeO [bit],
   @JobKnowledgeG [bit],
   @JobKnowledgeI [bit],
   @JobKnowledgeU [bit],
   @JobKnowledgeN [bit],
   @JobKnowledgeComment [varchar](255),
   @CommunicationSkillsO [bit],
   @CommunicationSkillsG [bit],
   @CommunicationSkillsI [bit],
   @CommunicationSkillsU [bit],
   @CommunicationSkillsN [bit],
   @CommunicationSkillsComment [varchar](255),
   @EducationO [bit],
   @EducationG [bit],
   @EducationI [bit],
   @EducationU [bit],
   @EducationN [bit],
   @EducationComment [varchar](255),
   @MotivationO [bit],
   @MotivationG [bit],
   @MotivationI [bit],
   @MotivationU [bit],
   @MotivationN [bit],
   @MotivationComment [varchar](255))
```

```
AS INSERT INTO [Applicant].[dbo].[Applicant]
  ([EvaluatorName],[ApplicantName],[PositionAppliedFor],[InterviewDate],

  [InterviewType],[ExperienceO],[ExperienceG],[ExperienceI],[ExperienceU],
  [ExperienceN],[ExperienceComment],[JobKnowledgeO],[JobKnowledgeG],[
  JobKnowledgeI],[JobKnowledgeU],[JobKnowledgeN],[JobKnowledgeComment],
  [CommunicationSkillsO],[CommunicationSkillsG],[CommunicationSkillsI],
  [CommunicationSkillsU],[CommunicationSkillsN],[CommunicationSkills
  Comment],
  [EducationO],[EducationG],[EducationI],[EducationU],[EducationN],
  [EducationComment],[MotivationO],[MotivationG],[MotivationI],
  [MotivationU],
  [MotivationN],[MotivationComment])
VALUES
  (@EvaluatorName,@ApplicantName,@PositionAppliedFor,@InterviewDate,
  @InterviewType,@ExperienceO,@ExperienceG,@ExperienceI,@ExperienceU,
  @ExperienceN,@ExperienceComment,@JobKnowledgeO,@JobKnowledgeG,
  @JobKnowledgeI,@JobKnowledgeU,@JobKnowledgeN,@JobKnowledgeComment,
  @dis:@CommunicationSkillsO,@CommunicationSkillsG,
  @CommunicationSkillsI,
  @CommunicationSkillsU,@CommunicationSkillsN,
  @CommunicationSkillsComment,
  @EducationO,@EducationG,@EducationI,@EducationU,@EducationN,
  @EducationComment,@MotivationO,@MotivationG,@MotivationI,
  @MotivationU,
  @MotivationN,@MotivationComment)
GO
```

When executed with no return parameters within an Update, Delete, or Insert statement, the return value is always the number of rows affected by the Command object. Any type of error will always return a -1.

Compile and Run

When the Web Service class is compiled, the class is turned into an assembly, copied to the assigned IIS virtual directory, and exposed through an .asmx endpoint. This IIS virtual directory contains the Web Service declaration that points requests to the compiled assembly. This declaration is contained in the .NET code behind page (a page created when you develop the application). This page is defined during development and contains the following information:

```
<%@ WebService Language="vb" CodeBehind="~/App_Code/Service.vb"
Class="Applicant" %>
```

This declaration stored in the .asmx file deployed to the IIS directory notifies and directs the Web Service handler to the class that contains the exposed methods to use when a specific SOAP message is received.

Anytime the .asmx page is called directly from a Web browser, the .NET Documentation Handler produces an HTML page that enables you to test and document the exposed Web methods, as shown in Figure 4.7.

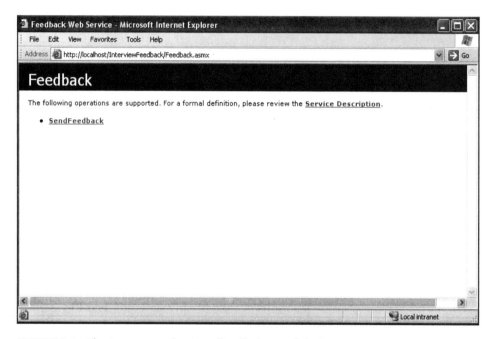

FIGURE 4.7 The Documentation Handler displays a default page.

The Documentation Handler is a standard .aspx page stored in the .NET Framework configuration directory named DefaultWsdlHelpGenerator.aspx. When a direct browser request is received, IIS maps to the .asmx file and then links to the associated Documentation Handler specified in the .NET machine configuration.

WHERE IS UDDI?

Like any network resource, Web Services would be impossible to find without some type of prior knowledge of either the location or specific functions exposed. XML Web Service directories like UDDI provide the central repository where a deployed service can publish descriptive information about itself. The UDDI standard defines a publishing methodology that allows either a developer or end user to find and use a Web Service. Published services within UDDI are responsible for providing business, service, and binding information that Web Service consumers can search and read. Within the intranet, Windows Server 2003 provides a standard-based UDDI implementation that is available through the URL http://@server-name:/UDDI. This brings up the default screen shown in Figure 4.8.

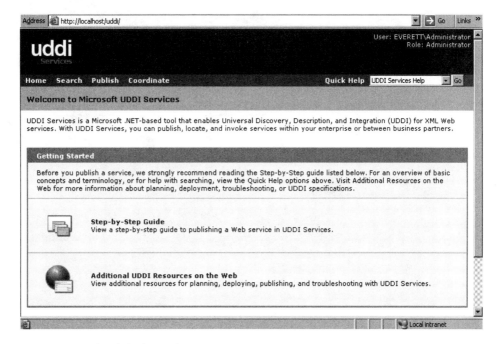

FIGURE 4.8 The default Windows Server 2003 UDDI screen.

UDDI is part of the .NET Framework's Microsoft.UDDI namespace. Once a Web Service is registered, UDDI clients and applications like InfoPath are then able to dynamically discover and implement these services using the methods exposed through the Web Service namespace. UDDI registries typically have two kinds of clients. The first is the business user that is publishing a service and its usage interface. The other is a client that needs to locate published services and then bind programmatically to the published interfaces and interact with the service.

Publishing a Service Provider

Web Services are attached to a specific provider. Providers are required to fully disclose their contact and business information. This provides a security level to consumers so they can determine specific security requirements or restrictions. The publishing screen is shown in Figure 4.9.

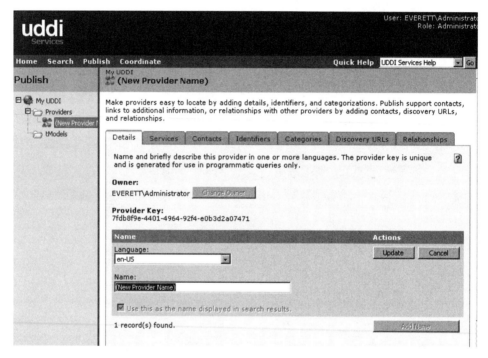

FIGURE 4.9 The UDDI provider registration screen.

A *business entity* is part of the UDDI structure that manages the overall provider. This additional security layer assigns a specific unique key or a Globally Unique Identifier (GUID) for registration and security.

Publishing the Service

Based on the provider registration, a set of available services can then be registered. Each service registration represents a single XML Web Service published within the UDDI structure. The default screen is shown in Figure 4.10.

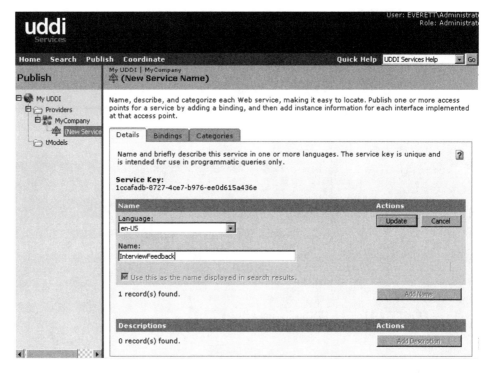

FIGURE 4.10   The UDDI service registration screen.

A service definition can include a variety of additional information that is used to fully describe the Web Service purposes. This includes not only the technical definition of ports and proxies, but also a human readable definition and description. Once a service is defined, the bindings are then registered. A binding represents each of the exposed Web Service end points of an .asmx file.

UDDI provides for multilanguage capabilities. This includes adding search information in a variety of languages

NOTE

Binding information provides the actual location information needed to access and address the Web Service. Shown in Figure 4.11, this information is used by end-user applications like InfoPath to programmatically bind to a specific Web Service instance.

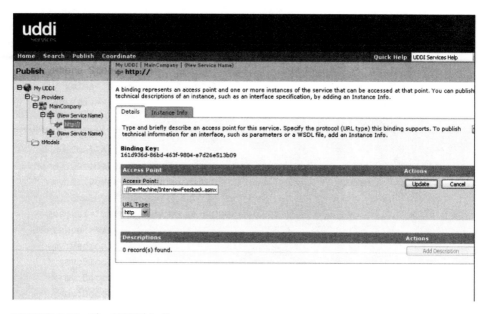

FIGURE 4.11 The UDDI binding screen.

Publishing the Instance Information

Once the bindings are entered, the next registration requirement is the entry of the specific instance information, as shown in Figure 4.12. Instance information is a pointer to the Technical Model (tModel) schema element. This element defines the type information and classification of the service. tModels are used to contain all the relevant technical information, function calls, and interface definitions supported by the Web Service.

The connection between the binding and the metadata is defined through the tModel instance. Similar to a dictionary or reference table in a database, the tModel contains the name, description, and a unique identifier. When called, the tModel provides the translation between the representation of the Web Service key and the actual interfaces.

The schema elements of the tModel, as shown in Figure 4.13, contain metadata information used to access specific type information or classification information for a registered Web Service. UDDI is responsible for storing this information and allows applications like InfoPath access to search through a variety of attributes and methods and then bind to the specific interface.

Generating Web Service Forms

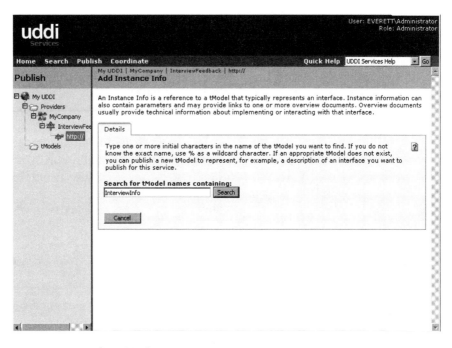

FIGURE 4.12 The UDDI instance entry screen.

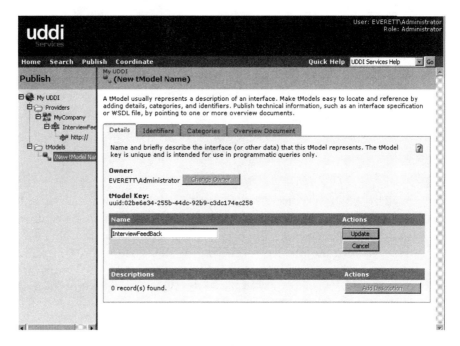

FIGURE 4.13 The UDDI tModel entry screen.

WHERE IS WSDL?

The only way that applications like InfoPath can access a specific SOAP endpoint is to know both the target URL value and the expected message format. Neither SOAP nor XML can fully describe this type of information. It's the job of WSDL to provide the SOAP service description using an XML schema to describe the expected message format and the service invocation requirements. WSDL defines Web Services as a series of network endpoints or virtual ports. The combination of these endpoints and an XML-based message description enables interface reusability. A WSDL document defines a series of XML elements that describe the Web Service interface. Table 4.1 shows the main WSDL document elements and their use.

TABLE 4.1 WSDL Document Definition Elements

Name	Description
Type	A container for type definitions using an agreed-upon type system
Message	An abstract definition of the data being communicated
Operation	A description of the actions supported by the service
Port Types	The abstract set of operations supported by the services
Port Type	A set of operations supported by one or more endpoints
Bindings	The protocol and data format required for a particular port type
Port	The definition of a single endpoint defined as a combination of bindings and network addresses
Service	A collection of related endpoints

The WSDL specification defines an XML-based format independent of SOAP and HTTP. WSDL is responsible for providing the remote invocation mechanism and message description to access Web Services. Within the .NET Framework, the .asmx handler automatically generates WSDL documents. For example, anytime the query string "?wsdl" is appended to an .asmx page, the Framework generates a default WSDL file. Figure 4.14 shows the WSDL for the interview feedback service that we created earlier.

```xml
<?xml version="1.0" encoding="utf-8" ?>
- <definitions xmlns:http="http://schemas.xmlsoap.org/wsdl/http/"
    xmlns:soap="http://schemas.xmlsoap.org/wsdl/soap/"
    xmlns:s="http://www.w3.org/2001/XMLSchema"
    xmlns:s0="http://tempuri.org/InterviewFeedback/SubmitFeedback"
    xmlns:soapenc="http://schemas.xmlsoap.org/soap/encoding/"
    xmlns:tm="http://microsoft.com/wsdl/mime/textMatching/"
    xmlns:mime="http://schemas.xmlsoap.org/wsdl/mime/"
    targetNamespace="http://tempuri.org/InterviewFeedback/SubmitFeedback"
    xmlns="http://schemas.xmlsoap.org/wsdl/">
 - <types>
   - <s:schema elementFormDefault="qualified"
       targetNamespace="http://tempuri.org/InterviewFeedback/SubmitFeedback">
     - <s:element name="SendFeedback">
       - <s:complexType>
         - <s:sequence>
             <s:element minOccurs="0" maxOccurs="1" name="EvaluatorName"
               type="s:string" />
             <s:element minOccurs="0" maxOccurs="1" name="ApplicantName"
               type="s:string" />
             <s:element minOccurs="0" maxOccurs="1" name="PositionAppliedFor"
               type="s:string" />
             <s:element minOccurs="0" maxOccurs="1" name="InterviewDate"
               type="s:string" />
             <s:element minOccurs="0" maxOccurs="1" name="InterviewType"
               type="s:string" />
             <s:element minOccurs="1" maxOccurs="1" name="ExperienceO"
               type="s:boolean" />
             <s:element minOccurs="1" maxOccurs="1" name="ExperienceG"
               type="s:boolean" />
             <s:element minOccurs="1" maxOccurs="1" name="ExperienceI"
               type="s:boolean" />
             <s:element minOccurs="1" maxOccurs="1" name="ExperienceU"
               type="s:boolean" />
             <s:element minOccurs="1" maxOccurs="1" name="ExperienceN"
               type="s:boolean" />
             <s:element minOccurs="0" maxOccurs="1" name="ExperienceComment"
               type="s:string" />
             <s:element minOccurs="1" maxOccurs="1" name="JobKnowledgeO"
               type="s:boolean" />
             <s:element minOccurs="1" maxOccurs="1" name="JobKnowledgeG"
               type="s:boolean" />
             <s:element minOccurs="1" maxOccurs="1" name="JobKnowledgeI"
```

FIGURE 4.14   The WSDL for the interview feedback Web Service.

The WSDL document contains a single <soap:binding> element that defines the type of Web Service. The WSDL 1.1 specification defines two SOAP message styles: RPC and document/literal. Within document-based binding, the <soap:Body> element contains one or more child elements called *parts*. There are no specific SOAP formatting rules regarding what this element can contain, and the content is based on mutual agreement between the sender and receiver. RPC messages contain a <soap:Body> element with the name of the method or remote procedure being invoked. This element, in turn, contains another element for each parameter of that procedure. Take a look at an example of a WSDL message for each of the two types of possible SOAP messages. Listing 4.4 shows a document/literal SOAP message, and Listing 4.5 shows an RPC SOAP message.

LISTING 4.4   A Document/Literal SOAP Message

```
<soap:Envelope xmlns:soap="http://schemas.xmlsoap.org/soap/envelope/">
<soap:Body>
<!- the following is an XML document described in the service'scontract
using XML Schema. In this example we know the document structure but
not the actual
processing specifics->
    <Example xmlns="http://example.org/soapformat">
      <invent>
        <Item>
          <Number>888-321-4567</Number>
          <Quantity>1200</Quantity>
        </Item>
        <Item>
          <Number>321-452-1200</Number>
          <Quantity>500</Quantity>
        </Item>
      </invent>
    </Example>
  </soap:Body>
</soap:Envelope>
```

LISTING 4.5   A RPC SOAP Message

```
<soap:Envelope xmlns:soap="http://schemas.xmlsoap.org/soap/envelope/">
<soap:Body>
<!- InventoryQuantity is the name of the procedure being invoked and
Number and Quantity
are parameters of the procedure. The two inventory elements are
namespace qualified but point to a different namespace area. ->
    <x:InventoryQuantity xmlns:x="http://example.org/soapformat/Example">
      <invent>
        <t:Inventory xmlns:t="http://example.org/soapformat">
          <t:Number>123-456-7890</t:Number>
          <t:Quantity>1200</t:Quantity>
        </t:Inventory>
        <t:Inventory>
          <t:Number>888-999-0120</t:Number>
          <t:Quantity>500</t:Quantity>
        </t:Inventory>
```

```
        </invent>
      </x: InventoryQuantity >
    </soap:Body>
</soap:Envelope>
```

The main difference between these two kinds of WSDL types is that within RPC you need to know the type and namespace requirements of the soap:zBody element. This means that the schema and RPC rules are required to validate the message. All Web Services within the .NET Framework are by default document/literal, although there is support for RPC types of services. InfoPath supports only document/literal style of Web Services.

If you attempt to connect InfoPath with an RPC-based Web Service, you will receive an error message.

NOTE

InfoPath and WSDL

InfoPath accesses Web Services like any other data source used to create a schema. Within InfoPath, once the Web Service is selected, the Web Services Adapter calls the WSDL and based on the returned values creates a set of schemas that can be mapped directly to the data source. An HTTP GET request is used to call the WSDL and return the Web Service structure. This structure is mapped to a set of fields that defines the message format sent based on the data filled into the form.

WHERE'S THE SOAP?

SOAP is a lightweight protocol intended for exchanging XML. The SOAP framework consists of an Envelope, Header, Body, and Fault that are part of the http://schemas.xmlsoap.org/soap/envelope namespace. This namespace provides the XML-based object protocols for the exchange of information within the .NET Framework. The Envelope defines a framework for describing what is contained in the message and how it should be processed; it is also a set of encoding rules for creating instances of application-defined types, and a method for representing remote procedure calls and receiving the response. The Header area defines the beginning of a specific set of Body segments that are contained within the Envelope. The Fault section provides a Body-level area to store and report errors.

All encoding with SOAP is in XML. For example, once an InfoPath form is created, any information entered into the form and then saved to the Web Service data source is submitted as part of a SOAP message that generates the network trace, as shown in Listing 4.6.

LISTING 4.6   The Network Trace Generated by an InfoPath Solution Communicating with the Web Service

```
POST /InterviewFeedback/Feedback.asmx HTTP/1.1\0d\0a
SOAPAction:
"http://tempuri.org/InterviewFeedback/Service1/SendFeedback"\0d\0a
Content-Type: text/xml; charset="UTF-8"\0d\0a
User-Agent: SOAP Toolkit 3.0\0d\0a
Host: localhost\0d\0a
Content-Length: 2265\0d\0a
Connection: Keep-Alive\0d\0a
Pragma: no-cache\0d\0a
\0d\0a
<?xml version="1.0" encoding="UTF-8" standalone="no"?><SOAP-
ENV:Envelope xmlns:SOAPSDK1="http://www.w3.org/2001/XMLSchema"
xmlns:SOAPSDK2="http://www.w3.org/2001/XMLSchema-instance"
xmlns:SOAPSDK3="http://schemas.xmlsoap.org/soap/encoding/" xmlns:SOAP-
ENV="http://schemas.xmlsoap.org/soap/envelope/"><SOAP-
ENV:Body><s0:SendFeedback
xmlns:s0="http://tempuri.org/InterviewFeedback/Service1">\0d\0a
\09\09\09<s0:EvaluatorName>Thom Robbins</s0:EvaluatorName>\0d\0a
\09\09\09<s0:ApplicantName>Joe Brown</s0:ApplicantName>\0d\0a
\09\09\09<s0:PositionAppliedFor>Manager</s0:PositionAppliedFor>\0d\0a
\09\09\09<s0:InterviewDate>8/12/03</s0:InterviewDate>\0d\0a
\09\09\09<s0:InterviewType>First</s0:InterviewType>\0d\0a
\09\09\09<s0:Experience0>true</s0:Experience0>\0d\0a
\09\09\09<s0:ExperienceG>false</s0:ExperienceG>\0d\0a
\09\09\09<s0:ExperienceI>false</s0:ExperienceI>\0d\0a
\09\09\09<s0:ExperienceU>false</s0:ExperienceU>\0d\0a
\09\09\09<s0:ExperienceN>false</s0:ExperienceN>\0d\0a
\09\09\09<s0:ExperienceComment>Has the
experience</s0:ExperienceComment>\0d\0a
\09\09\09<s0:JobKnowledge0>false</s0:JobKnowledge0>\0d\0a
\09\09\09<s0:JobKnowledgeG>false</s0:JobKnowledgeG>\0d\0a
\09\09\09<s0:JobKnowledgeI>true</s0:JobKnowledgeI>\0d\0a
\09\09\09<s0:JobKnowledgeU>false</s0:JobKnowledgeU>\0d\0a
\09\09\09<s0:JobKnowledgeN>false</s0:JobKnowledgeN>\0d\0a
\09\09\09<s0:JobKnowledgeComment>Possesses the job
knowledge</s0:JobKnowledgeComment>\0d\0a
\09\09\09<s0:Education0>false</s0:Education0>\0d\0a
\09\09\09<s0:EducationG>true</s0:EducationG>\0d\0a
\09\09\09<s0:EducationI>false</s0:EducationI>\0d\0a
\09\09\09<s0:EducationU>false</s0:EducationU>\0d\0a
\09\09\09<s0:EducationN>false</s0:EducationN>\0d\0a
```

```
\09\09\09<s0:EducationComment>Proper educational
components</s0:EducationComment>\0d\0a
\09\09\09<s0:CommunicationSkillsO>false</s0:CommunicationSkillsO>\0d\0a
\09\09\09<s0:CommunicationSkillsG>false</s0:CommunicationSkillsG>\0d\0a
\09\09\09<s0:CommunicationSkillsI>true</s0:CommunicationSkillsI>\0d\0a
\09\09\09<s0:CommunicationSkillsU>false</s0:CommunicationSkillsU>\0d\0a
\09\09\09<s0:CommunicationSkillsN>false</s0:CommunicationSkillsN>\0d\0a
\09\09\09<s0:CommunicationSkillsComment>Communicates
Well</s0:CommunicationSkillsComment>\0d\0a
\09\09\09<s0:MotivationO>false</s0:MotivationO>\0d\0a
\09\09\09<s0:MotivationG>true</s0:MotivationG>\0d\0a
\09\09\09<s0:MotivationI>false</s0:MotivationI>\0d\0a
\09\09\09<s0:MotivationU>false</s0:MotivationU>\0d\0a
\09\09\09<s0:MotivationN>false</s0:MotivationN>\0d\0a
\09\09\09<s0:MotivationComment>Motivation seems to be
high</s0:MotivationComment>\0d\0a
\09\09</s0:SendFeedback></SOAP-ENV:Body></SOAP-ENV:Envelope>
HTTP/1.1 100 Continue\0d\0a
Server: Microsoft-IIS/5.1\0d\0a
Date: Sat, 05 Jul 2003 18:42:05 GMT\0d\0a
X-Powered-By: ASP.NET\0d\0a
\0d\0a
HTTP/1.1 200 OK\0d\0a
Server: Microsoft-IIS/5.1\0d\0a
Date: Sat, 05 Jul 2003 18:42:07 GMT\0d\0a
X-Powered-By: ASP.NET\0d\0a
X-AspNet-Version: 1.1.4322\0d\0a
Cache-Control: private, max-age=0\0d\0a
Content-Type: text/xml; charset=utf-8\0d\0a
Content-Length: 324\0d\0a
\0d\0a
<?xml version="1.0" encoding="utf-8"?><soap:Envelope
xmlns:soap="http://schemas.xmlsoap.org/soap/envelope/"
xmlns:xsi="http://www.w3.org/2001/XMLSchema-instance"
xmlns:xsd="http://www.w3.org/2001/XMLSchema"><soap:Body><SendFeedbackRe
sponse xmlns="http://tempuri.org/InterviewFeedback/Service1"
/></soap:Body></soap:Envelope>
```

During the submission process, InfoPath automatically generates a SOAP message based on the WSDL received during the creation of the data source. The data source then creates and submits the SOAP message.

INFOPATH AND THE WEB SERVICE DATA SOURCE

During the design of an InfoPath form that will use the Web Service data source, a data structure is built on the operations selected within the Web Service. This results in forms that easily submit data or query data through a Web Service. Using a Web Service as the data source for an InfoPath form is essentially the same connection paradigm that we have illustrated in previous chapters. Several restrictions are placed on the Web Service data source to guarantee compatibility with existing Web Services. When you're submitting forms directly to Web Services, it is important to remember that developers cannot modify existing fields and groups within the data source. However, they can modify additional fields within the root of the data source that are considered outside the defined WSDL schema. InfoPath also allows you to do custom submissions using both script and managed code.

FORMS THAT SUBMIT DATA

ON THE CD

InfoPath enables you to design a form that can directly submit its data to a Web Service. (This feedback service application is available on the companion CD-ROM, in \Code\Chapter 4\FeedBackServiceSetup\WebService\Setup.exe.) This provides developers with an easy-to-use data-collection form that provides a direct submit or receive from a Web Service. Figure 4.15 shows the selection screen for deciding the type of connection.

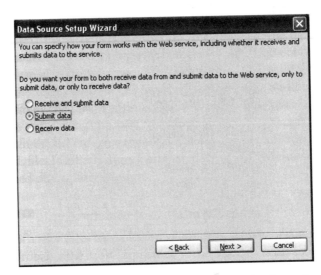

FIGURE 4.15   Defining the connection type for the Web Service.

Once the type of submission is defined for the InfoPath form, we can either search UDDI or enter the Web Service URL to the published WSDL, as shown in Figure 4.16.

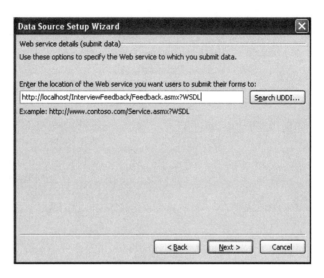

FIGURE 4.16 Providing the Web Service parameters.

Once the data source is found, InfoPath then brings down the WSDL and determines the valid operations defined by the Web Service, as shown in Figure 4.17.

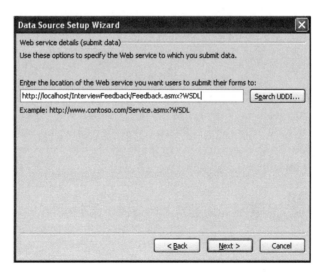

FIGURE 4.17 Defining the connection type for the Web Service.

Once these are defined, the data source is populated and the form may be laid out within the sections for data entry, as shown in Figure 4.18.

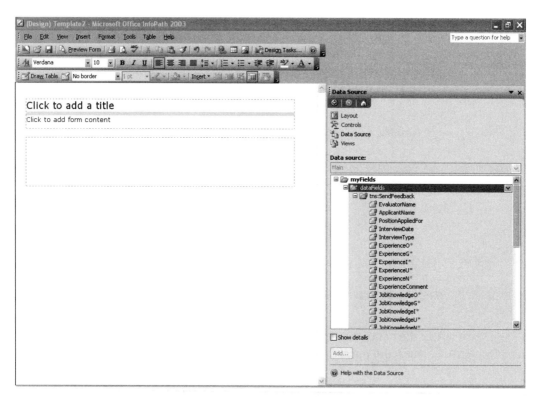

FIGURE 4.18 Designing the interview feedback form.

The individual data elements are appended to the default InfoPath namespace, as shown within the Properties tab in Figure 4.19.

By default, all submissions to a Web Service require that there be an available connection to the network and to the Web Service. However, InfoPath allows forms to be saved locally, and this can be used to provide offline access to data. This means that users can save either a completed or partially completed form to their local system. Once a connection is established to the server, users can then submit their forms to the specified Web Service.

FIGURE 4.19   Reviewing the default namespace assignment.

INFOPATH CONTROLS

When filling out a form, users enter information into various elements placed on the design surface. These elements are controls that provide a graphical representation of the underlying data source elements. When a form designer places controls on the form design surfaces, these controls become bound to the underlying data source. Most controls, including the text box, check box, and list box, are bound to fields. Fields are where the entered information is saved. If a control is not bound or if an error occurs within the binding, the information entered can't be saved because the underlying data source has no storage location. InfoPath provides five basic types of controls, as shown in Table 4.2.

TABLE 4.2 Controls Available Within InfoPath

Type	Name	Description
Standard	Text Box	The text box control is the most commonly used control on a form. Users can enter and type any kind of unformatted text into this control.
	Rich Text Box	Rich text boxes can contain formatted text. These controls also support image lists and tables using HTML formatting.
	List Box and Drop-Down List	These controls present a list of enumerated choices that a user can select. These choices can be populated from static lists, XML documents, Web Services, databases, and SharePoint lists.
	Date Picker	The date picker contains a box for users to enter data and a calendar button that allows them to select a date.
	Check Box	Check boxes allow users to enter yes/no or true/false values.
	Option Button	Option buttons let users select from a set of mutually exclusive choices. Groups of option buttons are bound to one-data source field, and each option saves a different value in the field.
	Button	Buttons are used to execute events that are tied to executable actions within a form.
	Section	Sections act as containers for other controls. They can include any of the other controls listed in the controls task pane.
Repeating and Optional Controls	Optional Section	Optional sections contain other controls and are used for including additional information that is not necessary for all users who are filling out a form.
	Repeating Section	These sections contain other controls and are used for presenting record-based data.
	Repeating Table	Repeating tables display information in a tabular structure where each item appears in a new row of the table.

$\rightarrow$

Type	Name	Description
	Master/Detail	A master/detail control is actually a set of two related controls. The master control is always a repeating table and the detail control can be either a repeating table or a repeating section.
	List (bulleted, numbered, and plain)	These controls provide any easy way to include simple repeating text elements.
File and Picture Controls	File Attachment	Files are uploaded and included in the form as part of the XML file. Before being added to the form element, they are converted to a Base 64 string.
	Picture	Pictures are included in a form as static elements. They allow users to insert new pictures as part of the form. These controls can store the picture as part of the form or as an address that is loaded at runtime. These are converted to Base 64 and then stored as part of the XML data source.
	Ink Picture	Ink pictures allow users of the Tablet PC to create and save ink-based drawings. This control is valid only when you're using a Tablet PC.
Advanced	Hyperlink	The hyperlink control is used link different URL based addresses together. They can point to any URL that exists within the Internet or intranet.
	Expression Box	Expression boxes are read-only text controls that perform calculations based on XPATH expressions.
	Vertical Label	A read-only label that appears at a 90-degree angle on a form. Often used for column heading in repeating tables.
	Scrolling Region	A container of other controls that retains a fixed size and scroll bars.
	Choice (Group, Repeating, Section)	These controls display choice controls. Each choice section provides a set of mutually exclusive options.
	Repeating Recursive Section	A control that contains other controls within itself. Used for creating hierarchical content and outline structures.
Custom	Custom	Enables adding ActiveX controls to an InfoPath form.

Buttons and expression boxes do not modify XML structure. These controls are presented through InfoPath using an XSLT transform for the view.

Control Inheritance

One of the defined business processes for the interview feedback form is that all candidates attend a defined number of interviews for each position they are being considered for. The problem with the current form design is that these interview stages may change based on organization, department, and even position. Hardcoding these values into the InfoPath form or Web Service will require programmer intervention whenever any of these specific elements change and will not allow the process to flow dynamically. The current schema definition defines the Interview Type field as a string that is associated with the text box control. Using control inheritance, you can easily change this to a drop-down list box control that is associated to a specific set of defined values, as shown in Figure 4.20.

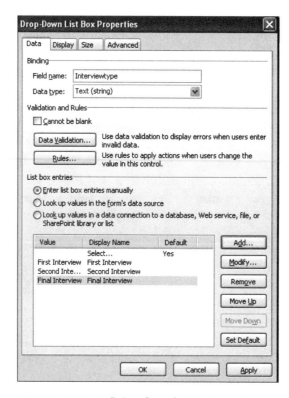

FIGURE 4.20 Defining the selection items for a drop-down control.

Within design mode, right-click on the control and select Change To on the shortcut menu. Then, select the appropriate control type. If the desired control type is not available, designers should check the field or group properties of the underlying data source. These properties are responsible for determining which control types are appropriate. The only exceptions are button, hyperlink, and the expression box control because they are considered special use controls. These are unable to change to any other type.

FORMS THAT QUERY FOR DATA

Another use of Web Services and InfoPath is to develop solutions that query data from a Web Service and return the data into a form. This solution type contains two InfoPath forms. The first provides a query view; the second is a data entry form that displays the queried data. Let's extend the interview feedback application, because the hiring manager wants to review submitted forms that show the notes entered about a candidate during the interview process. (You can find the interview feedback files on the CD-ROM in \Code\Chapter 4\Manager Feedback\Retrieve-Feedback.xsn.) The first step in retrieving this information is to extend the current Web Service using the WebMethods Framework to query and retrieve the appropriate data. Based on the defined workflow and database architecture, the applicant name is used as the query mechanism.

ON THE CD

Returning the Data Document

InfoPath is natively designed to work with generic XML payloads. The new method that we will add returns an XML data document to the front end. In looking at the code you will notice that a dataset is first used to retrieve the data from the database. The ADO.NET dataset is actually serialized using a specific XML format that contains an inline schema. Instead of returning the heavier dataset, we can simply convert it to an XML document as shown in Listing 4.7.

LISTING 4.7   Example of Converting a Dataset to an XML Document

```
<WebMethod()> Public Function GetApplicantFeedBack(ByVal ApplicantName
As String) As System.xml.XmlDataDocument
  'db connection
  Dim sqlConn As SqlConnection
  Dim sqlCmd As SqlCommand
  Dim strConstring As String
  Dim intUserID As Integer
```

```
strConstring = ConfigurationSettings.AppSettings("constring")
sqlConn = New SqlConnection(strConstring)
sqlConn.Open()
sqlCmd = New SqlCommand

With sqlCmd
  .Connection = sqlConn
  .CommandTimeout = 30
  .CommandType = CommandType.StoredProcedure
  .CommandText = "GetFeedbackByApplicant"
  .Parameters.Add("@ApplicantName", ApplicantName)
End With
  Dim ApplicantDA As SqlDataAdapter = New SqlDataAdapter
  ApplicantDA.SelectCommand = sqlCmd
  Dim ApplicantDS As DataSet = New DataSet
  ApplicantDA.Fill(ApplicantDS, "Evaluator")
  ApplicantDS.Namespace = "Http://localhost/Receivefeedback"
  Dim Info As System.Xml.XmlDataDocument = New
System.Xml.XmlDataDocument(ApplicantDS)
  Return Info
  sqlConn.Close()
End Function
```

InfoPath is unable to natively track changes to XML data. This is a feature provided by the dataset. However, InfoPath is able to work with the dataset object as long as you follow a few simple guidelines:

- InfoPath supports only one dataset within an edit form
- Constraints and relationships defined within a dataset cannot be disabled
- DeleteRule and UpdateRule properties are not supported

The Manager's Views

Using InfoPath, we can create a data source that points to the newly deployed Web Service. For this application, select the Receive data option for the data source, as shown in Figure 4.21. By default, this disables the automatic submit features within InfoPath.

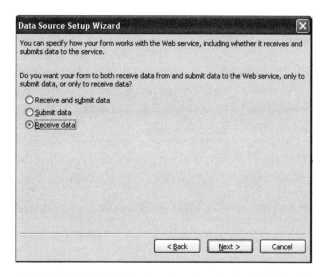

FIGURE 4.21 Selecting Receive data for the Web Service.

Once the data source is created, InfoPath attempts to retrieve a set of sample data with a query to the Web Service, as shown in Figure 4.22. The sample query enables the data source to retrieve and analyze a specific XML document and to determine the associated fields and controls within the data source.

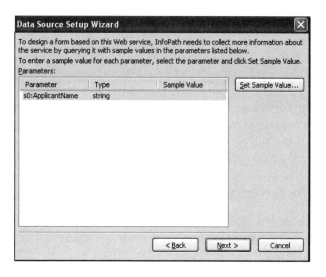

FIGURE 4.22 Defining sample data for the data source.

Once the data fields are retrieved, the data source is fully initialized. InfoPath defines two default data views. The query view is the default page available when the user opens the InfoPath form. This page provides the initial data capture that is used to retrieve Web Service data and load the Data View page. By default, the data entry view is also created. This view is initially created as a blank page to which form designers can add data source fields that are used to add new records. The initial view and the necessary code to manage view changes is maintained as part of the .xsf file and defined as part of the application manifest. Within the solution file, a script file called internal.js is auto-created; it contains the script code fired on the return of the Web Service data, as shown in Listing 4.8.

LISTING 4.8   Events Fired When Web Service Data Is Returned

```
// This file is automatically created and modified by Microsoft Office
InfoPath.
// Do not modify the contents of this file.
function SwitchToView0::OnClick()
{
  XDocument.View.SwitchView("Retrieve Info");
}
function SwitchToView1::OnClick()
{
  XDocument.View.SwitchView("Manager Lookup");
}
```

Once the Web Service Adapter returns the data, this event script is called and the results are displayed within the Manager Lookup view.

ENABLING CUSTOM SUBMISSION

Until now, we have focused on solutions that take advantage of the direct submission features of InfoPath. For some solutions, this won't be the correct implementation. InfoPath enables you to submit forms through either custom scripts or a generic HTTP POST.

Submitting with Custom Script

When an InfoPath document submits an XML document to a Web Service, the default behavior posts the contents of the individual nodes. This is a design feature that enables parameter-based field submission to the back-end Web Service. If the form designer wants to bypass this and submit the entire XML document, then he can enable a custom submit scripting routine by using the Submit options, as shown in Figure 4.23.

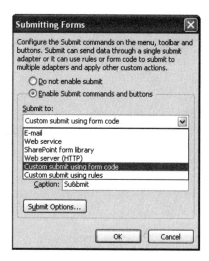

FIGURE 4.23 Enabling a custom submit function.

When enabled, XML submission occurs through the `OnSubmitRequest` function maintained as part of the application's solution file. For example, the script block shown in Listing 4.9 submits an entire XML request to a Web Service.

LISTING 4.9 Submitting the Entire InfoPath DOM to a Web Service

```
try{
  //Get a reference to the SendXMLNode secondary data source
  var objSendXMLNode = XDocument.GetDOM("SendXMLNode");
  objSendXMLNode.setProperty( "SelectionNamespaces",
    'xmlns:s1="http://mycompany.schema.com/schema" ' +
    'xmlns:sO="http://tempuri.org/" ' +
    'xmlns:dfs="http://schemas.microsoft.com/office/infopath/2003/data
FormSolution"' );

  //Remove any data from the SendXMLNode secondary data source
  var objData = objSendXMLNode.selectSingleNode(
  "/dfs:myFields/dfs:queryFields/sO:SendXMLNode/sO:theNode");
  var objCurrentData = objData.selectNodes("@* | node()");
```

```
objCurrentData.removeAll();
//Clone the XDocument
var objClonedDocument = XDocument.DOM.documentElement.cloneNode(true );
objData.appendChild( objClonedDocument );
//Call the "Query" method of the secondary data source to send the data
XDocument.DataObjects("SendXMLNode").Query();
//Report the results of the submit
XDocument.UI.Alert(
objSendXMLNode.selectSingleNode(
"/dfs:myFields/dfs:dataFields/s0:SendXMLNodeResponse/
s0:SendXMLNodeResult").text );
eventObj.ReturnStatus = true;
}
catch(ex)
{
eventObj.ReturnStatus = false;
}
```

Another custom submission option is to use a custom SOAP message, shown
in Listing 4.10. In this scenario, the form designer can define a custom message
using the SOAP library and HTTP.

LISTING 4.10   Defining a Custom SOAP Submission

```
try
  {
    //Create a SOAP object
    var objSOAPConnector = new ActiveXObject("MSOSOAP.HttpConnector30");

    //Set the EndPointURL property to point to the Web Service
    objSOAPConnector.Property("EndPointURL") =
    "http://server/WebService1/Submit.asmx";

    //Set the SoapAction property to point to the Web Service Method.
You can find this URI
  //in the WSDL file of the Web Service
  objSOAPConnector.Property("SoapAction") =
"http://tempuri.org/SendXMLNode";
  objSOAPConnector.Connect();
  //Begin construction of a SOAP message to send to the Web Service
  objSOAPConnector.BeginMessage();
```

```
  var objSOAPSerializer = new
ActiveXObject("MSOSoap.SoapSerializer30");
  objSOAPSerializer.Init( objSOAPConnector.InputStream );
  objSOAPSerializer.startEnvelope();
  objSOAPSerializer.startBody();
  //Construct the structure that marks the method name and parameter
name we're sending
  objSOAPSerializer.StartElement( "SendXMLNode", "http://tempuri.org/"
);
  objSOAPSerializer.StartElement( "theNode", "http://tempuri.org/" );
  //Write out the XML of the document
  objSOAPSerializer.WriteXml( XDocument.DOM.documentElement.xml );
  //Finish each element
  objSOAPSerializer.EndElement();
  objSOAPSerializer.EndElement();

  //Call EndMessage to complete the SOAP message and send it to the Web
Service Method.
  //This results in the Web Service Method being called.
  objSOAPSerializer.endBody();
  objSOAPSerializer.endEnvelope();
  objSOAPConnector.EndMessage();

  //Use a SoapReader to read the response from the Web Service Method
  var ResponseReader = new ActiveXObject("MSOSOAP.SoapReader30");
  ResponseReader.Load( objSOAPConnector.OutputStream );

  //If there was no error, return true
  if (ResponseReader.Fault != null)
  {
    eventObj.ReturnStatus = false;
  throw "Error submitting data: " + ResponseReader.Fault.xml;
  }
    eventObj.ReturnStatus = true;
}
catch (ex)
{
  XDocument.UI.Alert("Failed to submit document: " + ex.description);
}
```

In this example, the custom SOAP message is instantiated using the ActiveXObject method of the XDocument object model.

Submitting with HTTP

An existing InfoPath application often becomes a part of an existing Web-based application. This includes posting to specific pages and then allowing the page to do something with the data. When InfoPath posts to an HTTP address, the form data is actually contained as part of the binary stream. This means that as part of a post request, Web developers cannot access it within a Web page using either the form or variables collection. To access the posted data, developers use the readbinary method of the request object to retrieve the byte array that contains the data. Once retrieved, this data can be converted to a string and then processed on the Web page.

ASP.NET provides a low-level request/response API that enables developers to use the .NET Framework classes to service incoming HTTP requests. This is provided in the System.Web.IHTTPHandler interface and implements the Process Request method. These handler types are useful when the services provided by the high-level page framework abstraction are not required for processing an HTTP request.

Each incoming HTTP request received by ASP.NET is ultimately processed by a specific instance of a class that implements IHTTPHandler. The IHTTPHandler-Factory provides the infrastructure that handles the actual resolution of URL requests to IHTTPHandler instances. In addition to the default IHTTPHandlerFactory classes provided by ASP.NET, developers can create and register factories to support their own request resolution and activation scenarios.

Using InfoPath, you can have a form provide a post request using HTTP by editing the form properties and selecting HTTP with the URL of the page that you want to submit the request to, as shown in Figure 4.24.

FIGURE 4.24 Defining an HTTP request.

Within the page load event, we could add the code in Listing 4.11, which shows the submitted response of the interview feedback form in an ASP.NET Web Form DataGrid.

LISTING 4.11   Retrieving the Interview Information to an ASP.NET DataGrid

```
Dim binread As Byte()
    Dim bytecount As Integer

    bytecount = Request.TotalBytes
    binread = Request.BinaryRead(bytecount)

    'Converts the binary data to a string.
    Dim i As Integer
    Dim temp As Byte()
    Dim spost As String
    For i = 0 To (Request.TotalBytes - 1)
      spost = spost & Chr(binread(i))
    Next


    'Response.Write(spost)
    If spost = "" Then
      Page.Response.Write("Nothing to show")
    Else
      Dim stream As System.IO.StringReader
      Dim reader As System.Xml.XmlTextReader = Nothing

      stream = New System.IO.StringReader(spost)

      Dim ds As New System.Data.DataSet
      ds.ReadXml(stream)

      DataGrid1.DataSource = ds
      DataGrid1.DataBind()
    End If
```

This code grabs the binary stream of data and reads the request. This request data is then bound to the DataGrid object and displayed using an ASP.NET page.

SUMMARY

This chapter covered the process of creating Web Services and how they can be used within InfoPath. A variety of standards are part of Web Services, including WSDL, SOAP, and XML. One of the major advantages of using Visual Studio.NET is that it prevents developers from having to worry about the specific implementation. The WebMethods Framework and .NET enable developers to focus on the task of defining a business process. InfoPath allows you to consume these and then extend them to provide an easy-to-use collection source. One of the major advantages of using Web Services is that they allow you to develop a façade layer that can easily hide the specific implementation and sources of the repository data. However, as we will see in the next chapter, databases like Microsoft Access and SQL Server can also provide direct connectivity to InfoPath in creating an SQL data source.

5 Generating Database Forms

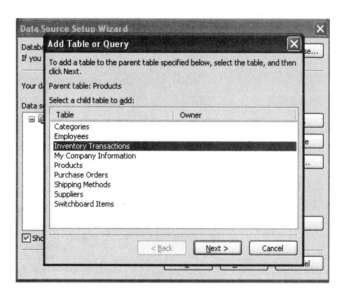

INTRODUCTION

Nobody would question that the success of XML is based on its simplicity and flexibility. These two advantages have given enterprises the choice of deploying XML solutions designed for human- and system-based consumers. The document-centric approach focuses on using XML to create a semi-structured set of documents that present irregular content designed for human consumption. Data consumer-using tools such as InfoPath and XHTML can read and interact with these types of documents. The data-centric approach focuses on using XML as a structured interchange language between machines or processes. Data is converted into XML and transported over a network connection as a SOAP message where a host system receives and then acts on the request.

Both types of implementation start and end with the data being stored in a relational database. A wide variety of tools that enable database access and retrieval using XML are available. These tools enable a sophisticated storage and retrieval of either structured or unstructured data. Even with the success of XML, the relational database is still the main repository for enterprise data. From large-scale enterprise solutions that reside in SQL Server 2000 to smaller departmental applications that use Microsoft Access 2003, a tremendous amount of information is contained within these data stores. InfoPath enables access and visibility into the data stored in both SQL Server and Microsoft Access as a data source that enables the development of rapid forms-based applications. This chapter covers InfoPath development of applications using a database as the source of forms-based applications.

DATABASE ARCHITECTURE

A database is similar to a data file that stores application data. Like the data file, a database doesn't present information directly to the user. The end user runs an application that is responsible for accessing the data and presenting it to the end user in an understandable format. The main difference between a data file and a database is that a database is a highly organized data structure. In a well-defined database, there is no storage of duplicate data. All related pieces of information are joined together to form objects. These objects, defined in records, represent a specific type of data relationship or data structure.

When working with data files, developers are required to write code that defines specific structures represented within a data file. The database contains a catalog of applications that determine how data is organized. Based on the credentials and connection information offered by the user, the catalog is responsible for dynamically presenting the requested data. Databases are organized into a holding file, which contains an optimized storage structure for data, and the Database Management System (DBMS), which is responsible for enforcing and maintaining the database schema.

The DBMS maintains the data relationships between the database elements and ensures that the data is stored according to a defined structure. Also, the DBMS provides recovery points in case of system failures. SQL Server 2000 uses a transaction log of each database transaction. This transaction log is a serial record of all modifications that have occurred in the database as well as the transactions for each of the modifications. This log records the start of each transaction and any changes made, as well as maintains enough information to undo the modification if necessary.

SOA has forced a shift in how databases are used to present and store data. Traditionally, databases were segmented into a separate application tier and provided only data storage. SOA has promoted them to first-class service providers and a strategic repository for business logic.

Which Is the Right Database?

Both SQL Server and Microsoft Access are relational databases used within many enterprises and application solutions. Each one is designed to solve a specific business need, and it is important to understand where they differ in feature and functionality. SQL Server 2000 is a true relational database management and analysis system designed to deliver a highly scalable line of business solutions, analysis, and data warehousing solutions. Microsoft Access is a relational database system designed for less scalable nonfault tolerant solutions and ideal for many offline scenarios. Designed with different architectures, the two databases can interoperate and this offers a hybrid solution that solves additional application integration issues. Table 5.1 shows some important differences between the two architectures that are important to remember when you're designing a database application.

Design considerations are import as well as the actual physical limitations. Table 5.2 outlines the basic physical limitations of both databases.

TABLE 5.1   Major Differences Between Microsoft Access 2003 and SQL Server 2000

Design Factor	Microsoft Access 2003	SQL Server 2000
Data Integrity	Provides no data logging and offers no recovery point to restore from. Is designed for smaller applications that are not considered mission critical.	Logs all transactions and provides point-in-time recovery. Is an ideal solution for mission-critical data.
Concurrency	Depends on the implementation; offers simultaneous access for reading data; a practical limit is less than 100 and that depends heavily on the available memory and disk space. This number also decreases depending on the amount of database querying.	Is an enterprisewide database that supports a variety of configurations that allow an almost unlimited number of users to access the database. The design of SQL Server is optimized for memory and disk space.
Management Features	Is easy for end users to administer and manage as the tools are built into the database. All management is done on a single database only.	Is more complex to administer but provides a rich set of tools that allow administration of both the database and data across the entire database catalog.
Database Size	As database size increases, the performance will decrease.	Database size isn't a factor in performance.

TABLE 5.2 Physical Limitations of Microsoft Access 2003 and SQL Server 2000

Feature	Microsoft Access 2003	Microsoft SQL Server 2000
Database Size	2 gigabytes minus the space needed for system objects	Terabytes
Number of Database Objects	32,768	2,147,483,647
Security	Based on user or workgroup information file	Integrated with Windows 2000 and NT security
Analysis Services (Data Mining, OLAP, Data Warehousing)	None	Built-in
SMP Support	None	Built-in
Clustering	None	Built-in

MICROSOFT SQL SERVER 2000

The SQL Server 2000 relational database engine is designed for highly scalable and reliable data storage. Figure 5.1 shows an overview of the component structure of SQL Server 2000. The database engine stores data in tables that represent an object of interest to the developer. Each table contains a schema that is modeled with columns and rows that represent a single occurrence of the object modeled by the table.

Applications submit either SQL statements or XPATH queries to the database engine that returns the results. SQL statements are based on the Transact-SQL (TSQL) dialect and return a tabular row set. TSQL is a sophisticated dialect of SQL that has a variety of enhanced features that are extensions to ANSI SQL 92. All database activities are done through a set of commands defined within TSQL. XPATH queries are first converted to TSQL and then converted back to a standard XML document before display to the user.

A SQL Server 2000 database consists of a collection of tables that store a specific set of structured data. Tables contain a collection of rows and records, and each column in the table is designed to store certain types of information based on the

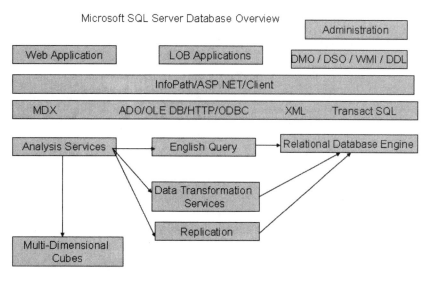

FIGURE 5.1 The SQL Server 2000 architecture.

defined schema. Tables have a variety of controls defined within their schema that the database designer can customize to ensure the data's business validity. Tables can also contain indexes that allow for quick retrieval of row information.

Declarative Referential Integrity (DRI) constraints are added to the table to ensure that interrelated data in different tables remains constant. A database can also store procedures that use the TSQL programming language to perform operations on the data. This includes storing views and inserting, updating, and deleting data within tables.

Database Design Considerations

When the developer is designing a database application, it is important to understand the exact business functions needed as well as the database concepts and features used for their representation. Database changes can become expensive from both a resource and time perspective. They often require a migration of the data to the new format and a re-design of applications and forms (like InfoPath) that are bound to the database. When designing a database application, architects, and developers should keep the following things in mind:

- The purpose of the database and how this will affect the design
- Database normalization rules that prevent mistakes in database design

- The protection of data integrity and object relationships
- Specific application and database security requirements
- Performance needs of the applications
- Maintenance requirements
- The estimated size and hardware configuration of the database

With these things in mind, let's create a database named CompanyInfo to manage the data within a company. (The database script can be found on the companion CD-ROM in \Code\Chapter 5\SampleDataBaseScript\Sample.sql.) This database contains a table named Customers that contains information about the company's current customers and their main point of contact. This table contains columns named CustomerID, CustomerName, CustomerPhone, Customer-Email, and CustomerContact. To ensure that no two customers share the same CustomerID, we add a constraint to the table. We also define a set of indexes because it is important for the business to quickly locate customer information based on their ID or name. Using the TSQL language, we define this schema structure with Listing 5.1.

LISTING 5.1 Creating the Customers Table

```
CREATE TABLE [dbo].[Customers] (
[CustID] [int] IDENTITY (1, 1)
  NOT FOR REPLICATION NOT NULL ,
[CustomerName] [varchar] (75)
  COLLATE SQL_Latin1_General_CP1_CI_AS NOT NULL ,
[CustomerPhone] [varchar] (12)
  COLLATE SQL_Latin1_General_CP1_CI_AS NULL ,
[CustomerEmail] [varchar] (50)
  COLLATE SQL_Latin1_General_CP1_CI_AS NULL ,
[CustomerContact] [varchar] (75)
 COLLATE SQL_Latin1_General_CP1_CI_AS NULL
) ON [PRIMARY]
GO
```

SQL Server can have as many as two billion rows per database and 1,024 columns per table. The number of rows and total size of the tables are limited only by the available storage. The maximum number of bytes per row is 8,060. Statements that are used to alter or create a database structure are part of the Data Definition Language (DDL). This is a subset of the TSQL dialect and is part of the database management system that is used to define all attributes and properties of a database. This language defines a set of constructs that include the CREATE TABLE statement to define all attributes and properties of the database, including row layout, column definitions, key columns, file location, and even storage strategy.

InfoPath and Database Connectivity

Connecting to SQL Server and Microsoft Access databases is done through the same design process that was used for Web Services and XML. The New option from the data connection link launches the Data Source Wizard, which allows you to either select or create a database connection object. Table 5.3 shows the Data Source Wizard's common underlying set of services that enable InfoPath to connect with external data sources.

TABLE 5.3   Adapter Sets Used by InfoPath

Connection Type	Adapter Used
XML Schema or XML Data File	XMLFileAdapter
Database (Microsoft SQL Server or Microsoft Access Only)	ADOAdapter
Web Service	WebServiceAdapter

Database connectivity is provided through either the ActiveX Data Object or an Open Database Connectivity (ODBC) Data Source Name (DSN) connection. Both of these provide a connection string to the underlying data source. The main difference is that the ADO connection object is optimized for both SQL and Microsoft Access and is the preferred method for database connectivity. The Data Source Wizard creates a reusable file that is stored in the user's My Data Sources folder and contains all the information needed to connect with the database.

The additional benefit of these connection files is that these files become a shared connection that is common to all Microsoft Office System 2003 applications. The Data Connection Wizard steps the user through the process of connecting to an OLE DB data source and persisting the connection into the Data Connection file. This wizard can also edit the connection information in existing data sources in case they change. The metadata stored within these files enables users to search for connections based on their descriptive data.

The Data Connection Wizard also provides access to an additional kind of common data source called the data retrieval service when you're connecting through Microsoft Excel 2003 and Office 2003 Web components. A data retrieval service is a Web Service installed on a Windows SharePoint Services (WSS) server used for connecting to and retrieving data. When the data retrieval service is used this way, the client application sends an HTTP request to the data retrieval service on WSS that is returned as an XML document containing the requested data. In addition to databases, WSS contains a data retrieval service for connecting to data in SharePoint lists.

When a form that is connected to a database is designed, we encounter the same restrictions as apply to a Web Service. InfoPath builds a data structure based on the database, and the resulting form can be used to submit data and query the existing database. Just as with a Web Service, the underlying data source matches the database and the existing fields or groups can't be modified except at the root group in the data source.

Defining the Data Source

When a new database connection is defined within Office, an Office Database Connection (ODC) file is created. This file contains the reusable connection information that is used to connect to the OLE DB provider used to obtain the data within a database. When we use a data source created for the MyCompany database and point to an invoice file, all the information needed to connect to the data source is maintained within the HTML file created during the creation of the connection. Listing 5.2 shows the connection file to the MyCompany database.

LISTING 5.2 An Office Database Connection File for the MyCompany Database

```
<html>

<head>
<meta http-equiv=Content-Type content="text/x-ms-odc; charset=utf-8">
<meta name=ProgId content=ODC.Table>
<meta name=SourceType content=OLEDB>
<meta name=Catalog content=CompanyInfo>
<meta name=Schema content=dbo>
<meta name=Table content=Invoice>
<xml id=docprops></xml><xml id=msodc>
<odc:OfficeDataConnection
  xmlns:odc="urn:schemas-microsoft-com:office:odc"
  xmlns="http://www.w3.org/TR/REC-html40">
  <odc:Connection odc:Type="OLEDB">
    <odc:ConnectionString>Provider=SQLOLEDB.1;Integrated
Security=SSPI;Persist Security Info=True;Data Source=ThomsDev;Use
Procedure for Prepare=1;Auto Translate=True;Packet
Size=4096;Workstation ID=THOMSDEV;
Use Encryption for Data=False;Tag with column collation when
possible=False;Initial Catalog=CompanyInfo</odc:ConnectionString>
    <odc:CommandType>Table</odc:CommandType>
```

```
<odc:CommandText>"CompanyInfo"."dbo"."Invoice"</odc:CommandText>
    </odc:Connection>
  </odc:OfficeDataConnection>
</xml>
<style>
  <!--
    .ODCDataSource
    {
    behavior: url(dataconn.htc);
    }
-->
</style>

</head>

<body onload='init()' scroll=no leftmargin=0
topmargin=0 rightmargin=0 style='border: 0px'>
<table style='border: solid 1px threedface;
  height: 100%; width: 100%' cellpadding=0
  cellspacing=0 width='100%'>
  <tr>
  <td id=tdName style='font-family:arial;
    font-size:medium; padding: 3px; background-color: threedface'>

  </td>
   <td id=tdTableDropdown style='padding: 3px; background-color:
threedface; vertical-align: top; padding-bottom: 3px'>

  </td>
  </tr>
  <tr>
  <td id=tdDesc colspan='2' style='border-bottom: 1px threedshadow
solid; font-family: Arial; font-size: 1pt; padding: 2px; background-
color: threedface'>

   </td>
  </tr>
  <tr>
  <td colspan='2' style='height: 100%; padding-bottom: 4px; border-top:
1px threedhighlight solid;'>
```

```
    <div id='pt' style='height: 100%' class='ODCDataSource'></div>
      </td>
    </tr>
</table>


<script language='javascript'>

function init() {
  var sName, sDescription;
  var i, j;

  try {
    sName = unescape(location.href)

    i = sName.lastIndexOf(".")
    if (i>=0) { sName = sName.substring(1, i); }

    i = sName.lastIndexOf("/")
    if (i>=0) { sName = sName.substring(i+1, sName.length); }

    document.title = sName;
    document.getElementById("tdName").innerText = sName;

    sDescription = document.getElementById("docprops").innerHTML;

    i = sDescription.indexOf("escription>")
    if (i>=0) { j = sDescription.indexOf("escription>", i + 11); }

    if (i>=0 && j >= 0) {
      j = sDescription.lastIndexOf("</", j);

      if (j>=0) {
        sDescription = sDescription.substring(i+11, j);
        if (sDescription != "") {
            document.getElementById("tdDesc").style.fontSize="x-small";
          document.getElementById("tdDesc").innerHTML = sDescription;
          }
        }
      }
    }
  catch(e) {
```

```
    }
  }
</script>

</body>

</html>
```

Once created, this connection can be used by InfoPath as well as opened within a Web browser and rendered through an Excel Web Component, as shown in Figure 5.2.

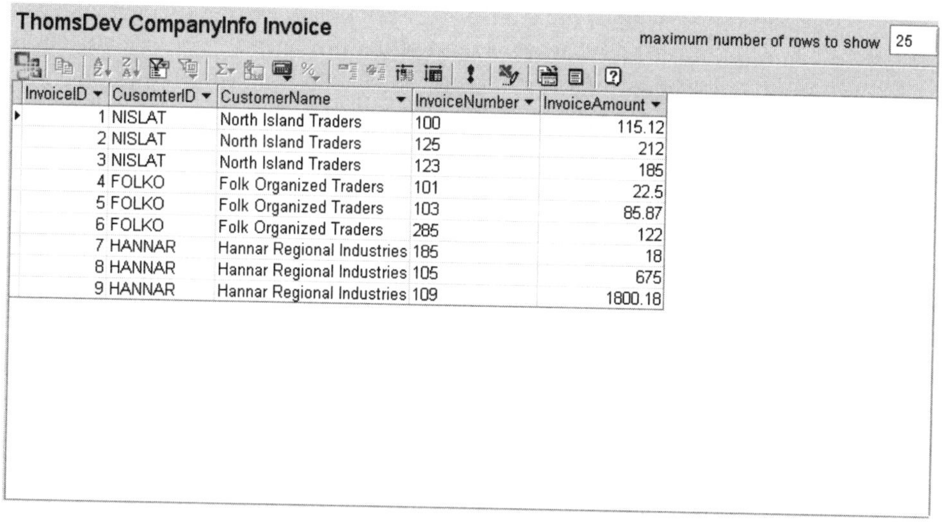

InvoiceID	CusomterID	CustomerName	InvoiceNumber	InvoiceAmount
1	NISLAT	North Island Traders	100	115.12
2	NISLAT	North Island Traders	125	212
3	NISLAT	North Island Traders	123	185
4	FOLKO	Folk Organized Traders	101	22.5
5	FOLKO	Folk Organized Traders	103	85.87
6	FOLKO	Folk Organized Traders	285	122
7	HANNAR	Hannar Regional Industries	185	18
8	HANNAR	Hannar Regional Industries	105	675
9	HANNAR	Hannar Regional Industries	109	1800.18

FIGURE 5.2 The ODC viewed through a Web browser.

The ADOAdapter is actually a subset of the OLE DB provider and existed before the .NET Framework. With the release of the Framework, this has become part of the System.Data.OleDB namespace. OLE DB is a COM-based data access object that provides access to all types of data and even provides access to a disconnected data store. OLE DB sits between the ODBC layer and the application. Within traditional ASP applications, OLE DB was the way that data was retrieved using the recordset object. InfoPath is not currently built using managed code, so the default provider types for database access are OLE DB and ADO.

OLE DB is the system-level programming interface for accessing data and is the underlying technology for ADO, as well as the source of data for ADO.NET. OLE

DB is an open standard for accessing all kinds of data, both relational and nonrelational. Natively, InfoPath exposes only the Microsoft Access and SQL Server portions of the provider. However, using the extensibility model through scripting or managed code, you can access other types of data using the built-in provider. For native code-based applications, ADO provides the COM-based application-level interface for all OLE DB data providers.

ADO also supports some behaviors not exposed through ADO.NET, such as scrollable, server-side cursors. However, because server-side cursors require holding database resources, their use might have a significant negative impact on the performance and scalability of applications. To send ADO recordsets through corporate firewalls, COM marshalling ports need to be opened. This is an additional security requirement that Web Services don't require because their XML-based payload uses HTTP as the transport mechanism. In these scenarios, the preferred method of a recordset object is to persist the source ADO recordset into an XML format and transmit the text instead. On the receiving end, these records are then re-hydrated into an ADO recordset.

Database Queries

InfoPath enables access to the relational data stored in SQL Server through the ADOAdapter. By default, this adapter is enabled for both the read and update of the underlying data source. Using InfoPath, this can be restricted to a query only view. The CompanyInfo database contains an invoice table that contains the current outstanding invoices. (This example is included on the companion CD-ROM, in \Code\Chapter 5\InvoiceLookup\InvoiceLookup.xsn.) Once connected to the data source, InfoPath renders the underlying data source fields, as shown in Figure 5.3.

Based on the selection of the data source fields, the underlying manifest.xsf solutions file maintains the generated SQL statement as part of the XML query element, as shown in Listing 5.3.

LISTING 5.3   An Example of a Persisted Database Connection

```
<xsf:query>
    <xsf:adoAdapter connectionString="Provider=SQLOLEDB.1;
    Integrated Security=SSPI;Persist Security Info=True;Initial
    Catalog=CompanyInfo;Data Source=ThomsDev;Use Procedure for
    Prepare=1;Auto Translate=True;Packet Size=4096;Workstation
    ID=THOMSDEV;Use Encryption for Data=False;Tag with column collation
    when possible=False" commandText="select
    "InvoiceID","CustomerID","CustomerName","InvoiceNumber",
    "InvoiceAmount" from "dbo"."Invoice" as "Invoice""
    queryAllowed="yes" submitAllowed="no"></xsf:adoAdapter>
</xsf:query>
```

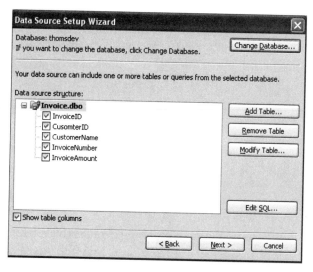

FIGURE 5.3 The tables available for query are shown.

In this solution, the query view acts as the view. When a user opens the solution, this is the page he will use to enter either the Customer ID or Customer Name. This generates a round-trip query to the database using the stored SQL statement. Once the query is complete, the code in the internal.js script is executed, the view switch is activated, and the data entry query is rendered. All fields within a data source are updateable. Selecting a field as read only within the Properties dialog box restricts the input capabilities of the underlying data source, as shown in Figure 5.4.

Defining an Expression

As part of the lookup, end users would like a total of the outstanding invoices owed by the customer. This can be done through code or using the expression box control. This control allows you to add an XPATH expression to the current form. One of the benefits of the expression control is that the existing schema isn't modified. Expressions are designed using the current schema and standard XPATH syntax, as shown here:

```
sum(dfs:dataFields/d:Invoice/@InvoiceAmount)
```

The actual rendering of this field is maintained in the XSL that is used to render the view and is stored within the InfoPath solution file, as shown in Listing 5.4.

FIGURE 5.4 Defining a read-only field.

LISTING 5.4 Rendering of an XPATH Field Within the InfoPath Solution File

```
<font size="2">Total Outstanding Invoices:
<span class="xdExpressionBox xdDataBindingUI
xdBehavior_Formatting" title="" tabIndex="-1"
xd:datafmt=""number","numDigits:auto;negativeOrder:1;""
xd:disableEditing="yes" xd:xctname="ExpressionBox"
xd:CtrlId="CTRL7"xd:binding="sum(dfs:dataFields/d:Invoice/@Invoice
Amount)"
style="WIDTH: 50%">
    <xsl:choose>

      <xsl:when test="function- available('xdFormatting:formatString')">
        <xsl:value-of select="xdFormatting:formatString(sum
        (dfs:dataFields/d:Invoice/@InvoiceAmount),"number",
        "numDigits:auto;negativeOrder:1;")"/>
      </xsl:when>
      <xsl:otherwise>
        <xsl:value-of select="sum(dfs:dataFields/d:Invoice/
        @InvoiceAmount)"/>
      </xsl:otherwise>
    </xsl:choose>
  </span>
</font>
```

Based on the values of the Invoice Amount field, the form will calculate a total for these fields and display it in the expression box. The last things this form does are to turn off any type of update and to remove or update the InfoPath repeating sections. By default, all repeating sections can add or delete rows. Because this is a read-only form, users don't need to do anything other than view the invoices. You can ensure this by using the repeating table properties. Uncheck the option to allow users to add and remove rows, as shown in Figure 5.5.

FIGURE 5.5 Turning off the ability to add or delete table rows.

Secondary Data Sources

InfoPath forms can host multiple data sources. One of the uses of a secondary data source is to load values for lookups and populate drop-down lists. Within the In-voice lookup, one of the requirements is that the lookup provide a list of existing customers. Having this list available will make it easier for the person who is using the form to search on a known set of values. You can make the list available by changing the existing text boxes on the query form to drop-down list boxes. List boxes by default can contain a fixed set of values, or they can be attached to a sec-ondary data source.

Using the Tools menu, create a secondary data source to the database. To constrain the values in the list box to a unique set, you just need to enter the following SQL statement:

```
select distinct "CustomerID","CustomerName" from "dbo"."Invoice" as
"Invoice"
```

Secondary data sources are also maintained as part of the manifest.xsf and stored in the solution file, as shown in Listing 5.5.

LISTING 5.5 An Example of a Persisted Secondary Data Source

```
<xsf:dataObjects>
  <xsf:dataObject name="Invoice" schema="Invoice3.xsd" initOnLoad="yes">
    <xsf:query>
      <xsf:Adoadapter connectionstring="provider=sqloledb.1;
      integrated security=sspi;persist security info=true;initial
      catalog=companyinfo;data source=thomsdev;use procedure for
      prepare=1;auto translate=true;packet size=4096;workstation
      id=thomsdev;use encryption for data=false;tag with column
      collation when possible=false" commandtext="select distinct
      "custoterid","customername" from "dbo"."invoice" as "invoice""
      queryallowed="yes":@/xsf:adoadapter:
    </xsf:query>
  </xsf:dataObject>
```

Once created, the secondary data source can then be bound to the form using the List Box Properties dialog box, as shown in Figure 5.6.

Executing Stored Procedures

Stored procedures are a precompiled collection of TSQL statements stored under a unique name and processed as a single unit. SQL Server supplies a variety of these that are used to manage and display information about the database and users. Stored procedures provided by SQL Server are called system stored procedures and are stored as part of the Master database. This database is responsible for controlling the operation of each instance of SQL Server. During the initial install of SQL Server, this database is installed automatically and keeps track of things like user accounts and remote servers. It is also responsible for tracking the ongoing processes, environmental variables, system error messages, and backups. One of the stored procedures maintained in this database is sp_who. This system stored procedure

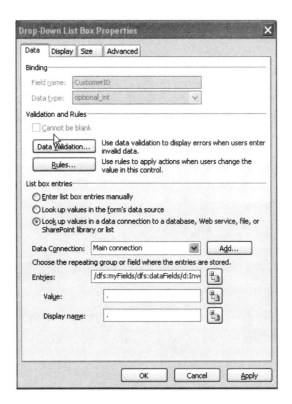

FIGURE 5.6 Assigning a secondary data source to a drop-down list box.

provides information about the current system users and processes, as shown in Figure 5.7.

Executing a stored procedure is similar to executing a prepared statement except that stored procedures exist as a permanent compiled object in the database. Also, from a developer perspective, stored procedures hide the complexity of SQL statements from an application. Stored procedures also assist in providing consistent implementation logic across applications. The SQL statements and logic needed to perform common tasks can be designed, coded, and tested once in a stored procedure. Each application needing to perform that task can simply execute the stored procedure.

This offers a centralized set of business logic and a single point of control for ensuring that business logic and rules are consistently enforced. Stored procedures also help to improve application performance. Each task implemented in the stored

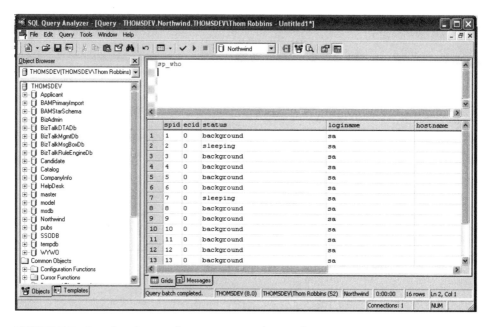

FIGURE 5.7 Running the sp_who system stored procedure.

procedure is part of a single execution plan on a server. All the execution and application logic is applied on the server before being returned to the client.

Every SQL Query has one or more associated execution plans. An execution plan consists of one or more component operations. SQL Server 2000 determines the best plan based on a cost based structure that is designed to provide the fastest response and lowest overhead.

NOTE

Stored Procedure Execution

The data source capabilities of InfoPath don't directly support the execution of stored procedures. The ADO Adapter object within the data source provides table-based access. Using scripts, we can extend the current Invoice Lookup solution to include the execution of a stored procedure that provides a total of all the outstanding invoices. (This example is included on the companion CD-ROM, in \Code\Chapter 5\InvoiceLookup\InvoiceLookup.xsn.)

ON THE CD

Using the CompanyInfo database, create a new stored procedure that totals the InvoiceAmount field:

```
CREATE PROCEDURE SumOfInvoices AS

Select Sum(InvoiceAmount) as TotalAmount from Invoice
GO
```

The CREATE PROCEDURE statement is used to define a stored procedure. This is used by the SQL Query engine to determine the type of execution plan for a set of statements. Using an algorithm defined within SQL Server, the database engine determines if a new stored procedure matches an existing execution plan or if a new one should be defined. This reduces the need of pre-compiling all stored procedures and extending the execution plan reuse within SQL Server.

The SELECT statement uses the SUM keyword as a way of totaling all the values within the InvoiceAmount field. By default, these types of queries are designed to return blank row names. Using the AS keyword enables the stored procedure to identify a row name for the return values.

Secondary Data Source Objects

Default data access within InfoPath is done through the data source object of the XDocument object. Executing the SumOfInvoices stored procedure uses this object. Create the secondary data source and then edit the SQL statement generated by the ADO Adapter, as shown in Figure 5.8.

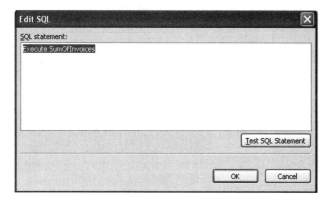

FIGURE 5.8 Updating the SQL statement field in InfoPath.

Replace the generated SQL statement with a call to the stored procedure. Using the EXECUTE keyword runs the stored procedure using the predefined execution path. When the data source is saved, ignore the error, as shown in Figure 5.9.

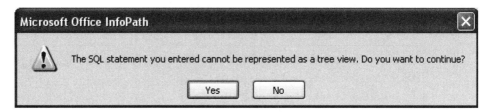

FIGURE 5.9   Ignore this error message when using a stored procedure.

Based on the use of XML, the ADO Adapter attempts to return all executable queries in a tree view or set of hierarchical data. When you execute stored procedures, the data returned from the stored procedures is not initially returned in a properly formatted XML string until the execution of the form. This secondary data source simply provides an entry in the XDocument object model that can be used to programmatically access the stored procedure execution.

Extending InfoPath

Within InfoPath, add a button control to the data entry page. The button control is a script component that is maintained as part of the XSL style sheet rendered for the page. This control provides a single OnClick event when pressed. Within MSE, enter the script shown in Listing 5.6 into the OnClick event.

LISTING 5.6   The `OnClick` Event for the Invoice Lookup Application

```
function GetTotal::OnClick(eventObj) {
  // Write your code here
  //Set the command for the data source's Query Adapter
  Document.DataObjects("TotalInvoice").QueryAdapter.Command = "execute
  SumOfInvoices";
   XDocument.DataObjects("TotalInvoice").Query();

  //Set the "SelectNamespaces" property so we can do
  // selectNodes calls on the DOM XDocument.DataObjects("TotalInvoice")
  .DOM.setProperty("SelectionNamespaces",'xmlns:dfs="_
```

```
http://schemas.microsoft.com/office/infopath/2003/dataFormSolution"
xmlns:d="http://schemas.microsoft.com/office/infopath/2003/ado/dataFi
elds"');

//Get a reference to the total var objTotalAmount
=XDocument.DataObjects("TotalInvoice").DOM.selectNodes("/dfs:myFields
/dfs:dataFields/d:row");
// Display the value
XDocument.UI.Alert("Total Customer Invoices: $" +
objTotalAmount.item(0).selectSingleNode( "@TotalAmount" ).text)
}
```

This function accesses the secondary data source created earlier in this chapter, within the XDocument DataObjects and returns the stored procedure values. The actual XML being returned by SQL Server is in the following format:

```
<dfs:myFields
xmlns:dfs=\"http://schemas.microsoft.com/office/infopath/2003/dataFormS
olution\">
<dfs:dataFields>
  <d:row
xmlns:d=\"http://schemas.microsoft.com/office/infopath/2003/ado/dataFie
lds\" TotalAmount=\"3235.67\"/>
</dfs:dataFields></dfs:myFields>
```

To access the SQL data returned as an XML structure, you need to define the SelectionNamespaces property. This property specifies a new set of XML namespaces used for an XPATH statement. When an XML document contains elements defined in an external namespace, this property specifies the namespaces to use for DOM navigation methods like SelectSingleNode.

MICROSOFT ACCESS 2003

Microsoft Access 2003 is architecturally different than SQL Server 2000. Access is designed to enable enterprisewide data access using a client/server model to corporate information. The client/server–based architecture is designed to provide the links to access and manipulate data regardless of its location and storage format. Using this type of data model as a pattern of database development allows SQL Server to act as the next scalable design pattern. Inherently, applications will grow and increase both in their size and complexity within their lifetime. Using the client/server application model, Access provides a simplified graphical user environment that rapidly enables application developers and end users to create applications. One of the benefits of platform architectures like .NET is that the common event model is used as the basis of all application design and development. This enables application users and developers to scale their applications quickly and easily.

Microsoft Access is a simplified relational database. The benefits of Access are really in that it allows users to easily create and modify database structures and applications using a variety of built-in wizards. In addition, the familiar look and feel of Microsoft Office makes Access an ideal solution for applications requiring the client/server architecture and less than two gigabytes of data storage.

Database Architecture

All database objects within Microsoft Access are maintained within a single .mdb file. At the top level is the Access user interface, which enables developers and end users to create and manage the relation components. The interface components and functions are stored within the Access relational Jet database. This database contains the following information:

Data Access Objects: A high-level object-oriented data access language that is both a DDL and Data Manipulation Language (DML) for Access.

Query Manager: A sophisticated query processor that builds SQL statements based on a cost-based optimizer that manages query objects and their result sets. This optimizer enables heterogeneous updateable joins using a query-on-query model. These joins are a unique feature of Microsoft Access that allows the creation of updateable queries against different tables in a different type of databases. For example, these joins allow you to update an Access table and a SQL Server data table with one query. The query manager is also responsible for deciding when to send queries to the Indexed Sequential Access Methods (ISAM) manager or the remote manager.

ISAM Manager: This manager provides access to various foreign ISAMs and has a native (local-to-Jet) ISAM called the Jet ISAM.

Remote Manager: The remote manager is responsible for receiving queries from the query manager and then makes the appropriate ODBC API calls to retrieve and pass data back to the query manager.

The lowest level of the Jet database is the ODBC layer. This layer enables Access to connect to any ODBC-compliant database. This is designed to enable Access to serve as the frontend for a variety of database sources like SQL Server and enhances the idea of enterprisewide connectivity.

The Jet Engine

Version 4 of the Jet Engine contained within Access 2003 is a mixture of both ANSI-89 Level 1 and ANSI-92 SQL syntax. In addition, when you use the OLE DB provider within Access, additional keywords and features that are not directly supported within ANSI SQL are exposed. The major differences between these two types of SQL syntax and Microsoft 2003 are as follows:

■ Different rules are applied to the "BETWEEN AND" SQL construct. This SQL feature has the following syntax:

```
Syntax: expr[1] [NOT] Between value 1 and value 2
```

■ Jet allows "value 1" to be greater than "value 2." With ANSI SQL, "value 1" must be equal to or less than "value 2"
■ Microsoft Jet SQL supports both the ANSI SQL wildcard characters and the Microsoft Jet-specific wildcard characters to use with the LIKE operator. The use of the ANSI and Microsoft Jet wildcard characters is mutually exclusive. ANSI SQL wildcards are available only when you're using Jet 4.X and the Microsoft OLE DB provider for Jet. When the ANSI SQL wildcards are used through Microsoft Access or DAO, they are interpreted as literals. When used through the OLE DB provider for Jet and Jet 4.X, they are not. Table 5.4 shows the major pattern match syntax requirements

TABLE 5.4   Pattern Match Syntax Requirements

Matching Character	Microsoft Jet SQL	ANSI SQL
Any Single Character	?	_ (Underscore)
Zero or More Characters	*	%

■ Microsoft Jet SQL is considered less restrictive and allows grouping and expression ordering. This enables ordered expressions

Access Components

Unlike SQL Server, which provides integrated security access within both the table and database structure, Access supports a workgroup information file that it reads on startup and that contains information about the users in the workgroup. This information includes user account names, password, and the groups of which they are members. This enables Access to function as a multi-user database and define permissions around the database attributes and objects that a specific user or group may have access to.

The structure of the Access database makes multi-user access very different than with SQL Server. When looking to provide an Access database to users in a networked environment, you should keep the following guides in place:

- Place the entire application on a network server and allow multiple users to open the database
- Split the database into two databases. This creates a back-end database, which contains the application tables, and a front-end database, which contains the application objects. The back-end database is then placed on a network server, whereas the front-end database is distributed to the application users. The benefit of this approach is the reduction of the network traffic needed to run the application. The downside is that all application access requires connectivity to the back-end database

When running in a multi-user environment, Access consists of several components. In addition to the access database, a multi-user Access database contains a workgroup information file and a locking database. The workgroup information file (.mdw) is the file that stores information about users in the workgroup. The other component is the locking information (.ldb) file for each database. This file resides in the same folder as the database.

The workgroup information (.mdw) file is a Microsoft Access database that stores information about users in a workgroup, including their account names, their passwords, and the groups that they belong to. It also stores preference information that each user can specify in the Tools Options dialog box.

The location of the workgroup information file in multi-user environments is important. It can either be placed on each local workstation or shared on a network server. However, if it's stored locally, you must take the steps necessary to update it when security settings change. The workgroup information file also stores a list of the most recently used databases. If the database design dictates that users must have their own lists of the most recently used database, then these need to be stored on the individual users' workstations and a schema for user-level security has to be designed.

The locking information (.ldb) file stores information about any records that are currently locked in the database. If the locking information file doesn't exist when the database is opened, the Microsoft Jet database engine creates it. There is one locking file created for every Microsoft Access database file that is opened in shared mode. Microsoft Jet gives the file the same name as the opened database but

ON THE CD

with an .ldb extension. For example, the sample Inventory.mdb has an associated locking information file called Inventory.ldb (see \Code\Chapter 5\Access Product\ProductActivity.xsn on the companion CD-ROM). The locking information file is stored in the same folder as the database. Microsoft Jet deletes the .ldb file when the database is closed.

Database Structure

Unlike with SQL Server, in Access a single MDB file matches a single database. This single file contains all the components that relate to the database. Table 5.5 shows the components that are stored as part of the database.

TABLE 5.5 Components Stored Within an Access 2003 Database

Component	Description
Tables	The tables are the backbone and the storage container of the data entered into the database. If the tables are not set up correctly with the correct relationships (see the next entry in the table), then the database may be slow, may give you the wrong results, or may not react the way you expect. Therefore, take a bit of time when setting up your tables. All actions—that is, queries, forms, and so on—must be based on or contained in a table. When opened, these tables look similar to a Microsoft Word or Microsoft Excel spreadsheet. They have columns and rows. Each column will have a field name at the top, and each row will represent a record.
Relationships	Relationships are the bonds built between the tables. They join tables that have associated elements. Before you can relationally join tables, there must be a common field between the two tables.
Queries	Queries are the means of manipulating the data to display in a form or a report. Queries can sort, calculate, group, filter, join tables, update data, delete data, and so forth. In the early stages of learning Access, you don't need to know SQL. Microsoft Access writes the SQL for you, after you tell it what you want, in the design view of the queries window.

$\rightarrow$

Component	Description
Forms	Forms are the primary interface where users enter data. The person who enters the data will interact with forms regularly. By using queries, properties, macros, and Visual Basic for Applications (VBA) , the programmer can set the forms to show only the data required. The ability to add, edit, and delete data can also be set. Forms can be set up very individually to reflect the use they are required for.
Reports	Reports are the results of the manipulation of the data entered into the database. Unlike forms, they cannot be edited. Reports are intended to be used to output data to another device or application; that is, printer, email, Microsoft Word or Excel.
Macros	Macros are an automatic way for Access to carry out a series of actions for the database. Access lets you select actions that are carried out in the order you enter. Macros can open forms, run queries, change values of a field, or run other macros.
Modules	A module is a window where developers write and store VBA. Advanced users of Microsoft Access tend to use VBA instead of macros.
Data Access Page	Data access pages are Web pages published from an Access database that have a connection to the database. These pages also allow you to connect to other data sources that can be pushed to the Web; these include Excel and SQL Server.

All components of Access are persistent. This design feature saves component changes when the database is closed and when a developer moves from one component to another. This is different that other Office applications such as Word, which saves the entire document only when it is closed.

Database Relationships

Tables contain definitions that relate to objects. These object definitions may require several tables of related data to fully describe them. Relationships are the object definitions that exist across tables. Once these relationships are defined using SQL, they allow data across multiple tables to be displayed.

Relationships work by matching data in key fields. Usually, these fields contain the same name in both tables. In most cases, these matching fields are the primary keys from one table that provide the unique identifier for each record and a foreign key in the other table. For example, an inventory management application can contain tables that describe products and the related purchase orders that together define an inventory item. Figure 5.10 shows the tables that are used to define the sample Inventory application.

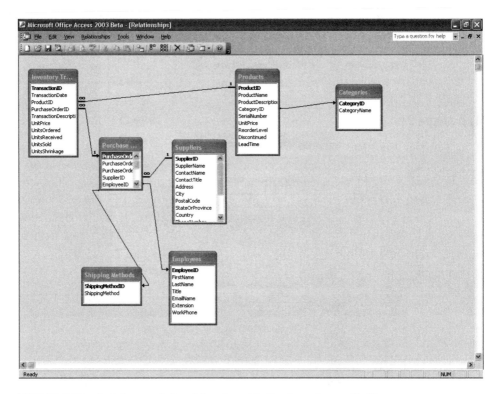

FIGURE 5.10   Database relationships stored in the Inventory.mdb file.

Database relational concepts for both SQL Server and Microsoft Access define different types of table relationships and consist of the following:

One-to-One: In a one-to-one relationship, each record in a table can have only one matching record in another table. This type of relationship is not common because most of the related information would be stored in a single table. Often, this type of relationship is used to divide tables with a large amount of fields, isolate sections of a table for security reasons, or store a subset of main tables.

One-to-Many: One-to-many relationships are the most common database type relationships. In this type of relationship, a single record in one table has many matching records in another table. The other side of the relationship is that many records are related to only a single record in the master table.

Many-to-Many: In many-to-many relationships, a single record has many matching records in another table, and in that table, a single record contains many matching records in the other table. This type of relationship is defined by the use of a third table called a *junction table*, which provides a primary key that consists of two fields from both tables. These types of relationships are really two one-to-many relationships, with a third table providing object context.

The Shape Provider

ON THE CD

Using the ADO Adapter within InfoPath, you can extend the Inventory Management Access Application to include InfoPath forms (this is included on the companion CD-ROM in \Code\Chapter 5\AccessProductActivity\ProductActivity.xsn). Using this application, you can add a form that provides product updates and transaction histories. This type of form uses the built-in relationships defined within the application to define the form. The base data source is defined from the initial products table, as shown in Figure 5.11.

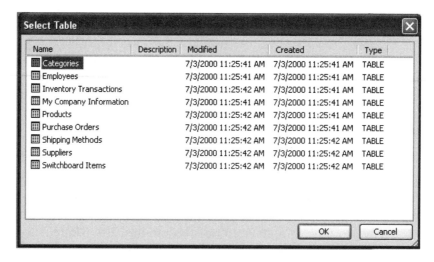

FIGURE 5.11 The listing of tables as seen in InfoPath.

Once the base table is selected, additional related tables are added to the data source, as shown in Figure 5.12.

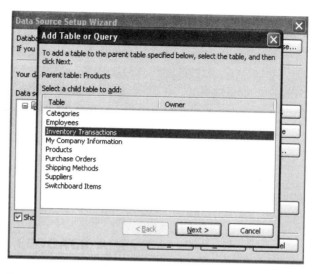

FIGURE 5.12 Using InfoPath to add additional tables to the data source.

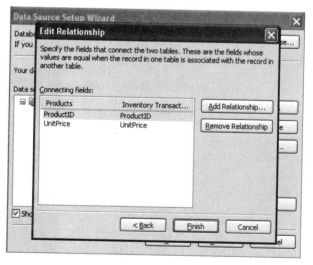

FIGURE 5.13 Selecting the related tables using InfoPath.

As related tables are added, the data source analyzes the existing table structure to determine if these tables have an existing relationship. These relationships are pulled into the data source and shown with the Data Source Wizard in Figure 5.13.

Doing this allows the data source to access both defined data sources and define new ones, as shown in Figure 5.14.

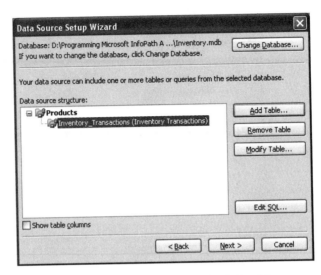

FIGURE 5.14 Reviewing the defined relationships within InfoPath.

Once all related tables are added, the data source adapter generates the SQL statement, as shown in Listing 5.7.

LISTING 5.7 The Shape Provider Statement Created by the Data Source Adapter

```
shape
{select [ProductID],[ProductName],[ProductDescription],[CategoryID],
[SerialNumber],[UnitPrice],[ReorderLevel],[Discontinued],[LeadTime]
  from [Products] as [Products]} as [Products]
  append
  ({select
[TransactionID],[TransactionDate],[ProductID],[PurchaseOrderID],
[TransactionDescription],

[UnitPrice],[UnitsOrdered],[UnitsReceived],[UnitsSold],[UnitsShrinkage]
  from [Inventory Transactions]}
  relate [ProductID] TO [ProductID],[UnitPrice] TO [UnitPrice]) as
[Inventory_Transactions]
```

The underlying Data Source Wizard uses the shape provider to generate a hierarchical recordset for display in InfoPath. The shape provider works by reading the parent and child relationships into a temporary table on the local machine;

using the cursor engine dynamically filters the child records to match the current parent record.

The shape provider allows tables to be joined based on relation, parameters or groups. The relation and parameter joins are similar to the SQL-based JOIN command except that both the child and parent records are read into the local cache before processing (instead of only selected fields). Initially, this type of query requires a higher overhead than a standard SQL JOIN, but once all the fields are cached locally, the overall performance increases.

The parameter-based shape hierarchy reads only the parent records and then fetches the matching child records on demand. This type of statement offers reduced initial overhead, but each new child query generates a database call, and a database connection is always maintained. The group-based hierarchy is the equivalent to the AGGREGATE SQL statement or performing an aggregate function on non-normalized data. This creates a non-updateable recordset that is presented within InfoPath, and all database records are fetched at the start of the connection. Once the data source is complete, the wizard provides summary information that can be used to determine whether the query is updateable, as shown in Figure 5.15.

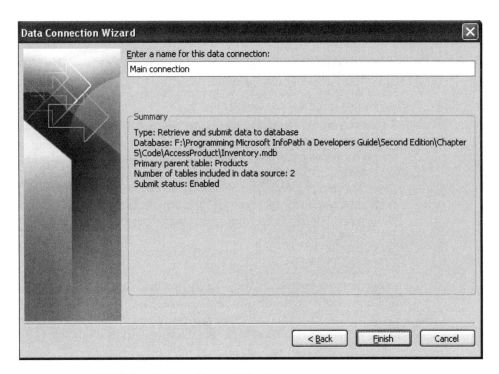

FIGURE 5.15 Finalizing the Data Source Wizard.

The completed data source provides the structured recordset within the data source window that matches the relationships defined during the wizard. Listing 5.8 shows the persisted data source maintained by InfoPath.

LISTING 5.8   SQL Query Persisted by the InfoPath Solution

```
<xsf:query>
<xsf:adoAdapter
connectionString="Provider=Microsoft.Jet.OLEDB.4.0;Password="";
  User ID=Admin;Data Source=D:Chapter 5\Inventory.mdb;Mode=Share Deny
None;
  Extended Properties="";Jet OLEDB:System database="";
  Jet OLEDB:Registry Path="";Jet OLEDB:Database Password=""
  ;Jet OLEDB:Engine Type=5;Jet OLEDB:Database Locking Mode=1;Jet OLEDB:
  Global Partial Bulk Ops=2;Jet OLEDB:Global Bulk Transactions=1;Jet
OLEDB:
  New Database Password="";Jet OLEDB:Create System Database=False;
  Jet OLEDB:Encrypt Database=False;Jet OLEDB:Don't Copy Locale on
Compact=False;Jet OLEDB:
  Compact Without Replica Repair=False;Jet OLEDB:SFP=False"
  commandText="shape {select
[ProductID],[ProductName],[ProductDescription],

  [CategoryID],[SerialNumber],[UnitPrice],[ReorderLevel],[Discontinued],
[LeadTime] from
  [Products] as [Products]} as [Products] append
  ({select
[TransactionID],[TransactionDate],[ProductID],[PurchaseOrderID],

  [TransactionDescription],[UnitPrice],[UnitsOrdered],[UnitsReceived],
[UnitsSold],
  [UnitsShrinkage] from [Inventory Transactions]}
  relate [ProductID] TO [ProductID],[UnitPrice] TO [UnitPrice]) as
  [Inventory_Transactions]" queryAllowed="yes" submitAllowed="yes">
</xsf:adoAdapter>
</xsf:query>
```

The manifest.xsf maintains the data source that contains the shape statement and based on query design executes that against the database. Using the relational shape provider within Access will cause forms to open more slowly as the size of the database increases.

SUMMARY

The success of XML has certainly not diminished the need for relational databases. They contain a wide variety of data within the enterprise. InfoPath, based on its extensible structure, can leverage these types of data sources and extend them to develop data-driven applications. This chapter has covered how, using SQL Server and Microsoft Access, InfoPath can leverage the ADO Adapter as a way of accessing these data sources.

Using a similar structure as we saw earlier with Web Services and XML, InfoPath accesses these relational data sources and returns information. Both SQL Server and Microsoft Access 2003 are powerful relational databases that are designed for very different types of environments. SQL, with its string enterprise wide connectivity and built-in scalability, is ideal for mission-critical applications. On the other hand, Microsoft Access is an ideal solution for client/server–based applications that don't have a string mission-critical need. Depending on the solution designed, they are both accessible from InfoPath. In the next several chapters, we will start to discuss how you can use both databases and Web Services to develop workflow solutions. These types of solutions provide an ideal application path for InfoPath-based solutions.

6 Building Workflow Enabled Applications

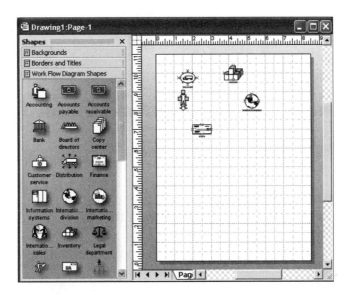

INTRODUCTION

All companies today are looking for ways to improve their overall operational efficiency. The rapid changes in technology and the globalization of major markets are requiring companies to find better ways to manage resources while lowering overall costs. These are two of the most important business drivers enabling companies to achieve long-term success. One way that many enterprises are finding they can meet these needs is by implementing workflow-enabled applications that automate existing business processes.

These applications are designed to model software applications against a specific business process with the goal that the applications should be flexible enough to change as the process is improved. They cover everything from simple task routing and approval to more advanced enterprise wide workflow and application integration. XML has become an important part of these types of solutions. Both its flexibility and ease of use make it the natural choice for these types of distributed applications. As an XML-based application, InfoPath makes an ideal front end for these types of applications.

As a standalone application, InfoPath allows you to design and implement simple workflow processes. When combined with other products in the Microsoft Office System 2003 and SOA design principles, the XML enablement makes InfoPath the ideal workflow-enabled platform. This chapter focuses on design principles and examples that show how these types of applications are developed using InfoPath to solve these types of business process automation issues.

DEFINING A WORKFLOW AUTOMATION SOLUTION

Before the invention of computers (otherwise known as the Dark Ages), workflow was a manual process. Each person involved in the process would receive a document, perform an action on the document, and then pass it to the next participant. The line manager was responsible for keeping the process moving forward and maintaining quality control. Within these processes, change was slow and error prone. With the introduction of technology, these types of paper-based processing became automated. The biggest benefit was that specific work items could be processed and changed at any number of processing points within the same application. Each of these steps or activities could easily be checked and reassigned based on any number of criteria.

Workflows are composed of a number of logical steps. Each individual step is known as an *activity*. Actions that execute within an activity may either involve human interaction (manual intervention) or be completely automated, executed using only system-based resources. Computing-based resources within a workflow help both the participants and the enterprise to deliver better worker productivity and efficiency while reducing overall processing errors. Figure 6.1 shows the similarity in the model between human- and computer-based workflow.

Workflows are, by definition, a sequence of events that result in the completion of an action. When they are automated, the workflow process enables documents, information, or tasks to be passed from one participant to another based on a procedural set of rules. The process-oriented nature of workflow applications is designed to coordinate smaller sets of work to accomplish a larger task.

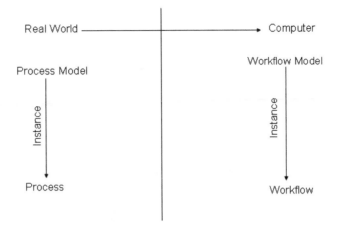

FIGURE 6.1   A similar model exists between human- and computer-based workflow.

The design of these types of systems follows a different approach than transaction-oriented systems do. Within a traditional application design, everything is done around the idea of a transaction. *Transactions* are defined as the completed execution of a program that certifies a set of pre-determined criteria. Transactions are always considered atomic, consistent, durable, and isolated. The main benefits of transactions are that they guarantee concurrency control and provide a consistent recovery point.

Here are some important considerations to keep in mind when you're designing a transaction-based application:

Atomic: This guarantees that the entire transaction is committed or ensures that none of it is committed.

Consistent: When applied, transactions don't violate any of the constraints defined by the database.

Durable: Once a transaction is committed, another transaction is required to undo the first.

Isolated: Each transaction is an independent and separate entity from any other. This guarantees that one transaction will not have an effect on another.

Workflow applications are designed very differently than transactional-based applications. In these types of applications, the logic is designed to enable multiple sessions to remain both active and incomplete for long periods without incurring either significant system overhead or requiring human intervention. It is important to understand that even though the overall workflow process doesn't adhere to the basic transactional model, certain activities could result in or spawn transactions.

Defining a Workflow Repository

The design of a workflow application is based on the process definition that defines the control flow for the application. These definitions are used to define resources, constraints, and the anticipated application flow. For simplicity, they are often developed using Visio as shown in Figure 6.2. For nontechnical business users, these definitions represent what actions are expected to occur during the execution of the workflow. Within the process definition, each process is composed of subprocesses that define a specific executable task. The physical design process of splitting the process into a series of tasks ensures that each step of the workflow is completely auditable. Each of the defined logical steps within a subprocess is known as an *activity* and, based on the specific business requirements, can be defined as either manual or automated.

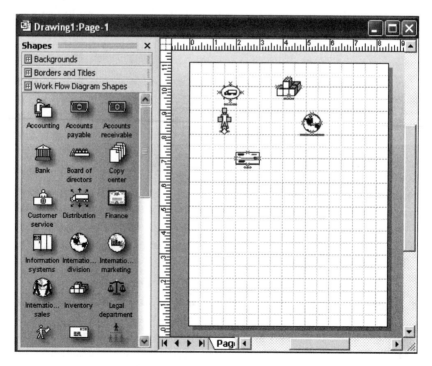

FIGURE 6.2 Visio can be used to build process definitions.

One of the most important benefits of any workflow application is to increase the efficiency and productivity of the participants. This doesn't mean that the entire subprocesses and workflow have to be automated. However, it is important to define the process definition so that you can determine the steps that are candidates for automation. This also ensures that documents within a process don't get lost.

The auditable nature of workflow applications ensures that documents can be tracked and are easy to find. The most common design pattern within these types of applications is the creation of a centralized repository to store documents or forms.

A type of application, collaborative workflow, focuses on teams working together toward common goals. Collaborative workflow is defined by a business process with a set of linked tasks. Workflow groups can vary from small project-oriented teams to widely dispersed people with common interests. This type of workflow has become one of the most important in any type of organization. Collaborative workflow is characterized by high business value but infrequent execution. Typically, the underlying process is rather complex and is created specifically for the task, often by customizing an existing process.

The increased importance of the knowledge worker has elevated the value of the collaborative processes within organizations. These types of workflow processes are intended to enhance the communications and effectiveness of these types of workers and to enable them to function faster and easier within an enterprise. The one major characteristic of this type of workflow that is different from many others is its semi-structured nature.

The nature of these types of workflow processes generally follows no fixed process map or well-defined roles. Depending on the process and the needs of the business requirements, people may fit into different roles at different points within the process. Often, the main drivers for these types of applications are the reduced cycle time and centralized repository of reusable information. Application throughput is not an important consideration, and process definitions are not considered rigid and can be amended frequently.

The Form Library

For InfoPath, the Form Library of Windows SharePoint Services (WSS) provides this type of centralized repository. The Form Library is a special-purpose WSS Document Library specifically based on an InfoPath Form Templates. The InfoPath Form Library is designed to provide the primary integration point between WSS and InfoPath, providing all the services needed to maintain, deploy, and share an InfoPath form. The form library is capable of displaying columns of information extracted from an InfoPath form. With these columns, the user can create custom views to organize forms and their content through property promotion. The form library also makes the extracted information available for searching as part of the SharePoint site. Form designers can use InfoPath to publish forms directly to the WSS library and to define custom views for their forms.

As a deployment location, users can open a form based on an InfoPath form by clicking on the Fill Out This Form button in a form library. When the user saves the completed form, it will automatically be saved back to the form library. If the user saves the form offline to work on later, he can still upload the completed form using the Upload Form command in the Form Library.

As data is accumulated, a WSS form library provides access to InfoPath's Merge Forms functionality through the Merge Forms view. The user uses checkboxes to select the documents he wants and then selects Merge Forms. Assuming the user has InfoPath installed, WSS will open a blank template in InfoPath and then merge each of the selected documents into that template. This operation does not change the original documents, but it allows you to view aggregate data from multiple documents easily.

A WSS Form allows the "promotion" of individual fields in an InfoPath document to columns in a WSS view. The contents of the promoted fields are displayed in a custom column. For example, say you were creating an FAQ-style form library where each document in the library contained one question, answer, and status field. Instead of depending on the filename to accurately reflect the contents of the document, you could promote the Question field to a WSS column. Users of the form library would be able to see the question covered by each document and pick the ones that meet their needs.

Using Forms-Based Libraries

A WSS Form Library can be created in several ways. In Chapter 2, we used the InfoPath built-in publishing wizard. WSS also provides a Web Administration view to create form libraries. This view allows users with the proper security permissions to directly create form libraries within the portal administration page.

Use the following steps when creating a new form library:

1. Open the WSS site and select Documents and Lists, as shown in Figure 6.3.

FIGURE 6.3 Select Documents and Lists to start creating a form library.

2. From within Documents and Lists, select the Create option, as shown in Figure 6.4.

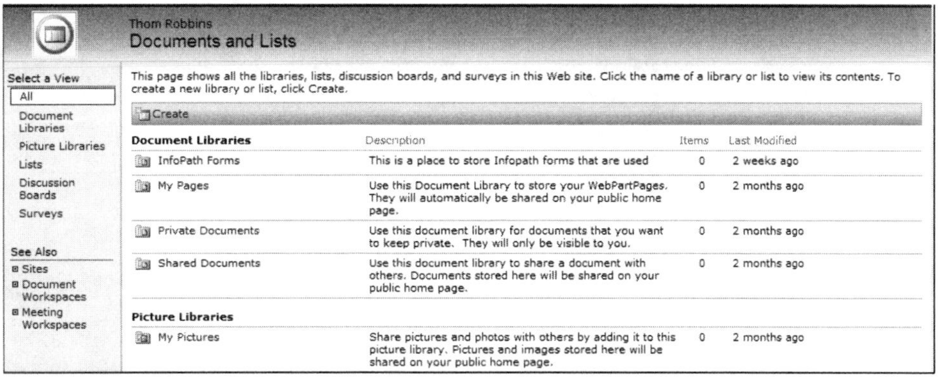

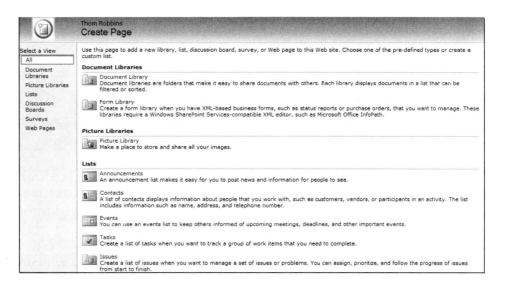

FIGURE 6.4   Select the Create option.

3. This Web page allows you to create all new document libraries. Select the Form Library option, which brings up the WSS Create Page, shown in Figure 6.5.

FIGURE 6.5   The WSS Create Page.

4. Enter the information to create the Sales Contact Page, which brings up the page creation properties, as shown in Figure 6.6.

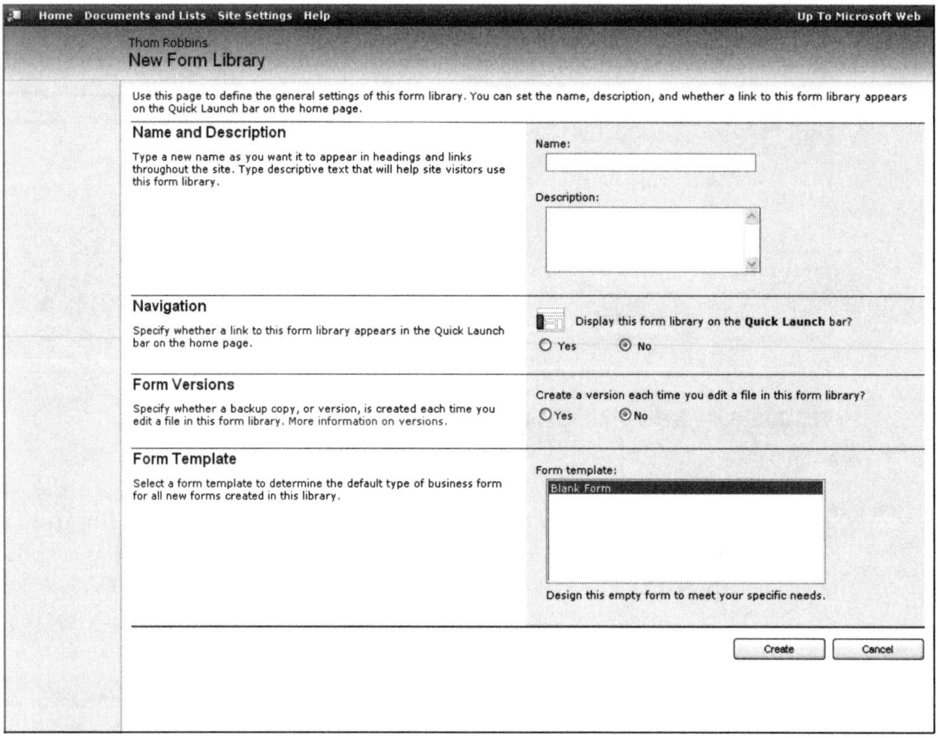

FIGURE 6.6 Page creation properties.

5. Once the page is created, you are redirected the default page, as shown in Figure 6.7, where you can then save the forms to these pages.

Often, workflow solutions provide a key competitive advantage in increasing customer satisfaction and retention, and enable organizations to better respond to changing market conditions. Because of the many benefits of workflow-based solutions, enterprises look to both optimize and protect them as critical assets. This often includes the ability to set security and user rights. WSS provides this for form libraries at both the site and library level as shown in Figure 6.8. The security model is designed to leverage either local security groups or Active Directory.

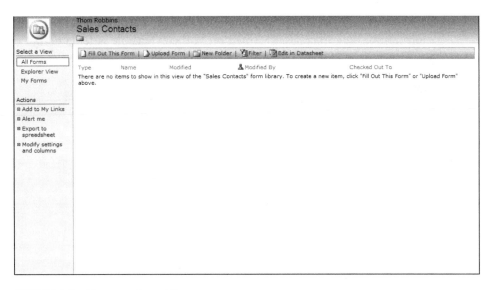

FIGURE 6.7   The new Form Library.

Use this page to add users to this site, list, or document library.

Step 1: Choose Users

You can enter e-mail addresses, user names (e.g., DOMAIN\name), or cross-site group names. Separate them with semicolons.

Users: Enter e-mail addresses and cross-site group names here

Address Book

Step 2: Choose Site Groups

Choose the site groups you want these users to have.

Site groups:
- Reader - Has read-only access to the Web site.
- Contributor - Can add content to existing document libraries and lists.
- Web Designer - Can create lists and document libraries and customize pages in the Web site.
- Administrator - Has full control of the Web site.

Next >

FIGURE 6.8   Setting security for a form library.

Exposing InfoPath Data

Once the form library is created, developers can store forms directly on the library and then expose key fields in the document as part of this. For example, we can create a Sales Contact form that can be stored in the WSS library (this can be found on

ON THE CD

the companion CD-ROM in \Code\Chapter 6\Sales Contacts\SalesContact.xsn).

This provides an ideal location for people to be able to store and retrieve contact information. We can create the form using the extensible schema definition (XSD), as shown in Listing 6.1.

LISTING 6.1   XSD Used to Create an InfoPath Form

```
<?xml version="1.0"?>
<xsd:schema
targetNamespace="http://schemas.mycompany.com/ns/sales/info"
xmlns:sales="http://schemas.mycompany.com/ns/sales/info"
xmlns:xsd="http://www.w3.org/2001/XMLSchema">

<xsd:simpleType name="roletypes">
  <xsd:restriction base="xsd:string">
  <xsd:enumeration value="Decision Maker"/>
  <xsd:enumeration value="Gatekeeper"/>
  <xsd:enumeration value="Influencer"/>
  <xsd:enumeration value="Champion"/>
  <xsd:enumeration value="User"/>
  <xsd:enumeration value="Other"/>
  </xsd:restriction>
</xsd:simpleType>

<xsd:element name="CompanyName" type="xsd:string"/>
<xsd:element name="ContactName" type="xsd:string"/>
<xsd:element name="ContactAddress1" type="xsd:string"/>
<xsd:element name="ContactAddress2" type="xsd:string"/>
<xsd:element name="ContactCity" type="xsd:string"/>
<xsd:element name="ContactState" type="xsd:string"/>
<xsd:element name="ContactZipCode" type="xsd:string"/>
<xsd:element name="ContactEmail" type="xsd:string"/>
<xsd:element name="ContactCellPhone" type="xsd:string"/>
<xsd:element name="ContactAssistName" type="xsd:string"/>
<xsd:element name="ContactAssistPhone" type="xsd:string"/>
<xsd:element name="ContactRole" type="sales:roletypes"/>
<xsd:element name="Comments" type="xsd:string"/>

<xsd:element name="salescontact">
  <xsd:complexType>
    <xsd:sequence>
      <xsd:element ref="sales:CompanyName"/>
      <xsd:element ref="sales:ContactName"/>
      <xsd:element ref="sales:ContactAddress1"/>
```

```
        <xsd:element ref="sales:ContactAddress2"/>
        <xsd:element ref="sales:ContactCity"/>
        <xsd:element ref="sales:ContactState"/>
        <xsd:element ref="sales:ContactZipCode"/>
        <xsd:element ref="sales:ContactEmail"/>
        <xsd:element ref="sales:ContactCellPhone"/>
        <xsd:element ref="sales:ContactAssistName"/>
        <xsd:element ref="sales:ContactAssistPhone"/>
        <xsd:element ref="sales:ContactRole"/>
        <xsd:element ref="sales:Comments"/>
      </xsd:sequence>
    </xsd:complexType>
  </xsd:element>
</xsd:schema>
```

The form shown in Figure 6.9 is based on the XSD just defined. This form is designed to store the Sales Contact information based on the data structure defined within the XSD.

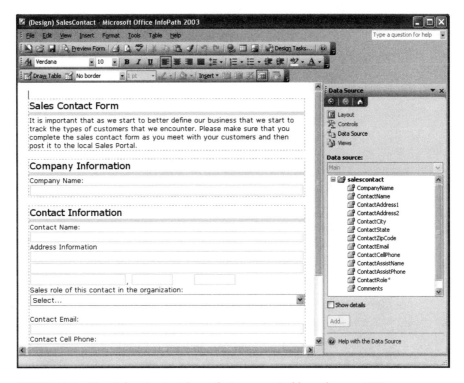

FIGURE 6.9 The Sales Contact form that we created based on an XSD.

Forms can promote their fields to the WSS site and show this as part of the actual design of the site. This provides a quick tickler for those users who are viewing the site and want to quickly review the information that has already been posted. Fields are exposed through the Forms Options dialog box and by selecting the fields from a drop-down list, as shown in Figure 6.10.

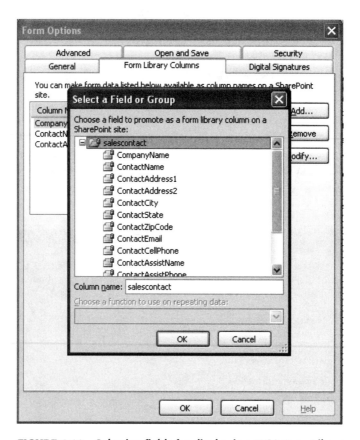

FIGURE 6.10   Selecting fields for display in a WSS Form Library.

Once saved, the solution file is modified to include a listProperties node that contains the promoted fields and is displayed when saved back to the portal site, as shown in Listing 6.2.

LISTING 6.2   The InfoPath Solution File Stores the Promoted Properties

```
<xsf:listProperties>
  <xsf:fields>
    <xsf:field name="CompanyName"
    columnName="{2FA32E08-4766-49B5-BF85-205BC6AC728C}"
node="/sales:salescontact/sales:CompanyName"
type="xsd:string"></xsf:field>
    <xsf:field name="ContactName"
columnName="{1E9FBA22-2D60-4CE3-8D87-8F1CF7788C57}"
node="/sales:salescontact/sales:ContactName"
type="xsd:string"></xsf:field>
    <xsf:field name="ContactAssistName"
columnName="{A8B29C59-86AC-4803-A47D-998E171A3486}"
node="/sales:salescontact/sales:ContactAssistName"
type="xsd:string"></xsf:field>
  </xsf:fields>
</xsf:listProperties>
```

Once the fields are selected, you can then publish the form to the WSS site. Use the following steps to define the default form published to the site using the InfoPath Publishing Wizard:

1. Within the form designer, select File Publish, as shown in Figure 6.11.

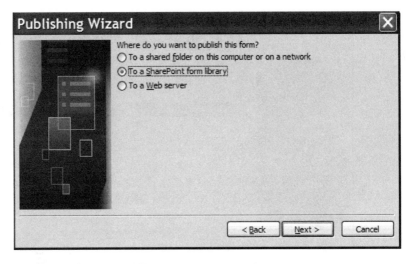

FIGURE 6.11   The InfoPath Publishing Wizard.

2. We have already created the Form library, so we will need to modify the existing library, as shown in Figure 6.12.

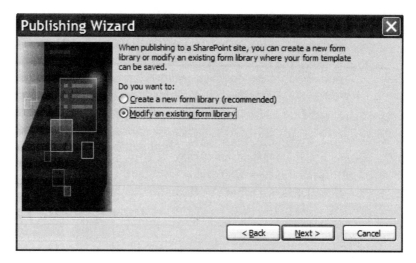

FIGURE 6.12 Selecting the form library to modify.

3. Enter the URL of the form library and then select it from the available list, as shown in Figure 6.13.

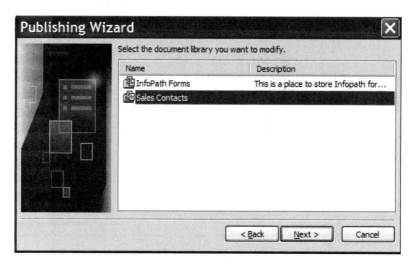

FIGURE 6.13 Selecting the available form libraries.

4. InfoPath form properties that are selected for promotion are automatically selected for WSS columns, as shown in Figure 6.14.

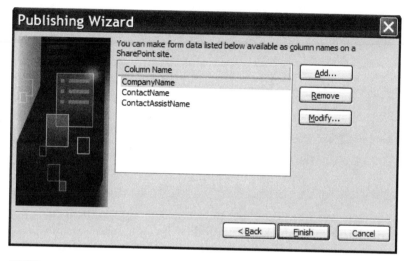

FIGURE 6.14   Selecting the properties to expose in the column list.

5. Once the form is published, you can notify users of the new form and location, as shown in Figure 6.15.

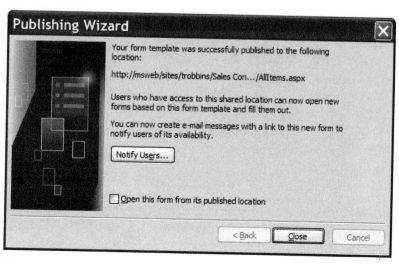

FIGURE 6.15   Completing the Publishing Wizard and notifying users.

6. Users can receive an email (as shown in Figure 6.16) that outlines and shows the form and its location.

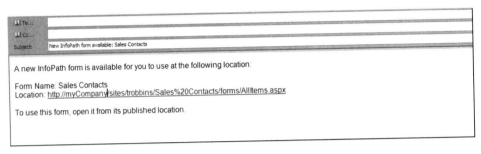

FIGURE 6.16   The notification email that invites users to use the form library.

Once the form is published to the WSS library, the form becomes the default template for the site. You can modify the basic menu to allow users to directly fill out the form from this site. Once the form is filled out, it can be directly saved back to the default site, as shown in Figure 6.17.

Once the form is saved, both the form and the promoted fields are viewable, as shown in Figure 6.18.

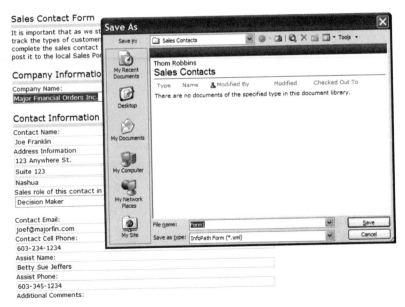

FIGURE 6.17   Saving an InfoPath form to the library.

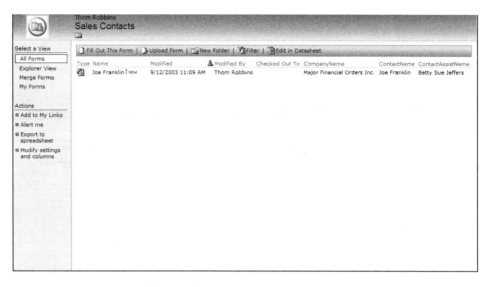

FIGURE 6.18   Reviewing the saved items.

Once an InfoPath form is saved to a form library, it should only be edited directly from the WSS site using the following steps.

1. Select the Modify Setting and Columns link from the Form Library, as shown in Figure 6.19.

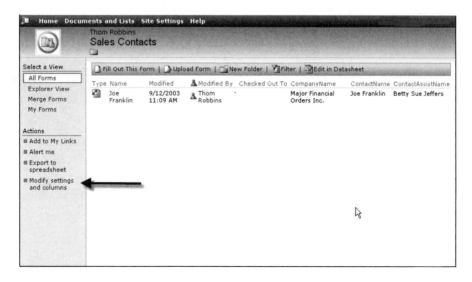

FIGURE 6.19   Modifying the WSS view.

2. Within General Setting, select the Edit Template link, as shown in Figure 6.20.

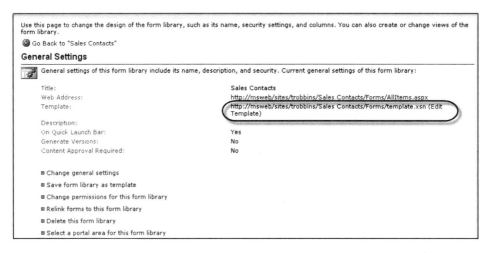

FIGURE 6.20   Editing the template.

One of the most important advantages of this type of workflow is that users can set up notifications that allow them to see when new items have been added. WSS allows portal users to set up alerts from any WSS portal page that will notify them when a new document has been added, as shown in Figure 6.21.

Alerts are not only limited to form libraries; they can be defined for anything within the repository.

NOTE

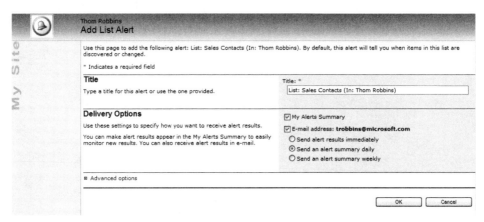

FIGURE 6.21   Defining a WSS alert.

The Need for Real Time

Activities within workflows can be executed either synchronously or asynchronously. With synchronous transactions, all participants are expected to wait for the completion of a process. In the real world, most business processes are not executed instantaneously. Most commonly, this is the result of a lack of either human- or machine-based resources. Typically, applications tend to require human intervention, so the cycle time for completion tends to get longer. As these cycle times get longer, these processes are often disconnected from the main application and run asynchronously. The asynchronous application model allows systems or users to start a process and not wait for the actual request to complete.

This is also the opposite design pattern of traditional transaction-based applications, in which all participants wait for the request to complete once a process is started. Such disconnected applications are often referred to as *asynchronous processing* because they are disconnected from the main process, and this allows each individual process to run at different speeds. Within a workflow application, this type of processing allows more flexibility in distribution and scaling workflow processes.

The benefits of asynchronous processing are as follows:

- Has faster response from front-end systems like Web pages or InfoPath forms, which the customer perceives as a faster system
- Makes load balancing of applications and requests easier
- Provides built-in fault tolerance
- Enables intermittently connected sub-systems

Within the asynchronous application model, the real benefit is the result of decoupling the application section. For the model to be effective, there must be some form of queue to hold pending requests, and each step of the process is responsible for communicating with these queues instead of directly with the previous or next step of the defined processes. This allows these types of applications a sense of isolation within the workflow processes.

One of the most common examples of asynchronous-based workflow is email. In today's world, this is the common way of completing various tasks and activities. Often, this is because people need information from other information workers in different departments, cities, and even time zones, or simply because they want the freedom to decide when they will complete a task. Email-based workflow is ideally suited for approval- and task-based routing.

In this scenario, an email-enabled form is submitted to users, who can review and complete the requested action. Email is used to notify them when they need to complete the task, and when the action is complete, users can notify the requestor that it's complete. Based on these types of scenarios, InfoPath provides a variety of built-in features.

InfoPath and Mail Enablement

The InfoPath object model allows you to send an InfoPath form as either an embedded message or as an attachment to an email message. In addition, InfoPath is client based, so it can interact with local applications such as Outlook 2003 as a way of generating and sending custom email messages.

The `MailEnvelope` Object

The `MailEnvelope` object enables you to send a custom email message within an InfoPath form. This object provides a number of custom properties that you can use programmatically to create a custom email message by using the system default mail editor and then attaching the current open InfoPath form to the message, as shown in Figure 6.22.

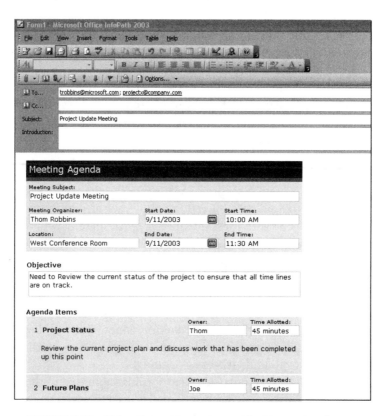

FIGURE 6.22 Using the `MailEnvelope` object to route a form.

It is important to remember that because of security concerns, InfoPath cannot directly send an email message. InfoPath can generate the envelope or message, but the user is required to actually complete the message send.

The `MailEnvelope` object is accessed through the MailEnvelope property of the Window object. The following example from the Meeting Agenda sample uses this property to set a reference to the `MailEnvelope` objects that are associated with the current window and to create the custom email message using the script shown in Listing 6.3. (This example is found in \Code\Chapter 6\Meeting\Agenda.xsn on the companion CD-ROM.)

LISTING 6.3   Creating a Custom Email Message Using the `MailEnvelope` Property

```
function SendMeetingAgendaBtn::OnClick(oEvent)
{
  var rgRecipients = new Array();
    var xmlRecipients =
getNodeList("/mtg:meetingAgenda/mtg:attendees/mtg:attendee
/mtg:emailAddressPrimary");
    var xmlRecipient;

    while (xmlRecipient = xmlRecipients.nextNode())
      rgRecipients.push(xmlRecipient.text);

    try
    {
      var oEnvelope = Application.ActiveWindow.MailEnvelope;

      oEnvelope.Subject = getNode("/mtg:meetingAgenda/mtg:subject").text;
      oEnvelope.To = rgRecipients.join("; ");
      oEnvelope.Visible = true;
    }
    catch(ex)
    {
      XDocument.UI.Alert(ex.description);
    }


}
```

The `ShowMailItem` Method

The `ShowMailItem` method enables you to programmatically create an email message using the default email editor and attaches the current InfoPath XML data as an attachment to the message. The main difference between this method and the

`MailEnvelope` object is that the InfoPath form is created as an XML attachment to the message, as shown in Figure 6.23.

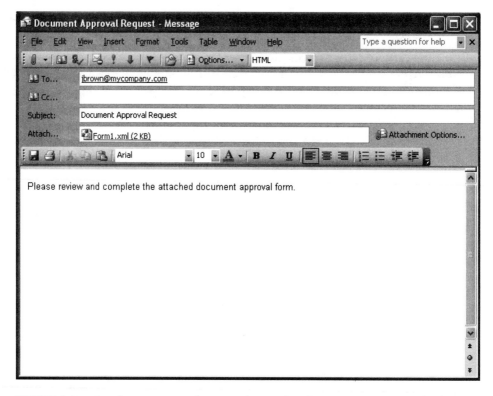

FIGURE 6.23 Sending an approval request form using the `ShowMailItem` method.

For those enterprises that block certain types of attachments, this method attaches the file to the generated email message with an XML extension. If this type of attachment is blocked, this method may not be an ideal solution.

Listing 6.4 uses the Document Approval form, generates the email message, and attaches the InfoPath XML data to it. (The Document Approval sample is found in \Code\Chapter 6\Document Approval\DocApproval.xsn on the companion CD-ROM.)

LISTING 6.4   Attaching an InfoPath Form to an Email Using the `ShowMailItem` Method

```
    var sendTos = "";
  for(var i
=0;i<=(XDocument.DOM.selectNodes("/approver:documentinformation/approve
r:Approvals/approver:ApproverEmail").length -1); i++) {
    sendTos = sendTos +
XDocument.DOM.selectNodes("/approver:documentinformation/approver:Appro
vals/approver:ApproverEmail").item(i).text + ";" ;
  }

  try
  {
    XDocument.UI.ShowMailItem(sendTos, "", "", "Document Approval
Request", "Please review and complete the attached document approval
form.");
  }
  catch(ex)
  {
  XDocument.UI.Alert(ex.description);
  }
```

CREATING AD HOC WORKFLOW

Ad hoc workflow processes allow the user to create and amend process definitions very quickly and easily to meet new circumstances as they arise. Within this type of workflow, it is possible to have as many different process definitions as there are users of the workflow. The main goal of ad hoc-based workflow is flexibility in areas where throughput and security are not the most important concern, and allowing the user's own experience to define the processes.

Within this type of process, the user is attempting to solve a specific domain-based problem or task that he needs to do by applying his own domain expertise to the problem. This can come in many different forms; based on both the person and organization, this may change. Ad hoc workflow is one of the most important types of workflow that an organization has in its workflow arsenal.

These processes often automate knowledge-intensive workflow that contains key bits of business and processing knowledge that often are lost, or, worse yet, that require additional work each time they are performed. Typically, these types of workflow have a low overall business value and low repetition rate. Often, they are known for not having a predefined structure, and for the next step in the process usually being determined by each user in the process. Each business process automated within this context is constructed individually whenever there is a need to perform a series of actions. Typical examples of this type of workflow applications are routing or "for your information" types of InfoPath form applications that include meeting- and task-based agendas.

Sales Call Report Example

Two of the most common problems in any sales-related organization are performing follow-ups and providing information back to both customers and managers. Typically, sales call follow-ups may include a variety of different process types and even workflow agents. The reality is that often even the most advanced Customer Relationship Manager (CRM) applications don't provide an easy-to-use tool for providing simple repetitive information. (The Sales Call Report example is found on the companion CD-ROM in \Code\Chapter 6\Sales Follow Up\ebr.xsn.)

ON THE CD

The form shown in Figure 6.24 is designed to solve this type of process and allow an easy-to-use ad hoc-based workflow that reduces the overall time it takes for a person to respond back to a customer. It provides a generic template that can be used by salespeople as a way of responding back to a customer. This solution also provides an offline component that can be used to easily capture existing knowledge and allow its reuse. One of the most important features of this type of application is the use of a custom task pane to help control, collect, and reuse the information entered by the user.

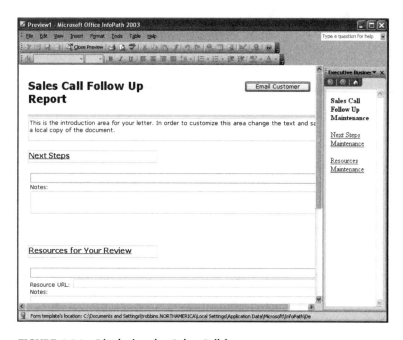

FIGURE 6.24 Displaying the Sales Call form.

Task Panes

Task panes allow you to define a process or amplify information within an InfoPath form. They often provide either a collection point or allow you to access external information within the form. They are simply HTML files that are made part of the solution and contained with the solution file. Task panes enable you to store and maintain a variety of information.

The task pane object model is maintained as part of the InfoPath object model and allows you to share the objects and script components that are maintained within the project. For example, within task panes, you can access both global variables and business-based functions using the window object of the task pane, as shown here:

```
\\accessing global variable
window.external.Window.XDocument.Extension.MyVariable
\\accessing function defined within the business logic
window.external.Window.XDocument.Extension.MyFunction()
```

InfoPath allows you to script external objects. Using the wscript object model, you can load the network name of the person that is filling out the form into a text box using this syntax:

```
var objNetwork = new ActiveXObject("WScript.network");
objMail.BCC = objNetwork.UserName;
```

This will, by default, generate a security error unless the form is fully trusted. This will be discussed further in Chapter 9.

Within the Sales Call example, the task pane is used to collect and store information that the user enters and then can be used to refresh the drop-downs with this information using the DataObjects function here:

```
function refreshDrops() {
XDocument.DataObjects("Next Steps").Query();
XDocument.DataObjects("Resources To Review").Query();
XDocument.View.ForceUpdate();
}
```

This function is then callable from the task pane and refreshes the current data sources, as shown here:

```
window.external.Window.XDocument.Extension.refreshDrops()
```

DESIGNING ADMINISTRATIVE WORKFLOW

The most important feature of an administrative type of workflow system is the defining the processes. Typically, a variety of definitions are running concurrently and they tend to involve numerous independent processes. Process definitions are usually created based on data entry forms; if the definition is too complex for the defined form, then a new one is designed for a new instance of the form solution. Flexibility is more important than productivity, and these systems tend to handle a lower number of transactions than production workflow. Administrative workflow is characterized by a low volume of transactions with a high repetition factor.

The Web Service Advantage

Within administrative workflow, Web Services play an important part in their definition and function. Web Services are often coupled with an InfoPath form as a way of defining the form and then enforcing the specific process. For example, let's create a Help Desk system (shown in \Code\Chapter 6\Help Desk\ASP 2.0 Web Service\Setup.exe on the companion CD-ROM) that shows how this works. Users are responsible for entering their requests through an InfoPath form that is based on a Web Service that controls the process, as shown in Listing 6.5.

ON THE CD

LISTING 6.5 Web Service for Submitting Help Desk Requests

```
<WebMethod()> Public Function InfoPathSubmitRequest(ByVal RequestName
As String, ByVal RequestPhone As String, ByVal RequestEmail As String,
ByVal RequestType As String, ByVal RequestComment As String) As Integer
        'create the DB connection
        Dim sqlConn As SqlConnection
        Dim sqlCmd As SqlCommand
        Dim strConstring As String

        strConstring = "Data Source=basexp;Initial
Catalog=helpdesk;Integrated Security=SSPI;"
        sqlConn = New SqlConnection(strConstring)
        sqlConn.Open()
        sqlCmd = New SqlCommand

        With sqlCmd
            .Connection = sqlConn
            .CommandTimeout = 30
            .CommandType = Data.CommandType.StoredProcedure
            .CommandText = "spInsertRequests"
```

```
                .Parameters.AddWithValue("@RequestName", RequestName)
                .Parameters.AddWithValue("@RequestPhone", RequestPhone)
                .Parameters.AddWithValue("@RequestEmail", RequestEmail)
                .Parameters.AddWithValue("@RequestType", RequestType)
                .Parameters.AddWithValue("@RequestComment", RequestComment)
                Return .ExecuteNonQuery()
            End With
            sqlConn.Close()
        End Function
```

The process is further enforced through the creation of a Web Service that supplies the list of available request types. The benefit of this is that as new request types are added, these are added separately to the database and automatically picked up through the form. Listing 6.6 shows a Web Service for connecting a secondary data source.

LISTING 6.6   Web Service for Connecting a Secondary Data Source

```
<WebMethod()> Public Function GetRequestTypes() As
System.Xml.XmlDocument
        'db connection
        Dim sqlConn As SqlConnection
        Dim sqlCmd As SqlCommand
        Dim strConstring As String

        strConstring = "Data Source=basexp;Initial
Catalog=helpdesk;Integrated Security=SSPI;"
        sqlConn = New SqlConnection(strConstring)
        sqlConn.Open()
        sqlCmd = New SqlCommand

        With sqlCmd
            .Connection = sqlConn
            .CommandTimeout = 30
            .CommandType = CommandType.StoredProcedure
            .CommandText = "spGetRequestType"
        End With

        Dim RequestDA As SqlDataAdapter = New SqlDataAdapter
        RequestDA.SelectCommand = sqlCmd
        Dim RequestDS As DataSet = New DataSet
        RequestDA.Fill(RequestDS, "RequestType")
```

```
        RequestDS.Namespace = "Http://localhost/RequestType"
        Dim Info As System.Xml.XmlDataDocument = New
System.Xml.XmlDataDocument(RequestDS)

        Return Info
        sqlConn.Close()
    End Function
```

Designing the InfoPath Form

The InfoPath form shown in Figure 6.25 is created using the Web Services, as we have done in previous chapters. The important thing is that a secondary data source is created to tie the request types to the form. This allows you to add new types and update the workflow without having to update the form.

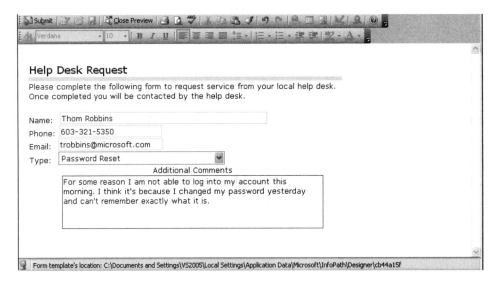

FIGURE 6.25 Displaying the Help Desk form.

If you are running this form in design mode, make sure that you have a copy of the Web Service running. This is a common mistake when you're designing InfoPath forms that use Web Services.

NOTE

Designing the Status Screen

Once the Web Service is completed, you can easily design and publish the form to allow users to enter their requests. Once requests are entered and submitted, they are shown on the Help Desk Scorecard Web page, as shown in Figure 6.26. This page allows the help desk personnel to view current status, respond to open requests and close completed ones.

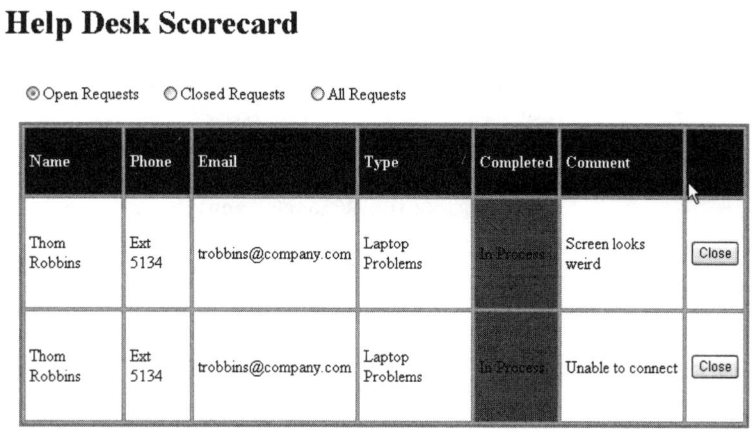

FIGURE 6.26 Displaying the Help Desk Scorecard.

The main part of the scorecard is calling the Web Service through an ASP.NET page. Once the Web Service is called, all data is shown through an ASP.NET 1.1 Web application that uses a data grid as shown in Listing 6.7.

LISTING 6.7 Retrieving Data for the Help Desk Scorecard

```
Public Function LoadRequests(ByVal TypeOfRequest As RequestType)
  Dim ws As New localhost.wsSubmit
  Dim xmlStatus As DataSet
  Select Case TypeOfRequest
    Case RequestType.AllRequests
      xmlStatus = ws.GetAllRequests
    Case RequestType.ClosedRequest
      xmlStatus = ws.GetRequests(RequestedStatus:=False)
    Case RequestType.OpenRequest
      xmlStatus = ws.GetRequests(RequestedStatus:=True)
  End Select
```

```
With DgRequests
  DataSource = xmlStatus
  DataBind()
  ' format the grid
  Select Case TypeOfRequest
    Case RequestType.AllRequests
      .Columns(GridColum.RCloseButton).Visible = False
    Case RequestType.ClosedRequest
      With DgRequests
        .Columns(GridColum.RCloseButton).Visible = False
        .Columns(GridColum.RCompletedBy).Visible = True
        .Columns(GridColum.RCompletedDate).Visible = True
      End With
    Case RequestType.OpenRequest
      With DgRequests
        .Columns(GridColum.RCloseButton).Visible = True
        .Columns(GridColum.RCompletedBy).Visible = False
        .Columns(GridColum.RCompletedDate).Visible = False
      End With

  End Select
  End With
End Function
```

During the actual process, all control is maintained within the Web Services. This ensures that any maintenance is always done on the Web Services and that forms do not need to be updated until the actual process has to change.

SUMMARY

This chapter has covered the basics of workflow design and process automation. You can design these types of applications in many ways. Often, developers can include a variety of design patterns. As we move into the next chapter, we will cover the more advanced features of workflow automation using BizTalk Server 2004.

7 Integrating with BizTalk Server 2004

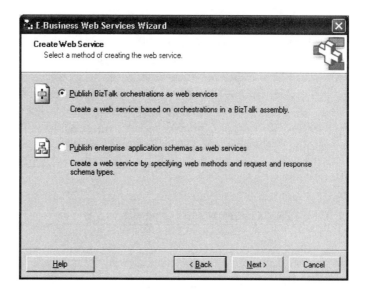

INTRODUCTION

True enterprise integration is more than just the process of exchanging random data across a network. Systems and applications naturally evolve. This evolution means more systems and applications are added, which starts exponentially increasing the complexity of enterprise integration. The goal of any successful enterprise integration strategy is to develop and maintain a unified set of business processes. Each individual processes is capable of collecting and distributing information both collectively and independently.

With XML acting as the underlying data exchange, BizTalk Server 2004 is a middleware solution that simplifies the task of enterprise integration. BizTalk allows you to design, maintain, and deploy integration components using the .NET Framework. Acting as a distributed software layer, BizTalk abstracts the complexity of the underlying applications into a single manageable interface. BizTalk Server 2004 solves three common enterprise integration scenarios: Enterprise Application Integration (EAI), Business Process Automation (BPA), and Information Worker integration.

During the development of enterprise solutions, it often becomes apparent that existing data collection mechanisms are tightly coupled to existing applications. As part of the application integration layer, BizTalk is designed to solve this problem by exposing a set of extensible XML Web Services. This allows developers to tie into existing systems, workflow, and process tracking information. When tied into InfoPath, this enables enterprises to build human-based workflows from the familiar interface of Microsoft Office.

This lets you present different XML formats in an interactive form that allows data to be read, completed, and submitted by users of BizTalk integration processes. This chapter provides an introduction to BizTalk Server 2004 and how you can use it to develop InfoPath-based solutions. We will also cover some of the design patterns for developing these types of composite-based applications.

WHAT IS BIZTALK SERVER 2004?

BizTalk Server 2004 is a full-featured integration server that enables the automation and management of business processes that connect internal systems with people and trading partners. It provides an orchestration engine along with a set of shared services that are designed to make it easier to orchestrate dynamic business processes inside and between organizations. BizTalk Server 2004 focuses on the following areas of integration:

- Business process management
- Human-based workflow
- Business rules
- Single sign-on
- InfoPath integration

A well-managed and orchestrated set of business processes provide operational and competitive advantages to enterprises. Business processes are a core value of any enterprise. Built on top of the *.NET Framework 1.1* and *Visual Studio 2003,* BizTalk Server 2004 is composed of two separate services:

BizTalk Orchestration: Allows the execution of a business processes

BizTalk Messaging: Transforms and routes data between business processes

These two services are combined as shown in Figure 7.1 to receive, route, process, and send messages. Orchestration provides the services needed to design, deploy, and manage business processes through an XML dialect called XLANG. The process files created with XLANG are used to manage the state of concurrent and long running business processes.

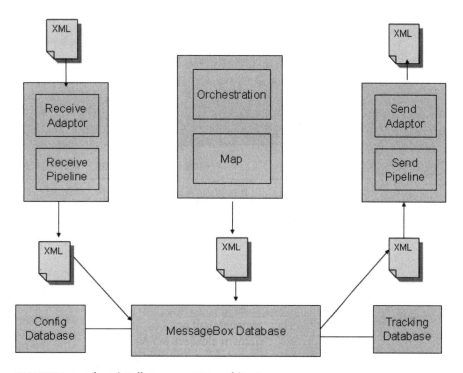

FIGURE 7.1   The BizTalk Server 2004 architecture.

BizTalk messaging enables the receiving of incoming documents and parses them to extract specific data and formatting information. This may include things such as key identifiers or specific routing instructions and rules used to deliver documents to their destinations. Messaging is also used to map and transform data formats and apply security to ensure data integrity.

THE ARCHITECTURE OVERVIEW

The combination of orchestration and messaging into a single subsystem enables a shared common data store for maintaining both process state management and messaging. During the actual execution of a process, the messaging components are designed to handle the transport and mapping, while the orchestration executes the actual process.

Because BizTalk Server 2004 must talk to a wide range of other software and platforms, it relies on a range of adapters. An adapter is an implementation of a communication mechanism, such as a protocol, for example, HTTP or Simple Mail Transport Protocol (SMTP). BizTalk Server 2004 provides a variety of built-in adapters. All adapters are built on a standard code base called the Adapter Framework. This framework provides a common way to create and run adapters. By default, all communications with a deployed business process occurs through an adapter.

The BizTalk Framework also provides an extensibility model that many third-party vendors can use to extend or write their own adapters for specific line of business applications.

BizTalk Server supports the following native adapters:

File Adapter: The file adapter is used to read and write files in the Windows file system. The receive adapter reads the file and creates a BizTalk Message object, so that the message can be processed by BizTalk Server. While the file is being read, it is locked to ensure that it is not modified while the message is being created.

HTTP Adapter: The HTTP adapter retrieves messages from the server and sends them to a destination URL on an HTTP POST request. The HTTP send adapter gets the message content from the body part of the BizTalk Message object. All other parts of the BizTalk Message object are ignored by the HTTP send adapter.

SMTP Adapter: The SMTP adapter is used to exchange information between a server running BizTalk Server and other applications by means of the SMTP protocol. BizTalk Server can send messages to other applications by creating an email message and then delivering it. Internally, the SMTP send adapter creates an SMTP-based email message and sends it to a target email address that is configured as a property of the SMTP adapter.

SOAP Adapter: The SOAP adapter is used by BizTalk Web Services when it receives and sends Web Service requests. The SOAP adapter enables the direct publishing of orchestrations as a Web Service. It also allows the consumption of external Web Services. When working with Web Services, the URL is used to identify the sending and receiving systems.

BizTalk Message Queuing Adapter (MSMQT):   The MSMQT adapter is the native Microsoft Message Queuing (MSMQ) adapter in BizTalk Server. MSMQ is a standalone reliable messaging service, with its own administration tools and message store. MSMQT works the same as MSMQ from a network perspective; the main difference is that instead of being sent to a queue, messages are sent to the BizTalk MessageBox database.

FTP Adapter: The FTP adapter enables the exchange of files between BizTalk Server 2004 and FTP servers.

SQL Adapter: The SQL adapter is used to exchange data between BizTalk Server and SQL Server databases. This adapter can pull individual records from one or more data tables, save the records as an XML message, and then pass the message to a line-of-business application through BizTalk Server. You can also use the SQL adapter to move large amounts of data to or from a SQL Server database or data warehouse as part of a complex BizTalk Server messaging or orchestration solution. In addition, you can use the SQL adapter to update and delete SQL Server tables by using parameterized SQL statements or stored procedures.

Base EDI Adapter: The EDI adapter enables sending and receiving messages using the American National Standards Institute (ANSI) X-12 and Electronic Data Interchange for Administration, Commerce, and Trade (EDIFACT) standards.

Adapters are added or configured through the BizTalk Administration Console, as shown in Figure 7.2. Enterprise Single Sign-On (SSO) enables users to sign on only once when interoperating with heterogeneous systems. This allows BizTalk adapters to provide the appropriate user ID and credentials to back-end systems based on the user's Windows credentials. Once authenticated by Windows, the user does not need to provide any additional credentials to connect to a back-end system.

SSO is only available for the HTTP and SOAP adapters. For the HTTP adapter, the send port and receive location can be configured to use SSO; for the SOAP adapter, only the receive location can be configured. By default, SSO is disabled and can be configured using the BizTalk Explorer Console. Authentication in SSO relies primarily on Windows and the Windows groups created in Active Directory.

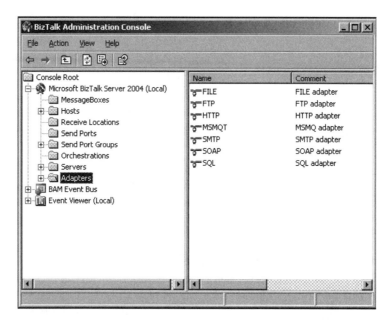

FIGURE 7.2 Managing the native adapters through the BizTalk Administration Console.

All operations completed by a user or administrator with SSO require that the user or administrator first be authenticated using Windows authentication.

Each of the specific receive location and send ports, which act as the addresses on an adapter, are configured using the BizTalk Explorer, as shown in Figure 7.3. BizTalk Explorer is available within the Visual Studio.NET 2003 IDE.

BizTalk Server 2004 is built using the .NET Framework 1.1. Development for this version of the .NET Framework is done with Visual Studio 2003. For ease of use, all samples in this chapter use Visual Studio 2003.

As a message is received through the receive adapter, it is then processed through a receive pipeline. This pipeline takes the incoming message, disassembles it from its native format into an XML document, and generates one or more messages that can be processed by the BizTalk Server. Table 7.1 shows the four stages of the receive pipeline and what occurs during each stage.

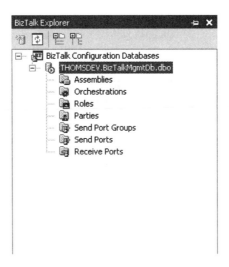

FIGURE 7.3 BizTalk Explorer, which is part of Visual Studio.NET 2003.

TABLE 7.1 Stages of the Receive Pipeline

Stage	Component	Description
Decode Stage	MIME/S-MIME Decoder	Decodes or decrypts the incoming messages. The decoder can handle messages and any attachments they contain in either MIME or Secure MIME (S/MIME) format. The component converts both kinds of messages into XML, and it can also decrypt S/MIME messages and verify their digital signatures.
Disassemble Stage		
	Flat file disassembler	Turns flat files into XML documents.
	XML disassemble	Parses incoming XML messages.
	BizTalk Framework disassembler	Accepts messages sent using the reliable messaging mechanism defined by the BizTalk Framework.

$\rightarrow$

Stage	Component	Description
Validate Stage		
	XML Validate	Validates the XML document produced in the disassemble stage against a specified schema or group of schemas. An error is returned if the document doesn't conform to one or more schemas.
Resolve Party Stage	Party Resolution	Attempts to determine the identity of the message sender and map it to an identity.

Outgoing messages can also go through multiple stages as defined by the send pipeline. Table 7.2 shows the stages and components for a send pipeline.

TABLE 7.2   Stages of the Send Pipeline

Stage	Component	Description
Pre-Assemble Stage	No Standard	An optional stage that provides hooks for custom components.
Assemble		
	Flat file assembler	Converts an XML message into a positional or delimited flat file.
	XML assembler	Enables adding an envelope and making other changes to an outgoing XML message.
	BizTalk Framework assembler	Packages messages for reliable transmission defined by the BizTalk Framework.
Encode	MIME or S/MIME Encoder	Packages outgoing messages in either MIME or S/MIME encoder.

MessageBox Database

At the core of the messaging and orchestrations is the MessageBox database, which stores all messages that an application can interact with. It also serves as a load-balancing mechanism used to distribute work to additional BizTalk Servers. When a BizTalk Server receives a message, the message is processed in a pipeline and then placed in the MessageBox database.

The incoming message has a context, that is, a set of properties associated with the message. For example, these properties may include the type of message or sender. BizTalk supports three types of properties: simple written properties, promoted properties, and predicate properties. Simple written properties are the base properties and messages defined within the system and business process. The promoted and predicate message properties are used to determine what business process is subscribed to this message and whether the business process has the permissions necessary to receive the message.

The MessageBox database uses a subscription to determine which messages are distributed to which servers. *Subscriptions* are a list of stored predicate and service information. The *predicate information* is the criteria that must be met by a message, and the *service information* is what to do with the message that meets the criteria.

Different business processes expect different types of messages at different times. Subscriptions are criteria that describe which of these message types the business process will receive. Each subscription is a query against the context properties of messages stored in the MessageBox database. The result of a subscription returns to its subscriber process only those messages that match the criteria that the subscription defines.

When a matching subscription is filled, a business process receives the message from the MessageBox database and processes the message on an available BizTalk Host instance. Each BizTalk Host is a logical container for items such as adapters, receive functions, and orchestrations. A BizTalk Host performs the following functions:

Receiving: These items do the initial processing of messages after they are picked up in a receive location. When a host contains a receiving item, such as a receive location or pipeline, it functions as a security boundary, and the message decoding and decrypting occur directly in the host pipeline.

Sending: These items do the final processing of messages before they are sent out of the send port. When a host contains a sending item, such as a send port or pipeline, the host provides a security boundary, and the signing and encryption of a message occurs in the host pipeline.

Processing: These items process messages based on the instructions defined in an orchestration.

One BizTalk host can contain multiple items that send, receive, and process messages. However, for security and management, it is always recommended to separate trusted and nontrusted items by creating separate BizTalk hosts.

BizTalk Server 2004 natively supports two types of hosts. *In-process hosts* are those that the server can create and control. These hosts can receive and send messages and are used to process orchestrations. The second are *isolated hosts,* which are used to represent external processes like an ISAPI extension. These are created externally by adapters like the HTTP and SOAP adapter to host these external process types. When you view these as part of the tracking process, they are considered isolated and will always show as unknown because BizTalk is unable to access their current process state.

Messages normally are targeted at an orchestration, but it is also possible for a message to go directly to the send pipeline, which uses BizTalk 2004 purely as a messaging system. Each orchestration creates subscriptions to indicate the kinds of messages it wants to receive. When an appropriate message arrives in the Message-Box, that message is dispatched to its target orchestration, which takes whatever action the business process requires. The result of this processing is typically another message, produced by the business process and saved in the MessageBox.

This message, in turn, is processed by a send pipeline, which may convert it from the internal XML format used by BizTalk Server 2004 to the format required by its destination. The message is then sent out via a send adapter, which uses the appropriate mechanism to communicate with the application for which this message is destined.

For example, a business process may subscribe to "Requisitions", which defines a certain message type, or the subscription may be more business oriented, as in a subscription for "Capital Asset Purchases Greater than $10,000." Alternately, the subscription criteria may contain a location rather than a message type. For example, a business process may subscribe to all messages, regardless of type, that originate from a specific company.

Business processes are implemented as one or more orchestrations, each one consisting of executable code created using the .NET Framework. You don't create orchestrations by writing code; instead, a business analyst or developer graphically organizes a defined set of shapes to express the conditions, loops, and other behavior of a business process. Business processes can also use the Business Rules Framework, which provides a simpler interface to express business processes.

Business Rules Framework

The Business Rules Framework provides developers and designers with a mechanism for coupling business policies and logic with complex business processes. It combines an inference engine with a declarative model that allows the separation of implementation details from the business logic in rules. This allows you to update rules and policies that contain them without having to update code as you would in a traditional development cycle.

The Business Rules Composer, as shown in Figure 7.4, is a graphical interface that allows developers, business analysts, and administrators to develop and apply policy-based rules. Rule conditions are often based on data sources that have detailed, difficult-to-read binding information. This may tell the developer little or no information about what the data source actually refers to. The Business Rules Framework allows you to create vocabularies of rules that are tied to domain-specific terminology that can be associated with rule conditions and actions. Developers can bind business logic, change policies, and deploy these policies. Exposed as a set of functionality available within the Microsoft.RulesEngine namespace, they can be programmatically managed and edited.

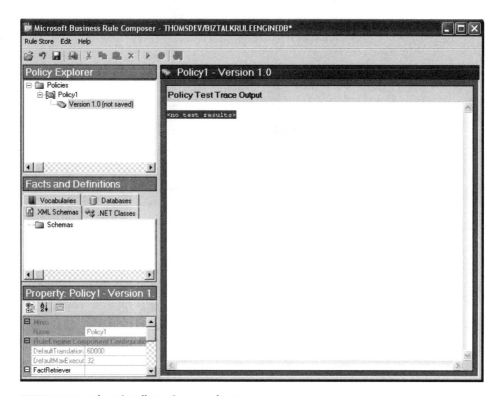

FIGURE 7.4 The BizTalk Business Rules Composer.

Figure 7.5 shows a set of rules. As a best practice, follow these guidelines when developing rules:

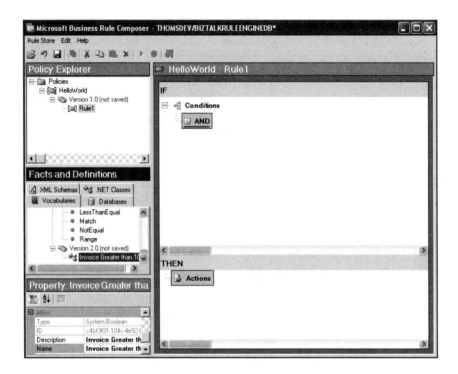

FIGURE 7.5 A defined rule set within the Business Rules Composer.

1. Identify existing or new business logic that is to be represented as IF-THEN statements in the rules.
2. Identify the data facts that the business logic will be applied to. The rules engine can use data exposed through assemblies, classes, XML documents, or databases.
3. Create a policy and then define the rules to present the business logic. Associate the rule, condition, and action with the facts identified previously.
4. Test the policy to verify proper behavior.
5. Deploy the policy to a host application.

6. Create a policy inside an application or Web Service using the name of the defined policy as a parameter, as shown here:

```
Dim xd as System.XML.XMLDocument
xd = incomingXMLMessage
xmldoc = new TypedXMLDocument("MyMessageType", xd)
myPolicy = new Microsoft.RuleEngine.Policy("MyPolicyName")
myPolicy.Execute(xmldoc)
myPolicy.Dispose()
OutgoingXMLMessage = xmldoc.Document
```

7. Pass the data facts to the policy object and execute the policy.
8. Review the results of the executed policy.

XLANG

Orchestrations are used to design, execute, and manage a business processes. The logic necessary for this is maintained in an XML file format called an XLANG orchestration.

Within BizTalk Server 2004, XLANG allows you to import and export orchestrations to the Business Process Execution Language for Web Services 1.1 (BPEL4WS) specification. The BPEL4WS language is a standard, platform-independent language for formally describing Web Service behaviors and processes that was jointly developed by Microsoft and IBM to provide a standard mechanism for universal interoperability. The BPEL4WS language defines both business protocols and executable business processes to facilitate automation and integration of enterprise application and business-to-business processes, while improving their scalability.

BPEL4WS takes advantage of several XML specifications: WSDL 1.1, XML Schema 1.0, and XPATH 1.0. BPEL4WS employs WSDL messages and XML Schema type definitions for its data model, and XPATH for data manipulation. All external resources and partners are represented as WSDL services. BPEL4WS also provides extensibility to accommodate future versions of these standards.

BPEL4WS supports both synchronous and asynchronous peer-to-peer message exchanges within stateful, long-running interactions involving two or more parties. It also specifies precisely the mutually visible message exchange behavior of each of the parties involved in the protocol, without revealing internal implementations. In this way, businesses can retain privacy, and process implementations can be changed without affecting the public business protocol.

Because BPEL4WS clearly describes business protocols in a platform-independent manner and describes all cross-enterprise business behaviors, participants can understand and conform to a business protocol without having to work out ad hoc agreements, which have historically added most of the difficulty to establishing cross-enterprise automated business processes. Remember the conversion restrictions, shown in Table 7.3, when you're importing or exporting business processes.

TABLE 7.3 Conversion Table for XLANG to BPEL4WS

Type	XLANG's	BPEL4WS
Literals	String, character	XPATH string
	Integer, real	XPATH number
	Boolean "true," "false"	XPath true(), false() functions
	Literal constant	XSD equivalent
Variables	Variable reference	bpws:getContainerData(%varName%, part,%locationPath%)
	Message reference (.NET type)	bpws:getContainerData (%msgName%, part, %locationPath%)
	Message-part reference	bpws:getContainerData(%msgName%, %locationPath%)

Type	XLANG/s	BPEL4WS
	Distinguished-field reference	bpws:getContainerData (%msgName%, %partName%, %locationPath%)
	Message data-property reference	bpws:getContainerProperty (%msgName%, %propertyQName%)
Operators	Unary +	Ignored
	Unary -	XPATH unary -
	Unary !	Path not(...) function
	Binary &&, ||	XPATH "AND," "OR" operators
	Binary ==, !=, <=, <, >=, > Binary +, -, *, % with both	XPATH "=," "! =," "<=," "<," ">=," ">" operators
integral operands		XPATH "+," "-," "*," "mod" operators

In addition, the following XLANG constructs are disallowed in BPEL4WS:

- Message context-property reference
- Service-property reference
- Port-property reference
- Service link-property reference
- Unary—with non-integral type
- Unary ~
- Cast operator
- Binary / with integral operands
- Binary +, -, *, %, / with non-integral operands
- Binary <=, <, >=, > with nonstring operands
- Bitwise operators &, ^, |
- Shift operators <<, >>
- Checked expression
- Intrinsic expression
- Pre- and post-increment and decrement ++, --
- Object invocation (with or without and/or ref parameters)
- new operator

XLANG has been a core component of BizTalk since the first product release but has been substantially enhanced within the new version. XLANG is now an extension of the managed runtime environment of the .NET Framework. This inclusion provides enhanced support for communication, transactions, long-running processes, and state management. These new managed orchestrations appear as a palette in Visual Studio.NET 2003, as shown in Figure 7.6. This palette allows developers to visually create, edit, and modify workflow processes directly within the development environment.

An additional extension to XLANG is a tracking engine. The Business Activity Monitor (BAM) allows business decision-makers to monitor business processes and track potential process bottlenecks. Using the dashboard interface of WSS, the business user can monitor, interact with, and even change existing BizTalk processes. The main feature of BAM is to provide a platform for continual process improvement that is easy to configure and manage.

FIGURE 7.6 The XLANG components available within Visual Studio.NET 2003.

INTEGRATION WITH THE .NET FRAMEWORK

The direct integration of BizTalk into the Visual Studio.NET 2003 IDE adds a new set of project types within Visual Studio.NET 2003, as shown in Figure 7.7.

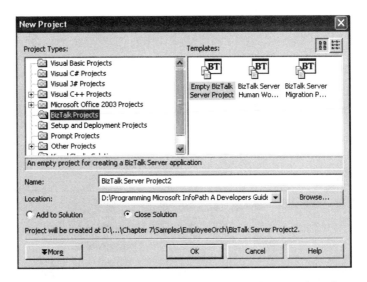

FIGURE 7.7 Available BizTalk project types within Visual Studio.NET.

For example, if we created an orchestration that converted patient registration information collected within InfoPath to update a back-end mainframe, we would start within an empty BizTalk project. (This can be found in \Code\Chapter 7\ PatientOrchestration\NewPatientOrchestration.sln on the companion CD-ROM.) This project type creates a blank project with default references to managed assemblies needed to create an orchestration. These default assembly references include the following:

ON THE CD

- Microsoft.BizTalk.DefaultPipelines
- Microsoft.BizTalk.GlobalPropertySchemas
- System
- System.Xml

The Microsoft.BizTalk.DefaultPipelines is a reference to the BizTalk Pipelines module. The reference defines a .NET or COM component that links to the various processing stages of either the sending or receiving message. Each portion of these components specifies a messaging stage. For example, these stages include encoding/decoding, assembly/disassembly, and encryption/decryption. The pipeline designer allows the developer to modify, change, or augment the specific order of the processing stages.

The Microsoft.BizTalk.DefaultPipelines namespace defines the default pipelines, which are XMLReceive, PassThruReceive, XMLTransmit, and PassThruTransmit. The default pipeline reference can process documents using the PassThruReceive and PassThruTransmit function. The default processing order for the BizTalk Pipeline is shown in Table 7.4.

TABLE 7.4   Default Pipeline Processing Order

Pipeline	Order
XML Receive Pipeline	Decrypter
	Decoder
	Disassembler
	Validator
	Party Resolution
XML Transmit Pipeline	Assembler
	Encoder
	Encrypter

Defining Messages

Pipelines are used to process messages that are defined as an XML Schema (XSD). These schema definitions define and maintain the specific message formats and structures that are used during the orchestration. You add XSDs within Visual Studio.NET by using the Add New Item, as shown in Figure 7.8.

The schema as shown in Figure 7.9 represents the XML data that is being submitted by the InfoPath form. This schema represents the data that is saved as part of the form and defined within the InfoPath solution. The problem is that the data needed to post to the back-end mainframe system is actually a different format, as shown in Figure 7.10.

Once both of the schemas are completed, it is important to review and validate both sources to ensure that there are no semantic problems with the XSDs. In many ways, reviewing and comparing a specific message instance is a lot easier than reviewing the schema tree and data types. Creating XSD can be a very complex process that includes describing all the possible formats and variations within a specific document type. Visual Studio.NET 2003 allows you to generate an instance of

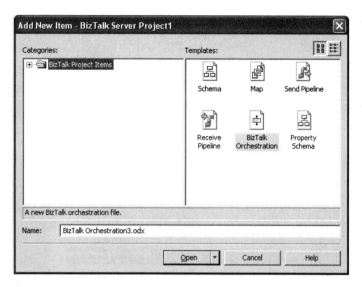

FIGURE 7.8   Adding a new schema item.

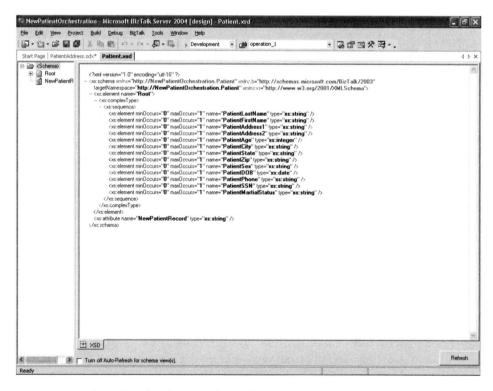

FIGURE 7.9   The InfoPath inbound schema definition.

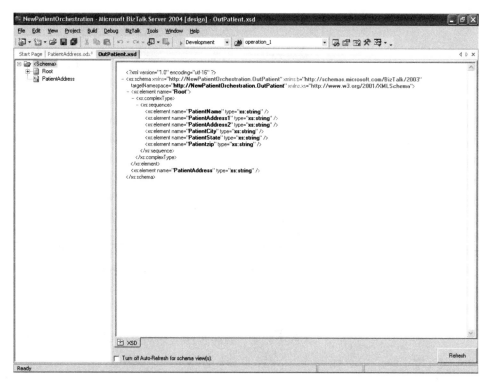

FIGURE 7.10 The mainframe-required schema definition.

the XML document to review the specific format structure. Within the Solutions Explorer, right-clicking on the schema and selecting Generate Instance creates a reference document for schema definitions.

Generating a default XML instance is not a foolproof way of validating a schema, but it will help you quickly validate the XML document for accuracy and data type inconsistencies.

Orchestration Design

Messages are the basic unit of communication within an orchestration. Messages consist of one or more parts with context data that describes their properties and content. BizTalk orchestration uses messages to provide the context for interchange between business process participants. Typically, orchestration is broader in scope than a traditional workflow.

Each participant is autonomous, and the responsibility for routing a work item is determined by each cooperating participant. BizTalk orchestration extends the definition of the traditional interaction diagram to include definition and control for decisions, concurrent actions, transactions, and supporting actions. The result of a completed orchestration is an XLANG executable file that represents the description of the business processes.

Within the Visual Studio.NET 2003 Integrated Device Electronics (IDE), new orchestrations are added in the same way as all other BizTalk items—through the Solutions explorer and the New Item menu. This adds a file with an .ODX extension that contains the XLANG structures. Within the IDE, the orchestration page provides a visual interface that presents the underlying XLANG structure.

This interface is broken into three sections that define an orchestration, as shown in Figure 7.11. First is the actual design surface or palette. This area is the visual surface where toolbox items are dropped and configured to define the process flow. Using this surface, developers can drop the send and receive ports that define the inbound and outbound message handler. The second is the orchestration

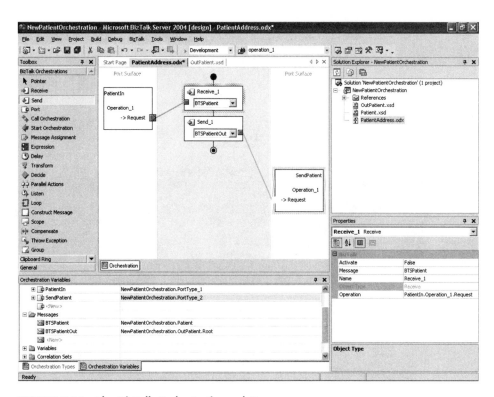

FIGURE 7.11   The BizTalk Orchestration palette.

designer, which uses the Orchestration Types window to define the specific port types, correlation types, and role links that are available for use within the orchestration. Using this window, we can define the specific inbound and outbound operations defined for the orchestration. Finally is the Orchestration Variable window, which shows the orchestration properties, parameters, ports, messages, variables, correlation sets, and role links available for the orchestration. This window is used to define and correlate the specific message to either the inbound or outbound port.

Mapping Schema Definitions

Within the orchestration designer, the transform shape enables the flow of data from one message to another. This can be done either through a direct assignment or a mapping process. The NewPatientOrchestration requires a specific map because a data translation is needed to build the outbound message. The transform shape provides access to the BizTalk Mapper, which allows the assignment of specific source and destination attributes, and provides both transformation and translation of specific schema elements and attributes.

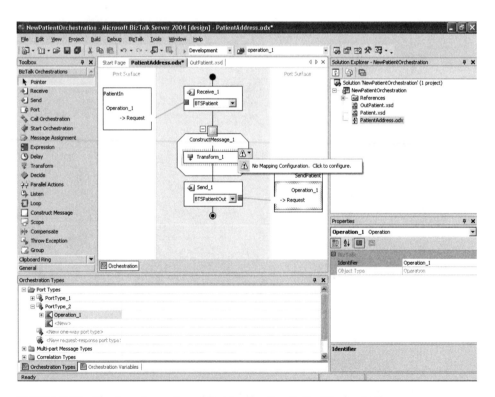

FIGURE 7.12   The transformation object for the NewPatientOrchestration.

You initialize and define maps by placing the transform shape onto the design palette, as shown in Figure 7.12, and then defining the schema for the source and destination documents. This configuration is then loaded into the BizTalk Mapper, where the actual element and attribute flow from one message to another is defined.

Within a map, functoids are used to manipulate the data flow. Functoids are used to map data elements and attribute into different elements and attributes across different structures. Within BizTalk Server 2004, they have become part of the Visual Studio.NET 2003 toolbox palette and appear as part of the data map. Functoids are divided into the categories, as shown in Table 7.5.

TABLE 7.5   Categories of Functoids Available for Mapping

Functoid Category	Description
Advanced Functoids	Use the Advanced functoids to configure various types of data manipulation, such as implementing custom script, value mapping, and managing and extracting data from looping records.
Conversion Functoids	Use the Conversion functoids to returns a hexadecimal value when given a decimal value. This closely matches engineering functions such as DEC2HEX. Conversion functoids can also be used to convert a character to its ASCII value or a value to the corresponding ASCII character.
Cumulative Functoids	Use the Cumulative functoids to perform various types of accumulation operations for values that occur multiple times within an instance message.
Database Functoids	Use the Database functoids to extract data from a database.
Date and Time Functoids	Use the Date and Time functoids to add date, time, date and time, or add days to a specified date, in output data.
Logical Functoids	Use the Logical functoids to either perform specific logical tests at runtime or to determine whether output instance data is created at runtime.
Mathematical Functoids	Use the Mathematical functoids to perform calculations by using specific values, called arguments, in a particular order, or structure.

$\rightarrow$

Functoid Category	Description
Scientific Functoids	Use the Scientific functoids to convert a numeric value to a scientific value. For example, the Cosine functoid takes a value in radians from a field or record and returns the value of the cosine.
String Functoids	Use the String functoids to manipulate data strings by using string functions. For example, the String Find functoid finds one text string within another text string, and returns the position of the first character of the found string. Similarly, the String Concatenate functoid combines two or more input parameters into a single output field.

When working on a map, we can drag functoids directly onto the design palette. For example within the NewPatientOrchestration, we dragged the string concatenation onto the map and dragged the source and destination elements between the two, as shown in Figure 7.13. Within a map, input links correspond to input parameters and lead to a functoid from the left, and an output link corresponds to the output parameters and leaves the functoid from the right.

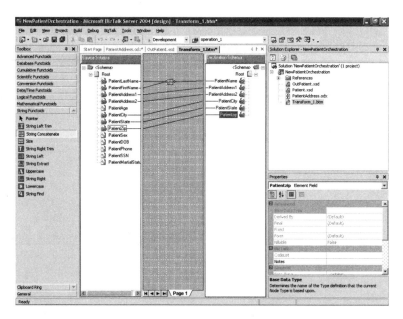

FIGURE 7.13 Functoids and mapping within BizTalk.

Deploying the Solution

Once the map and orchestration are completed, the solution is ready for deployment. All projects within BizTalk Server 2004 are deployed into a managed .NET Framework 1.1 assembly as a DLL. This is done by building the solution and then deploying it using the E-Business Web Services Wizard, as shown in Figure 7.14.

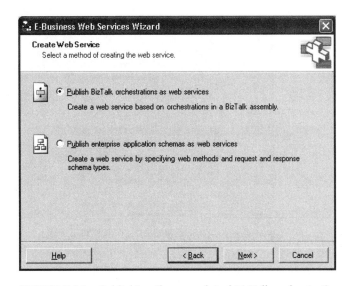

FIGURE 7.14   Publishing the completed BizTalk orchestration.

This wizard provides the option of deploying either an orchestration or enterprise schema as a Web Service. When deploying an orchestration, the wizard starts with the compiled DLL and generates the necessary namespace, Web Service name, communication patterns, and request/response objects to build and deploy an ASP.NET Web Service Project. The wizard identifies the defined ports, location, and schema within the compiled assembly to generate the necessary WSDL file that provides the Web Service definition.

Any orchestration that uses only a single Web port is published as a single .asmx file that defaults to the orchestration name. The NewPatientOrchestration used more than one Web port, and the default naming context is the name of the orchestration with an underscore followed by the Web port name. For example, once the NewPatientOrchestration was deployed, the Web port names NewPatient Orchestration_Outbound.asmx and NewPatientOrchestration_Inbound.asmx were assigned. These are the names that InfoPath will use to bind to the orchestration using the InfoPath Web Service adapter, as shown in Figure 7.15. Once InfoPath is bound to the specific Web Service, InfoPath can submit and receive data from these defined BizTalk Services.

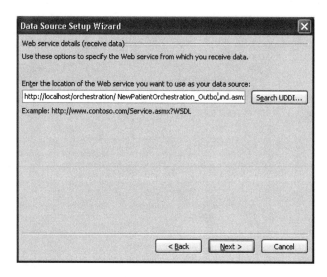

FIGURE 7.15   Binding the InfoPath form to the Web Service.

SUMMARY

InfoPath provides the ideal solution for gathering frontend information. It is designed to help streamline the process of gathering and reusing information throughout an enterprise. InfoPath provides a set of tools that enable the creation of dynamic forms to gather and share information across a wide range of business processes. Because of the native format of XML, BizTalk Server 2004 uses InfoPath as an easy-to-use interface. This chapter has shown how you can use the process management features of BizTalk Server 2004 to generate an XML Web Service that can easily be consumed by InfoPath.

In the next chapter, we move back into the client side. We will take a look at how we can create smart client applications that can take advantage of these server-side orchestrations.

8 Integrating Smart Client Applications

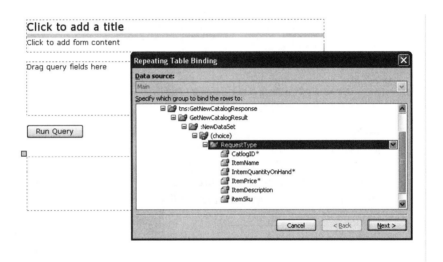

INTRODUCTION

Smart client applications by their definition run on the local device. The fact they are locally resident means they can run offline and leverage CPU, disk, and other system resources for better application performance. Technically, smart client applications are built using .NET Windows Forms, .NET Compact Framework, Office 2003, Information Bridge Framework, or Visual Studio Tools for Office. Like any type of enterprise application, seamless communication with back-end systems is a key requirement. Smart clients provide this through their use of the .NET Framework and XML as the standard mechanism for data interchange.

As a smart client technology, Microsoft Office-based solutions have been an integral part of the enterprise infrastructure for many years. Traditionally, one problem with the Office application has been sharing the collected data across disparate systems. The Office data binaries and presentation layer are tightly coupled and exposed through a limited series of COM-based automation layers. Office 2003 has solved this problem with a default integration of XML and the .NET Framework. This effectively decouples the data and presentation from Office applications. In addition, the use of custom XML Schema makes the data structures easily portable. This enables a clean separation of the data and business logic from other aspects of the actual document presentation.

This chapter covers how smart client applications, such as InfoPath, are built and can exchange data with Windows Forms, Web Services, and the rest of the Office system family. We will also cover how these types of solutions enable a broad set of functionality that can be both connected to and disconnected from the enterprise data stores.

THE SMART CLIENT APPLICATION

The term *information worker* is used to describe an individual in an enterprise who participates in the flow of information or an execution of business processes. These workers often perform a variety of repetitive but highly specialized tasks during their normal job functions. Often, they are accessing data from a variety of back-end data sources across multiple applications. These types of individuals are perfect candidates for using smart client applications. Being part of the mainstream business, they are looking for better and familiar ways to access large volumes of information easily and quickly. Many of the dynamic features of the Microsoft .NET Framework coupled with the familiar interface of Office have emerged as ways for enterprises to serve this type of application requirement.

The goal of smart client applications is to enable application users access to their enterprise data remotely and allow these users to continually update how and what types of information is shared with the Internet, partners, and disparate systems. This type of application paradigm affects all levels of an enterprise and enables companies to complete the shift to a loosely coupled distributed application environment. This type of application infrastructure provides the following key advantages:

- Smart clients are based on an application model that provides an enhanced user experience through customization and personalization
- Application scalability is a natural by-product of this type of application design
- The component-based design processes of SOA provide easier application maintenance and reduced support costs
- The advanced toolsets enable application developers to shorten software development cycles

■ The local footprint of an application with proper design enables applications to run without network connectivity

The ultimate goal of smart client technologies like InfoPath is to enable the design and implementation of a variety of solutions—ultimately, turning exposed data into business endpoints that Information Workers can use.

What Is a Smart Client?

Fundamentally, smart clients are any type of locally deployed application designed to consume XML and interact with server side resources. The use of XML and Web Services enables the aggregation of multiple data sources using a standardized framework. Smart clients like InfoPath are then used to provide the common metaphor for frontend data collection and XML is used for local data persistence. Unlike traditional browser-based applications, smart clients are solutions that don't depend on a constant connection to the server for processing. Actually, most processing and application logic is expected to occur on the local client.

Web Service Integration

One important aspect of the XML integration is the use of Web services. This integration allows the retrieval of data from enterprise data stores. For example, using the code in Listing 8.1 (This sample can be found in \Code\Chapter 8\Catalog\ClientCatalog\ClientCatalog.sln on the companion CD-ROM.). We can create a Web Service that retrieves catalog information from a WebMethod using an ADO.NET Dataset.

ON THE CD

LISTING 8.1   Web Service That Returns a Catalog Dataset to the Client

```
<WebMethod()> Public Function GetNewCatalog() As DataSet
        'create the DB connection
        Dim sqlConn As SqlConnection
        Dim sqlCmd As SqlCommand
        Dim strConstring As String

        strConstring = "Data Source=basexp;Initial
                        Catalog=Catalog;Integrated Security=SSPI;"
        sqlConn = New SqlConnection(strConstring)
        sqlConn.Open()
        sqlCmd = New SqlCommand

        With sqlCmd
            .Connection = sqlConn
            .CommandTimeout = 30
```

```
            .CommandType = CommandType.StoredProcedure
            .CommandText = "spGetCatlogInfo"
    End With

    Dim RequestDA As SqlDataAdapter = New SqlDataAdapter
    RequestDA.SelectCommand = sqlCmd
    Dim RequestDS As DataSet = New DataSet
    RequestDA.Fill(RequestDS, "RequestType")
    Return RequestDS

    sqlConn.Close()
End Function
```

The dataset is an ADO.NET object that is part of the System.Data namespace. Its strength is that it can act as a disconnected XML based collection used to aggregate data from one or more data sources. By default, when data is loaded the dataset infers an XML schema. When loading from a SQL database, the SQLDataAdapter serves as the bridge between the database and SQL Server. This bridge is provided by the Fill method. This method transforms the streamed data into the data source using Transact SQL statements.

When the SQLDataAdapter fills the dataset, it creates the necessary tables and columns to match the filled data. In Listing 8.1, the catalog data is filled with the data from a SQL stored procedure that is then used to infer the XML Schema structure. The catalog dataset contains a single datatable object that is used to represent the catalog data. When the WebMethod is called directly from the browser, it returns the XML representation, as shown in Figure 8.1.

When using a dataset, InfoPath interprets it as an XML structure that contains an inline schema. This schema is used to create the form's main data connection. To create the InfoPath form that displays this information and access the catalog dataset, follow these steps:

1. Start InfoPath and select Design a form from the main menu.
2. In the Design a new form section in the task pane, select New from Data Connection option.
3. In the Data Connection Wizard, select Web Services as the type of data connection for the form, then select Next.
4. Select Receive data to specify how the form works with the Web Service and click Next.
5. In the text field, type the URL location of the Web service and click Next.
6. Select the GetnewCatalog Web Service method as the operation used to receive data and click Next.
7. Keep the default name of Main query as the data connection to use to receive data from the Web Service.

```
<?xml version="1.0" encoding="utf-8" ?>
- <DataSet xmlns="http://tempuri.org/wsCatalog/CatalogInfo">
  + <xs:schema id="NewDataSet" xmlns="" xmlns:xs="http://www.w3.org/2001/XMLSchema" xmlns:msdata="urn:schemas-
    microsoft-com:xml-msdata">
  - <diffgr:diffgram xmlns:msdata="urn:schemas-microsoft-com:xml-msdata" xmlns:diffgr="urn:schemas-microsoft-com:xml-
    diffgram-v1">
    - <NewDataSet xmlns="">
      - <RequestType diffgr:id="RequestType1" msdata:rowOrder="0">
          <CatalogID>1</CatalogID>
          <ItemName>Classic Black Shoes</ItemName>
          <ItemQuantityonHand>100</ItemQuantityonHand>
          <ItemPrice>49.9500</ItemPrice>
          <ItemDescription>Classic black shoes are for the stylish people that always want to look their best</ItemDescription>
          <ItemSku>1345634576</ItemSku>
        </RequestType>
      - <RequestType diffgr:id="RequestType2" msdata:rowOrder="1">
          <CatalogID>2</CatalogID>
          <ItemName>Big Time Fedora</ItemName>
          <ItemQuantityonHand>300</ItemQuantityonHand>
          <ItemPrice>12.5000</ItemPrice>
          <ItemDescription>The fedora always shows that you want to look you best no matter what.</ItemDescription>
          <ItemSku>1324353678</ItemSku>
        </RequestType>
      </NewDataSet>
    </diffgr:diffgram>
  </DataSet>
```

FIGURE 8.1   XML that contains a dataset returned from the Catalog Web Service.

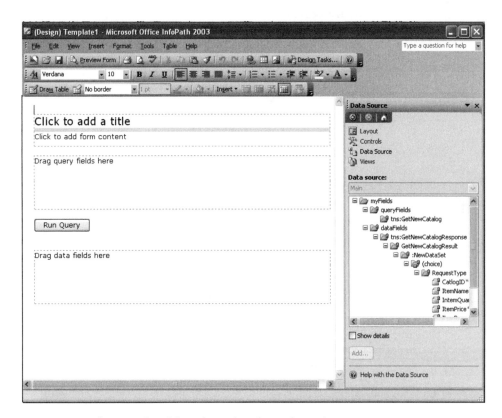

FIGURE 8.2   The completed form bound to the Web Service.

Once these steps are completed, the InfoPath form contains a data source that is linked to the expressed inline schema, as shown in Figure 8.2.

During the creation of the data source, InfoPath reads the Web Services Description Language (WSDL) generated by the Web Service. This is used to create the XSD schema that is used to define the form's data source structure. The schema is stored with the form template and contains the XSD shown in Listing 8.2.

LISTING 8.2 The InfoPath Form Template Points to the Web Service Location

```xml
<?xml version="1.0" encoding="UTF-8" standalone="no"?>
<xsd:schema elementFormDefault="qualified"
targetNamespace="http://schemas.microsoft.com/office/infopath/2003/data
FormSolution" xmlns:xsd="http://www.w3.org/2001/XMLSchema"
xmlns:dfs="http://schemas.microsoft.com/office/infopath/2003/dataFormSo
lution" xmlns:tns="http://tempuri.org/WebService2/Service1">
    <xsd:import namespace="http://tempuri.org/WebService2/Service1"
schemaLocation="schema1.xsd"/>
    <xsd:element name="myFields">
        <xsd:complexType>
            <xsd:sequence>
                <xsd:element name="queryFields">
                    <xsd:complexType>
                        <xsd:sequence>
                            <xsd:element ref="tns:GetNewCatalog"/>
                        </xsd:sequence>
                    </xsd:complexType>
                </xsd:element>
                <xsd:element name="dataFields">
                    <xsd:complexType>
                        <xsd:sequence>
                            <xsd:element
ref="tns:GetNewCatalogResponse"/>
                        </xsd:sequence>
                    </xsd:complexType>
                </xsd:element>
                <xsd:any namespace="##other" processContents="lax"
minOccurs="0" maxOccurs="unbounded"/>
            </xsd:sequence>
            <xsd:anyAttribute namespace="##other"
processContents="lax"/>
        </xsd:complexType>
    </xsd:element>
</xsd:schema>
```

Based on this XSD, InfoPath will by default create a repeating choice group if the data source is dropped onto the InfoPath form, as shown in Figure 8.3.

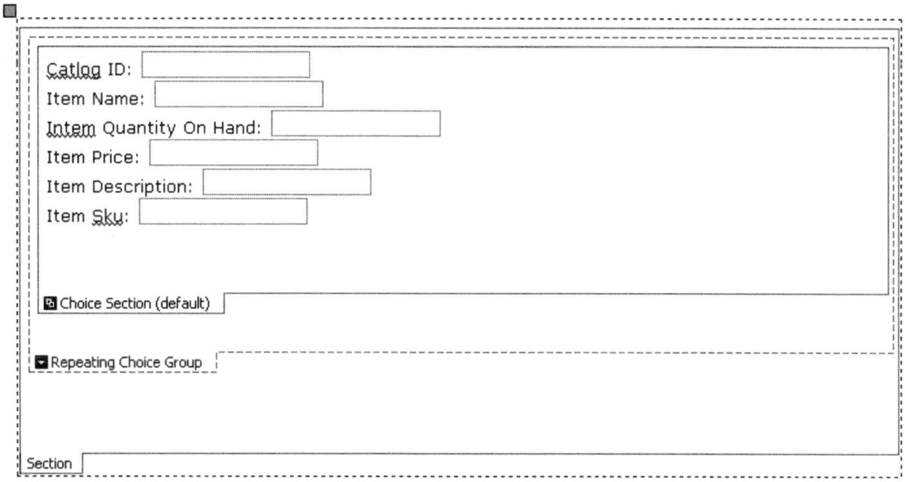

FIGURE 8.3   The default structure of the catalog Web Service.

This is because the XSD requires that the Web Service return zero or more catalog records. By default, the Choice Group is used by InfoPath to express this type of data structure. In reality, this form is going to be used to only retrieve data. For better presentation and end-user experience, this should be shown as a repeating table. The transformation of this default structure is controlled by the form bindings, as shown in Figure 8.4.

Once the proper bindings are set and the default view is created, the form is displayed, as shown in Figure 8.5.

It is important to remember that the WSDL parser that is used by InfoPath is not designed to support multiple dataset instances. As a result, InfoPath executes a special set of checks to validate the dataset instance. Even though you can design a form against a Web Service that has multiple dataset instances, only one of these instances can exist while the form is being edited. However, if we wanted to get around this, we could create a wrapper class that converts the dataset to an XML-DataDocument using the code in Listing 8.3.

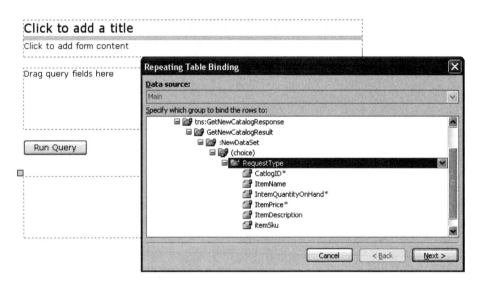

FIGURE 8.4 Setting the bindings for a repeating table.

The Official My Company Catalog

Run Query

This catalog is updated nightly from our warehouses and provides the most current information of all stock items that we have on hand.

Catalog Name	Quantity on Hand	Price	Item Description	Order Number
Classic Black ...	100	49.9500	Classic black shoes are for the stylish people that always want to look their best	1345634576
Big Time Fed...	300	12.5000	The fedora always shows that you want to look you best no matter what.	1324353678

FIGURE 8.5 An InfoPath form that shows the catalog information.

LISTING 8.3 Converting a Dataset to an XMLDataDocument

```
<WebMethod()> Public Function InfoPathGetNewCatalog() As _
    System.Xml.XmlDocument
    Dim ds As DataSet

    ds = GetNewCatalog()
    ds.Namespace = "Http://localhost/Catalog"
```

```
    Dim Info As System.Xml.XmlDataDocument =New _
System.Xml.XmlDataDocument(ds)
    Return Info

End Function
```

The catalog form created here represents a connected InfoPath form. This means that as long as the Web Service is available, the form functions. However, if this form is opened and if the user can't connect with the Web Service, InfoPath displays the error message shown in Figure 8.6.

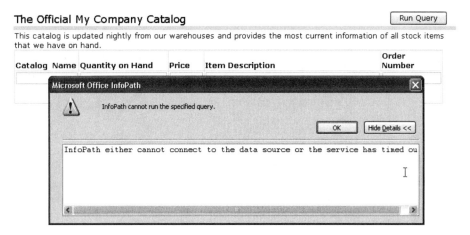

FIGURE 8.6   When users can't connect to the Web Service, InfoPath displays this message.

This is a major problem if we need to take the current solution mobile or need to provide any type of offline access. In this scenario, an InfoPath form that relies on connectivity to a Web Service may not be the best answer.

Using XSLT

Using the .NET Framework, we can leverage XML-based transformations that are used within the InfoPath .solution (.xsn) file as a way of providing offline data. As a side benefit, we can leverage the initial dataset as a way of accessing our data. Essentially, an .xsn file is nothing more than a compressed .cab file that contains a list of files. If we export the current applications into a file directory, as shown in

Figure 8.7, we can see that they are simply a series of XML and XSLT files. In building this solution, we can work outside the InfoPath IDE and later repackage the files into an XSN for distribution.

XSLT is used extensively within InfoPath as a way of rendering client data. It takes an XML file as input, applies a series of commands, and outputs a formatted file. The XML file shown in Listing 8.4 contains the contact information shown in Figure 8.7.

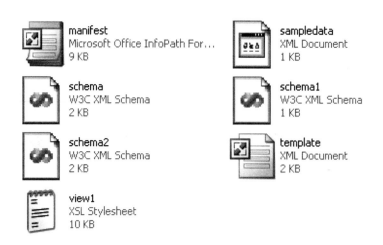

FIGURE 8.7 Exported lists of files that make up an InfoPath solution.

LISTING 8.4 XML File Showing Customer Contact Information

```xml
<?xml version="1.0" encoding="utf-8" ?>
<?xml-stylesheet type="text/xsl" ?>
<customers>
  <customerinfo>
    <customername>Main Street Auto</customername>
    <address1>123 Anywhere St</address1>
    <address2>Suite 123</address2>
    <city>Nashua</city>
    <state>NH</state>
    <zipcode>03110</zipcode>
    <contactname>Mary Roberts</contactname>
    <currentbalance>1200</currentbalance>
  </customerinfo>
```

```
<customerinfo>
  <customername>Second Street Manufacturing</customername>
  <address1>456 Main Street</address1>
  <address2>Building 12</address2>
  <city>Bedford</city>
  <state>NH</state>
  <zipcode>03060</zipcode>
  <contactname>Marvin Robbins</contactname>
  <currentbalance>750</currentbalance>
</customerinfo>

<customerinfo>
  <customername>East Side Excavating</customername>
  <address1>12 East St</address1>
  <address2>Suite 8512</address2>
  <city>Keene</city>
  <state>NH</state>
  <zipcode>03801</zipcode>
  <contactname>Chris Russo</contactname>
  <currentbalance>1600</currentbalance>
</customerinfo>
</customers>
```

The file now contains customer information and their current balances, which can be seen in Figure 8.8.

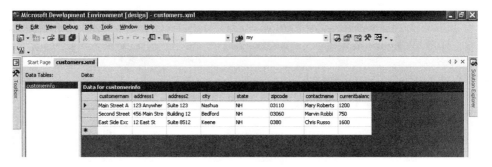

FIGURE 8.8   A sample XML file entered using Visual Studio.NET.

Using XSLT, we can create the XML transformation shown in Listing 8.5, which results in the creation of an HTML page.

LISTING 8.5 XSLT Applied to the Customer Data That Generates an HTML Page

```
<?xml version="1.0" encoding="UTF-8" ?>
<xsl:stylesheet version="1.0"
xmlns:xsl="http://www.w3.org/1999/XSL/Transform">

<xsl:template match="customers">
<html><body>
<h1>Current Customer List</h1>
<table width="800">
<xsl:apply-templates/>
</table>
</body></html>
</xsl:template>

<xsl:template match="customerinfo">
<tr>
  <td><xsl:number/></td>
  <xsl:apply-templates/>
</tr>
</xsl:template>

<xsl:template match="customername |address1 |address2 |
              city | state |
            zipcode | contactname | currentbalance">
  <td><xsl:value-of select="."/></td>
</xsl:template>
</xsl:stylesheet>
```

This transformation produces an HTML page that contains the data that we are looking to show about the list of customers and is shown in Figure 8.9.

Current Customer List

1	Main Street Auto	123 Anywhere St	Suite 123	Nashua	NH 03110	Mary Roberts	1200
2	Second Street Manufacturing	456 Main Street	Building 12	Bedford	NH 03060	Marvin Robbins	750
3	East Side Excavating	12 East St	Suite 8512	Keene	NH 0380	Chris Russo	1600

FIGURE 8.9 View of the transformed customer data.

XSLT and Visual Studio

Visual Studio has a variety of built-in tools that allow you to create XSLT and apply transformations. It is important to remember that InfoPath makes extensive use of XSLT to both show views and apply other types of data actions. InfoPath and Visual Studio both use XML and XSLT.

If we revisit the catalog example using the Web Service (shown in Listings 8.1 and 8.2), we could extend this to take advantage of a client-based solution that extracts the data from the dataset and then caches the data locally. Using XSLT, we could extend this solution to include some transformations that show an HTML document, InfoPath document, and Word 2003 document. (This example is available on the companion CD-ROM in \Code\Chapter 8\Catalog\OfflineCatalog.xsn.)

HTML Formatting

Using the built-in HTML formatting and copying the stylesheet within InfoPath, we can create the XSLT shown in Listing 8.6, which renders the document in HTML.

LISTING 8.6   Rendering an InfoPath Form to an HTML Document

```
<?xml version="1.0" encoding="UTF-8"?>
<xsl:stylesheet version="1.0"
xmlns:my="http://schemas.microsoft.com/office/infopath/2003/myXSD/2003-
09-12T22:55:52" xmlns:xsl="http://www.w3.org/1999/XSL/Transform"
xmlns:msxsl="urn:schemas-microsoft-com:xslt"
xmlns:xd="http://schemas.microsoft.com/office/infopath/2003"
xmlns:x="urn:schemas-microsoft-com:office:excel"
xmlns:xdExtension="http://schemas.microsoft.com/office/infopath/2003/xs
lt/extension"
xmlns:xdXDocument="http://schemas.microsoft.com/office/infopath/2003/xs
lt/xDocument"
xmlns:xdSolution="http://schemas.microsoft.com/office/infopath/2003/xsl
t/solution"
xmlns:xdFormatting="http://schemas.microsoft.com/office/infopath/2003/x
slt/formatting"
xmlns:xdImage="http://schemas.microsoft.com/office/infopath/2003/xslt/x
Image">
  <xsl:output method="html" indent="no"/>
  <xsl:template match="NewDataSet">
    <html>
      <head>
        <meta http-equiv="Content-Type" content="text/html"></meta>
        <style controlStyle="controlStyle">BODY{margin-
left:21px;color:windowtext;background-color:window;layout-grid:none;}
```

```
.xdListItem {display:inline-block;width:100%;vertical-align:text-top;}
.xdListBox,.xdComboBox{margin:1px;}
.xdInlinePicture{margin:1px; BEHAVIOR: url(#default#urn::xdPicture) }
.xdLinkedPicture{margin:1px; BEHAVIOR: url(#default#urn::xdPicture)
url(#default#urn::controls/Binder) }
.xdSection{border:1pt solid #FFFFFF;margin:6px 0px 6px
0px;padding:1px 1px 1px 5px;}
.xdRepeatingSection{border:1pt solid #FFFFFF;margin:6px 0px 6px
0px;padding:1px 1px 1px 5px;}
.xdBehavior_Formatting {BEHAVIOR: url(#default#urn::controls/Binder)
url(#default#Formatting);}
.xdBehavior_FormattingNoBUI{BEHAVIOR: url(#default#CalPopup)
url(#default#urn::controls/Binder) url(#default#Formatting);}
.xdExpressionBox{margin: 1px;padding:1px;word-wrap: break-word;text-
overflow: ellipsis;overflow-
x:hidden;}.xdBehavior_GhostedText,.xdBehavior_GhostedTextNoBUI{BEHAVIOR
: url(#default#urn::controls/Binder) url(#default#TextField)
url(#default#GhostedText);}
.xdBehavior_GTFormatting{BEHAVIOR: url(#default#urn::controls/Binder)
url(#default#Formatting) url(#default#GhostedText);}
.xdBehavior_GTFormattingNoBUI{BEHAVIOR: url(#default#CalPopup)
url(#default#urn::controls/Binder) url(#default#Formatting)
url(#default#GhostedText);}
.xdBehavior_Boolean{BEHAVIOR: url(#default#urn::controls/Binder)
url(#default#BooleanHelper);}
.xdBehavior_Select{BEHAVIOR: url(#default#urn::controls/Binder)
url(#default#SelectHelper);}
.xdRepeatingTable{BORDER-TOP-STYLE: none; BORDER-RIGHT-STYLE: none;
BORDER-LEFT-STYLE: none; BORDER-BOTTOM-STYLE: none; BORDER-COLLAPSE:
collapse; WORD-WRAP: break-word;}.xdTextBox{display:inline-block;white-
space:nowrap;text-overflow:ellipsis;;padding:1px;margin:1px;border: 1pt
solid #dcdcdc;color:windowtext;background-
color:window;overflow:hidden;text-align:left;}
.xdRichTextBox{display:inline-block;;padding:1px;margin:1px;border:
1pt solid #dcdcdc;color:windowtext;background-color:window;overflow-
x:hidden;word-wrap:break-word;text-overflow:ellipsis;text-
align:left;font-weight:normal;font-style:normal;text-
decoration:none;vertical-align:baseline;}
.xdDTPicker{;display:inline;margin:1px;margin-bottom: 2px;border: 1pt
solid #dcdcdc;color:windowtext;background-
color:window;overflow:hidden;}
.xdDTText{height:100%;width:100%;margin-
right:22px;overflow:hidden;padding:0px;white-space:nowrap;}
```

```
    .xdDTButton{margin-left:-21px;height:18px;width:20px;behavior:
url(#default#DTPicker);}
   .xdRepeatingTable TD {VERTICAL-ALIGN: top;}</style>
        <style tableEditor="TableStyleRulesID">TABLE.xdLayout TD {
  BORDER-RIGHT: medium none; BORDER-TOP: medium none; BORDER-LEFT:
medium none; BORDER-BOTTOM: medium none
}
TABLE.msoUcTable TD {
  BORDER-RIGHT: 1pt solid; BORDER-TOP: 1pt solid; BORDER-LEFT: 1pt
solid; BORDER-BOTTOM: 1pt solid
}
TABLE {
  BEHAVIOR: url (#default#urn::tables/NDTable)
}
</style>
        <style languageStyle="languageStyle">BODY {
  FONT-SIZE: 10pt; FONT-FAMILY: Verdana
}
TABLE {
  FONT-SIZE: 10pt; FONT-FAMILY: Verdana
}
SELECT {
  FONT-SIZE: 10pt; FONT-FAMILY: Verdana
}
.optionalPlaceholder {
  PADDING-LEFT: 20px; FONT-WEIGHT: normal; FONT-SIZE: xx-small;
BEHAVIOR: url(#default#xOptional); COLOR: #333333; FONT-STYLE: normal;
FONT-FAMILY: Verdana; TEXT-DECORATION: none
}
.langFont {
 FONT-FAMILY: Verdana
}
</style>
      </head>
      <body>
        <div><xsl:apply-templates select="." mode="_1"/>
        </div>
        <div> </div>
      </body>
    </html>
  </xsl:template>
  <xsl:template match="NewDataSet" mode="_1">
```

```
        <div class="xdSection xdRepeating" title="" style="MARGIN-BOTTOM:
6px; WIDTH: 542px" align="left" xd:CtrlId="CTRL8" xd:xctname="Section"
tabIndex="-1">
  <div><xsl:apply-templates select="RequestType" mode="_2"/>
      </div>
      <div> </div>
      <div> </div>
      <div> </div>
    </div>
  </xsl:template>
  <xsl:template match="RequestType" mode="_2">
      <div class="xdRepeatingSection xdRepeating" title=""
style="MARGIN-BOTTOM: 6px; WIDTH: 100%" align="left" xd:CtrlId="CTRL9"
xd:xctname="RepeatingSection" tabIndex="-1">
      <div>Catalog ID: <span class="xdTextBox" hideFocus="1" title=""
xd:CtrlId="CTRL10" xd:xctname="PlainText" tabIndex="0"
xd:binding="CatalogID" style="WIDTH: 130px">
          <xsl:value-of select="CatalogID"/>
        </span>
      </div>
      <div>Item Name: <span class="xdTextBox" hideFocus="1" title=""
xd:CtrlId="CTRL11" xd:xctname="PlainText" tabIndex="0"
xd:binding="ItemName" style="WIDTH: 130px">
          <xsl:value-of select="ItemName"/>
        </span>
      </div>
      <div>Item Quantityon Hand: <span class="xdTextBox" hideFocus="1"
title="" xd:CtrlId="CTRL12" xd:xctname="PlainText" tabIndex="0"
xd:binding="ItemQuantityonHand" style="WIDTH: 130px">
          <xsl:value-of select="ItemQuantityonHand"/>
        </span>
      </div>
      <div>Item Price: <span class="xdTextBox" hideFocus="1" title=""
xd:CtrlId="CTRL13" xd:xctname="PlainText" tabIndex="0"
xd:binding="ItemPrice" style="WIDTH: 130px">
          <xsl:value-of select="ItemPrice"/>
        </span>
      </div>
      <div>Item Description: <span class="xdTextBox" hideFocus="1"
title="" xd:CtrlId="CTRL14" xd:xctname="PlainText" tabIndex="0"
xd:binding="ItemDescription" style="WIDTH: 130px">
          <xsl:value-of select="ItemDescription"/>
        </span>
```

```
        </div>
        <div>Item Sku: <span class="xdTextBox" hideFocus="1" title=""
xd:CtrlId="CTRL15" xd:xctname="PlainText" tabIndex="0"
xd:binding="ItemSku" style="WIDTH: 130px">
            <xsl:value-of select="ItemSku"/>
          </span>
        </div>
        <div> </div>
        <div> </div>
        <div> </div>
      </div>
    </xsl:template>
  </xsl:stylesheet>
```

InfoPath Formatting

Earlier, we talked about how when a Web Service is not connected to the Catalog Web Service, an InfoPath form like the one shown in Listing 8.6 that is bound to a Web Service would generate an error. If we create a second solution that uses a local copy of the data, we can create an XSLT that takes the data from the dataset, then applies an XSLT style sheet to it and outputs an InfoPath-compatible set of XML. The key in this is to use processing instructions such that, when placed in the XML, the system will review to determine the type of editor to use for accessing this file. The XSLT to format a file to match our InfoPath document contains the code in Listing 8.7.

LISTING 8.7 XSLT Style Sheet Used to Format the InfoPath Saved XML

```
<?xml version="1.0" encoding="UTF-8" ?>
<xsl:stylesheet version="1.0"
xmlns:xsl="http://www.w3.org/1999/XSL/Transform" >
<xsl:output method="xml" omit-xml-declaration="no"/>

<xsl:template match="/">
<xsl:processing-instruction name="mso-
infoPathSolution">solutionVersion="1.0.0.1" productVersion="11.0.5329"
PIVersion="1.0.0.0"
href="file:///D:\Programming%20Microsoft%20InfoPath%20A%20Developers%20
Guide\Chapter%208\Samples\Catalog\OfflineCatalog.xsn" language="en-
us"</xsl:processing-instruction>
<xsl:processing-instruction name="mso-
application">progid="InfoPath.Document"</xsl:processing-instruction>
```

```
<catalog:catalogData
xmlns:catalog="http://schemas.mycompany.com/ns/offline/info">
<xsl:for-each select="NewDataSet">
  <catalog:catalogInfo>
    <catalog:CatalogID><xsl:value-of
select="CatalogID"/></catalog:CatalogID>
    <catalog:ItemName><xsl:value-of
select="ItemName"/></catalog:ItemName>
    <catalog:ItemQuantityonHand><xsl:value-of
select="ItemQuantityonHand"/></catalog:ItemQuantityonHand>
    <catalog:ItemPrice><xsl:value-of
select="ItemPrice"/></catalog:ItemPrice>
    <catalog:ItemDescription><xsl:value-of
select="ItemDescription"/></catalog:ItemDescription>
    <catalog:ItemSku><xsl:value-of select="ItemSku"/></catalog:ItemSku>
  </catalog:catalogInfo>
</xsl:for-each>
</catalog:catalogData>

<</xsl:template>
</xsl:stylesheet>
```

Formatting for Word 2003

Microsoft Word 2003 is also completely XML-enabled and can use a similar type of processing set of instructions to consume XML. Word uses the WordML XML-based model that defines its XML structure. Using the XSLT transformation shown in Listing 8.8, we can transform the same dataset into a Word 2003 XML document.

LISTING 8.8 Transforming an XML Document into a Word Document

```
<xsl:stylesheet version="1.0"
xmlns:xsl="http://www.w3.org/1999/XSL/Transform"
xmlns:o="urn:schemas-microsoft-com:office:office"
xmlns:w="http://schemas.microsoft.com/office/word/2003/2/wordml">

<xsl:template match="/">
<xsl:processing-instruction name="mso-
application">progid="Word.Document"
</xsl:processing-instruction>

<w:wordDocument
xmlns:w="http://schemas.microsoft.com/office/word/2003/2/wordml">
```

```
<o:DocumentProperties>
  <o:Title>My Company Catalog Information</o:Title>
</o:DocumentProperties>

<w:body>
   <xsl:for-each select="NewDataSet/RequestType">
     <w:p>
        <w:r>
        <w:t>
          <xsl:value-of select="ItemName"/>
        </w:t>
        <w:t>
          <xsl:value-of select="ItemQuantityonHand"/>
        </w:t>
        <w:t>
          <xsl:value-of select="ItemPrice"/>
        </w:t>
        <w:t>
          <xsl:value-of select="ItemDescription"/>
        </w:t>
        <w:t>
          <xsl:value-of select="ItemSku"/>
        </w:t>
        </w:r>
     </w:p>
   </xsl:for-each>
  </w:body>
</w:wordDocument>

</xsl:template>
</xsl:stylesheet>
```

A TABLET PC AS A SMART CLIENT

The Tablet PC operating system is a Windows XP Tablet PC Edition that is a superset of the traditional desktop application. One of the main advantages of this device is that it is built on top of the Windows XP platform and provides users with the same features as the traditional desktop with enhanced features targeted for mobility. As a superset of Windows XP, the Tablet PC provides additional capabilities that can be used to extend these types of devices. Installing the .NET Framework by default, Windows XP Tablet PC Edition allows you to take full advantage of managed code and VB.NET and C# applications—without having to worry about redistributing the .NET Framework.

In addition to being able to take full advantage of the exciting new capabilities of the Tablet PC platform with ink, pen, and handwriting recognition APIs, you can have the full power of Windows and all the existing Windows APIs, components, developer tools, and applications that run on Windows XP. The Tablet provides additional capabilities that extend these types of devices. The benefit of using the Tablet PC with InfoPath is that this combination can take advantage of these advanced functions and provide additional capabilities over the traditional PCs, as seen in Figure 8.10.

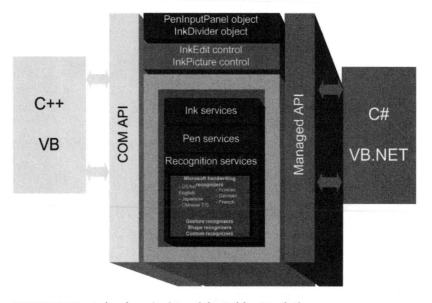

FIGURE 8.10 A developer's view of the Tablet PC platform.

The Ink Control

One of the main features of InfoPath when used with the Tablet is that you can directly enable the ink on the form. (This is available on the companion CD-ROM in \Code\Chapter 8\Tablet\Ink Form\ink.xsn.) One of the advantages of this is that you can show the file and collection annotations. The ink control is actually one feature of the Tablet SDK. This feature is available only when you're using a Tablet PC. Figure 8.11 shows an InfoPath form that uses the ink control.

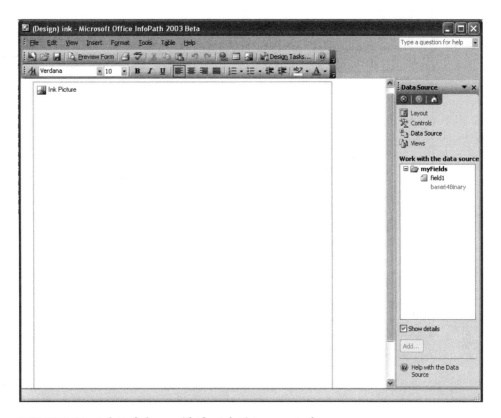

FIGURE 8.11   InfoPath form with the Ink Picture control.

Figure 8.12 shows what happens when this form is loaded and ink is added.

What Is Base 64?

When you use inking within InfoPath, the contents of saved XML are converted and stored in Base 64. The Base 64 Content-Transfer-Encoding is designed to represent arbitrary sequences of octets in a form that is not humanly readable. The encoding and decoding algorithms are simple, but encoded data is only about 33% larger than un-encoded data. This is important to remember because encoding images can substantially increase the size of your files. This encoding is identical to the

FIGURE 8.12 A completed ink form.

one used in Privacy Enhanced Mail (PEM) applications that are defined as part of Request for Comments (RFC) 1421. The only change that Base 64 encoding made to this RFC is that it eliminates the "*" mechanism for sending embedded clear text.

Within Base 64, a 65-character subset of ASCII that allows 6 bits per printer character, is used. The extra character, "=", is used to signify a special processing instruction.

The Base 64 encoding process represents 24-bit groups of input bits as output strings of four encoded characters. You create the 24-bit input group of an encoded file by concatenating three 8-bit input groups. These 24 bits are then treated as four concatenated 6-bit groups, each translated into a single digit in the Base 64 alphabet. The encoding rules guarantee that the bit stream is ordered with the most significant bit first.

Each 6-bit group is used as an index into an array of 64 printable characters. Any character referenced by the index is placed in the output string. These characters, identified in Table 8.1, are selected as part of the index. The value set automatically excludes characters with special meaning, such as FTP, CR, and LF.

TABLE 8.1 The Base 64 Alphabet

Value	Encoding	Value	Encoding	Value	Encoding	Value	Encoding
0	A	17	R	34	i	51	z
1	B	18	S	35	j	52	0
2	C	19	T	36	k	53	1
3	D	20	U	37	l	54	2
4	E	21	V	38	m	55	3
5	F	22	W	39	n	56	4
6	G	23	X	40	o	57	5
7	H	24	Y	41	p	58	6
8	I	25	Z	42	q	59	7
9	J	26	a	43	r	60	8
10	K	27	b	44	s	61	9
11	L	28	c	45	t	62	+
12	M	29	d	46	u	63	/
13	N	30	e	47	v		
14	O	31	f	48	w	pad	=
15	P	32	g	49	x		
16	Q	33	h	50	y		

The resulting output stream is required to be presented in lines that don't exceed 76 total characters each. Within Base 64, the decoding software automatically ignores any characters not found in Table 8.1. When the actual stream is decoded, these are considered transmission errors.

ON THE CD

When the sample Ink Form (included on the CD-ROM in \Code\Chapter 8\Tablet\Ink Form\saved.xml)is saved, the resulting XML file contains the Base 64 encoded field, as shown in Figure 8.13.

```
<?xml version="1.0" encoding="UTF-8"?><?mso-infoPathSolution solutionversion="1.0.0.1" productversion="11.0.5329" PIvers
    <my:field1 xmlns:xsi="http://www.w3.org/2001/XMLSchema-instance">R0lGODlhJAJVAvCAAAAAAIAAAACAAICAAAAAgIAAgACAgICA
9mmf9mzP9m//+ZAP+ZM/+ZZV+Zmf+ZZP+Z///MAP/MM//MZv/Mmf/MzP/M////AP//M///Zv//mf//zP///yH5BAEAAPBALAAAAAAkAlUCAAj/AP8JHE1wOMK
y/3JOwaGXKhDYd6dpzytdyaLPPPsxK61k13thRyycR+ChHsWbBdE9+x13wKygc/FGsfZgKNLwxUb21Tjq1/FW/KLwcOse31rTsHx/pqvXaoX3/3IRZOo4Lkt<
beuJGRyrJd8cSIwa0kpzvE1UAvmIIWU0GfvV5UK9L7SLv02Ve9ZgSe29oINbjkAj+OFRwjCNU0RtEHDxnIBcrUoh2741eOnImpFvmqR9aUBYj/SiQVLppcQH<
NF9/VHhTh+EOQNQNDbusrxFSr6Qaqjaxv5xwhMWJN6eT8Qfcv6HzsmOtJCX1c/wprRAAn0Q87mAwtpY/f3UR40hoyALOHfJki1GEZNcdsHNS4Hv/SQSvuDMmhMMi
3QBx+5EM8IMjIxfFKwjltzJ/lgIqnoEMVCIoUQJKMgIdzYLvFHEkvIhH6w1BABmISVBRLX1TUiBehImC2xWcWpRN5iK2gFFa22EuUFIVKnnOv/kgp9cFhzhZ0
21ENiVFNQWNgvypqhLERfkmsnJEMKTFLTVi7NrEdvwBygoBuNIEK1GFBDngH7xUxWWx11GqtgTBuEgRmDxyJjirVA/xCh4CKhJhJKSpE3VHglv/OZZwexC1GZi
HRox6WbhqhK5cSK0yQ2fFXIFfDyU4b2wJhJBo7rBZ6WE0g1TqB1ExCyRHRPy7wLxAi2wchfQho12G5J1a4rLVowhupOhgYiRP5iYCYEvxS1QT/yrgn0cjAOBi
4w1Z96qZDvUR6fd7C5cO6PE5myNwfKEH6SeLju4gTx1X04Df/uIVLw5yMBCz8S1DwZqAnfrPkgLVJw6Xk+6upBy7/1AkEKO3N1Xj6fcy7iiLv/RA2gIApaoO-
KJJ6a4Yosvxjhjj7fmuGOPPwY5ZJFHJr1kk09GOWWvv2a5ZZ2dfhj1mmWemuwabb8Y5Z25135r1nn38GOmihhya6aKOPRjpppZdmummnn4Y6aqlop6a6aquvxj
</my:field1>
</my:myFields>
```

FIGURE 8.13 Notepad view of the Base 64 encoded form.

Reusing Base 64 with a Smart Client Application

Using Visual Studio, we can take the saved Base 64-encoded XML and convert that into a bitmap image that can be shown in a Windows Form application, as shown in Listing 8.9.

LISTING 8.9 Converting Base 64-Encoded XML into a Bitmap

```
Public Class Form1

    Private Sub BtnConvert_Click(ByVal sender As System.Object, _
            ByVal e As System.EventArgs) Handles BtnConvert.Click
        Dim retnbit As Bitmap
        Dim rdr As New Xml.XmlTextReader("saved.xml")

        rdr.WhitespaceHandling = Xml.WhitespaceHandling.None

        ' Read the file. Stop at the Base64 element.
        While rdr.Read()
            If "my:field1" = rdr.Name Then
                Dim base64txt = rdr.ReadElementString()
                retnbit = BitmapFromBase64(base64txt)

                Exit While
            End If
        End While

        PicImage.Image = retnbit

    End Sub
```

```
Public Function BitmapFromBase64(ByVal base64 As String) As
System.Drawing.Bitmap
    Dim oBitmap As System.Drawing.Bitmap
    Dim memory As New
    System.IO.MemoryStream(Convert.FromBase64String(base64))
    oBitmap = New System.Drawing.Bitmap(memory)
    memory.Close()
    memory = Nothing
    Return oBitmap
End Function

End Class
```

When applied against the existing saved XML form, this decodes the image and converts it into a bitmap like that shown in Figure 8.14.

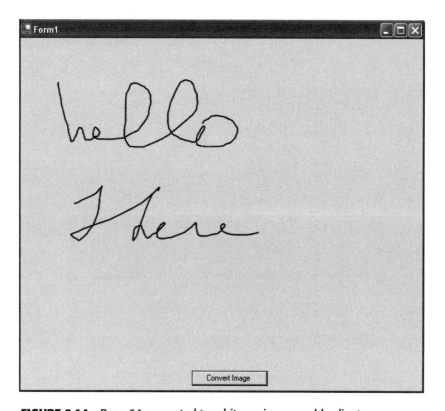

FIGURE 8.14   Base 64 converted to a bitmap in a reusable client.

SUMMARY

Within this chapter, we have covered the advantages and design patterns that we use when developing smart client applications. This solution is only one of many places that an InfoPath solution can be used. However, like many of the solutions we have discussed, it can easily be extended into other applications such as Microsoft Office and even a Windows Form. This becomes even more important as you start to develop client applications designed for the Tablet PC. This platform provides additional extensibility that can easily be used within your applications.

It is important to understand all the topics that we have covered up to this point because we begin to discuss security in the next chapter. Design patterns are an important part of the application development cycle. Of course, one of the most important concepts of any application design is to ensure that all data is protected against both unwanted and unintentional access.

9 Securing Solutions

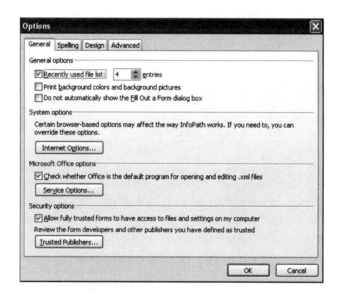

INTRODUCTION

It's unfortunate, but most application solutions are developed without security in mind. This introduces security flaws early in the development cycle that are not always caught. There are many reasons for this. For example, it may be the result of developers trying to learn the specific application domain and being unaware of how to adequately protect the systems and data. What is often interesting is that during a standard development cycle, at least one, if not more, application prototypes are done. The purpose of these is to provide possible answers about a possible approach to solving the business issues, but often the last thing developers worry about is application security.

As applications are completed and deployed, it becomes apparent that security is more than just adding a username and password screen. Security issues can actually be magnified through the deployment of a distributed system that follows SOA design patterns. The multitude of services and possible interactions can increase the difficulty of developing a secure solution. In a service-oriented environment, each of the individual service components is capable of requiring security. This can easily increase the complexity of a given application as the services and components are scaled across multiple application domains and enterprise infrastructures.

Security can be implemented in a variety of ways within the types of applications that we have covered. InfoPath and the .NET Framework are two of the most important aspects, and each provides a piece of a cohesive strategy that if properly designed can effectively secure and protect your service-based infrastructure. This chapter focuses on ways security should be implemented within these types of applications and many of the specific concerns that you should address when developing distributed applications.

WHAT DOES SECURITY MEAN?

Security is designing and implementing ways to protect important corporate assets. The definition of *assets* can cover a wide range of physical items like corporate data or Web pages, but also may include others things such as a company's reputation. Defining application security is a process that includes infrastructure deployment issues, business requirements, and even legal requirements. It is important to remember that it is an ever evolving and never ending part of the development process.

The definition of a secure infrastructure contains a variety of individual elements that work together to create a secure infrastructure. Each of these smaller interdependent pieces composes the core of what security is about. Following is a list of these concepts that you should keep in mind when designing secure applications:

Authentication: Authentication addresses the question of who you are. This is the process that any application or operating system uses to determine the unique identity of a security principal. Authorization includes challenge response, Kerberos, or even custom-designed security schemes that can be implemented to answer this question.

Authorization: Authorization addresses the question of what an authenticated principal is able to do. This process determines the specific resources and operations an authenticated client is permitted, within the scope of the application or operating system. Authorized resources include Web Services, databases, and InfoPath. Within these resources, authorization is extended to include smaller elements like the individual properties and methods.

Accountability: Accountability addresses the question of what you did when accessing a resource. This process provides a tracking mechanism or event log of what actions occurred. By definition, this is the result of the completion of a security-restricted action.

Data Integrity: Data integrity addresses the question of whether data is protected from unauthorized modification. This becomes an extremely important concern as data passes across enterprise borders or unfamiliar networks. Many times, this is a common scenario for the use of digital signatures and even cryptography to ensure that the data isn't viewable or modifiable.

System Availability: System availability addresses the question of whether systems are highly available for legitimate authenticated users. A complete discussion about this topic is beyond the scope of this book and extends to protecting specific infrastructure assets from Denial of Service Attacks (DOS) and other common attacks that attempt to spoof or overwhelm a system.

THE INFOPATH SECURITY MODEL

Every application is responsible for providing some level of security control. The approach used within InfoPath is to protect both the running application and the local machine from any security breaches that can harm or cause misuse of application data. InfoPath provides two fundamental levels of security. First, as a client-based application, it's responsible for adhering to locally defined security policies and privileges. Under no circumstances should it provide any type of attack surface for the local machine. Second, as a data-focused application, InfoPath provides additional levels of security to ensure that any data it may be responsible for is protected. All forms within InfoPath have a security level associated with them. By default InfoPath will attempt to open forms at their associated security level. If the assigned security level within the form is higher than what can be granted the form will not open.

When developing an InfoPath form, the security concerns are similar to those of Web applications within Internet Explorer. Fundamentally, the security level of a form depends entirely on where the form template (.xsn) is located and not on where the user stores or opens the associated XML data file. Users can determine the location of the form template they are working with by looking at the status bar in InfoPath, as shown in Figure 9.1. The most common threats that a malicious InfoPath form may pose can include the following.

Form template's location: C:\Documents and Settings\Thom Robbins\Local Settings\Application Data\Microsoft\InfoPath\a613db16cb4

FIGURE 9.1 Determining the security level for an InfoPath form.

- Malicious use of ActiveX controls
- Malicious use of properties and methods of the InfoPath object model
- Potential disclosure of sensitive information from the local computer or remote data sources.

InfoPath forms can be deployed with varying levels of security. The level of security is dictated by the level of access to external resource that a form needs. As a default security precaution, all forms are initially restricted from accessing local system resources and components not marked safe for scripting. When an InfoPath form is created in the designer the set of files created includes the manifest.xsf file. This file contains a root element that contains the global metadata for the current InfoPath solution. This element is called the xDocumentClass element and is shown in Listing 9.1

LISTING 9.1 The XDocumentClass Stored in the Manifest.xsf File

```
<xsf:xDocumentClass solutionVersion="1.0.0.15"
productVersion="11.0.6357" solutionFormatVersion="1.100.0.0"
publishUrl="C:\Books\Programming Microsoft InfoPath a Developers
Guide\Second Edition - master\Chapter 9\Code\Resource
Request\ResourceRequest.xsn" name="urn:schemas-microsoft-
com:office:infopath:ResourceRequest:-myXSD-2003-10-05T18-48-30"
trustSetting="automatic"
xmlns:xsf="http://schemas.microsoft.com/office/infopath/2003/solutionDe
finition" xmlns:msxsl="urn:schemas-microsoft-com:xslt"
xmlns:xd="http://schemas.microsoft.com/office/infopath/2003"
xmlns:xsi="http://www.w3.org/2001/XMLSchema-instance"
xmlns:my="http://schemas.microsoft.com/office/infopath/2003/myXSD/2003-
10-05T18:48:30" xmlns:xhtml="http://www.w3.org/1999/xhtml"
xmlns:xdUtil="http://schemas.microsoft.com/office/infopath/2003/xslt/Ut
il"
xmlns:xdXDocument="http://schemas.microsoft.com/office/infopath/2003/xs
lt/xDocument"
xmlns:xdMath="http://schemas.microsoft.com/office/infopath/2003/xslt/Ma
th"
xmlns:xdDate="http://schemas.microsoft.com/office/infopath/2003/xslt/Da
te">
```

Part of this global data is information about the form deployment. This can be either a URL or a URN location for the form template. Both of these provide a unique identifier for the InfoPath form; however, they will affect how a form is used within the security model.

The URL-based template location is the default when publishing a form from InfoPath to a Web server, WSS, or a file share. Within the `xDocumentClass`, this is specified in the `publishUrl` attribute. These forms are considered sandboxed. This means that they have highly restricted access to system resources. In comparison with a Web page, the URL-based form template has the same level of permission as a Web page opened from the same location.

The URN-based form template is used for forms that require higher-level access to system and external resources. Typically, this will include ActiveX control or other components. By default, a URN based form will receive the same permission as application running locally. Within the `xDocumentClass` of the InfoPath template, they specify a Uniform Resource Indicator (URI) in the name attribute. This type of InfoPath form can request full trust from the system if the require-FullTrust attribute of the xDocumentClass is set to "yes."

EXAMINING SECURITY LEVELS

At runtime, the location of the template plays a major role in determining the security level that is applied to the form. By default, this is used to assign the initial security level of either restricted, domain, or full trust. Within InfoPath, the security settings are available within the Tools—Form Options—Security Tab, as shown in Figure 9.2.

Restricted

The restricted level does not permit any communication outside of the form template. It is an ideal solution for self-contained forms that can be opened anywhere. This is the most restrictive security level and is intended to prevent the transmission of harmful forms or scripts to a computer.

When running in this security mode, the following features are automatically disabled:

- Custom task pane
- Data connection (except for the email submit)
- ActiveX controls
- Managed code
- Roles
- Workflow

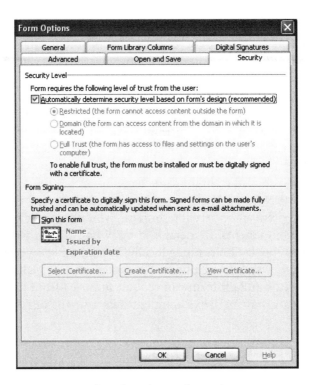

FIGURE 9.2 The InfoPath security settings

Domain

The main reason to make a distinction between Restricted and Domain security was to allow Form templates without script or data connections to be opened anywhere. The domain security level restricts a form to a particular Internet zone. The form is allowed to communicate with other data inside its own domain, but it cannot retrieve data from other domains. This specifically is designed to prevent cross-domain scripting attacks. In these types of security attacks, malicious code is downloaded from an untrusted server that may access sensitive data.

Domain form templates still require that they be opened from their published location. However, by using the Send Form as Attachment option in the File menu, a Domain form template can be mailed out as an attachment. This attachment, when received and opened, functions as a link to the actual published location. The form template at the published location is what actually is opened in the InfoPath Editor, rather than the one that was clicked on. At that point, the published form template is copied locally and will appear as a selection in the Fill Out a Form dialog every time InfoPath is launched.

Typically, form templates stored on a Web server or running in a WSS site on the local network run in the Intranet zone. Unlike with IE, in which the security for HTML generated by XML/XSLT is based on the URL of the XML, InfoPath security is based on the URL of the form template rather than on the individual XML files. You can use an InfoPath form template from any URL with XML files from the same or different domains.

Forms based on an URL are considered sandboxed. When the form is opened, it is placed in the local system cache and denied access to local system resources. For example, like a Web page, it cannot write to the local hard drive. This type of form inherits its default permissions from Internet Explorer (IE) security settings that are applied to the original location of the form template. Security zones within IE are used to determine specific access rights. These zones are defined by the URL and can control cross-domain permissions based on the default location where the form template is hosted. When you're running the InfoPath IDE, these types of forms contain an URL template location that is displayed on the bottom left of the InfoPath IDE.

Full Trust

Full trust is the highest security level that can be granted an InfoPath form. Because of security concerns, full trust is only applied to an InfoPath form deployed to a local machine. In addition, full trust is only granted used when working with a digitally signed form that matches a trusted publisher on your computer or by installing the form and setting the requireFullTrust attribute to "yes." Otherwise the maximum default trust level is Domain. Once full trust is given to an InfoPath form, its code can access object model calls such as file save, and many of the more restrictive security prompts won't appear. Forms with full trust are based on a URN and are able to do the following.

- Access external objects
- Access Microsoft Active X controls not marked safe for scripting
- Execute Custom business logic contained in the Component Object Model (COM) component
- Provide additional object model access

The InfoPath object model associates every property and method with a security level. This level determines whether the property or method is directly callable from a form template. All form templates are defined into three possible security levels. The higher the trust factor of a solution, the more resources it can access. These levels are defined in Table 9.1.

TABLE 9.1 Form Template Security Levels

Security Level	Description
1	Callable by any form template.
2	Called only from templates running in the same domain that is granted cross-domain permissions.
3	Cannot be called by InfoPath 2003 form templates unless they are fully trusted. This level is the highest security restriction that can be placed on a property or object.

Any member of the InfoPath object model set to a security level 3 means that it can be used only from a fully trusted from. For example, the HTML Window property is used to return a reference to an HTML Window object running in a custom task pane. This property is an inherited property of the TaskPane objects that is available only when you're using a custom task pane. The following code example is available only within a fully trusted form:

```
var objHTMLWindow;
objHTMLWindow = XDocument.View.Window.TaskPanes(0).HTMLWindow;
objHTMLWindow.parentWindow.TaskPaneSwitchView();
```

If you use any property or object model member with a security level of 3 in any form that is not fully trusted, this results in a "permission denied" error.

NOTE

Creating a Fully Trusted Form

To enable level 3 access to trusted forms on your computer, you must first define the security options for fully trusted locally installed forms. This systemwide option is available from the Tools Options menu, as shown in Figure 9.3.

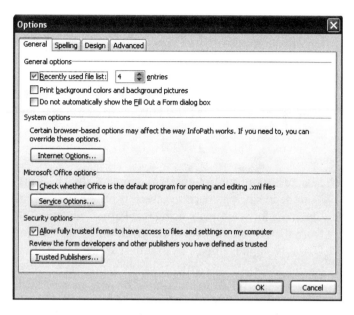

FIGURE 9.3 Systemwide InfoPath option to enable trusted forms.

This option defines a set of trusted publishers. Once enabled, this option will automatically grant full trust to any form that is installed and signed by a trusted authority. Once enabled, you create and then register the specific form on the local machine in two ways. Although slightly different, they generally following the following steps:

1. Modify the form so that it is URN-based rather than URL-based.
2. Add the `requireFullTrust` attribute to the .xsf file and set its value to "yes."
3. Register the fully trusted solution on the target computer using the `RegisterSolution` method of the InfoPath `ExternalApplication` object.

It is possible and often desirable to create a URN-based form that is fully trusted. The difference between a URN-based form that is not fully trusted and a fully trusted form is that the requireFullTrust attribute is set to "no" in a not fully trusted form. These InfoPath solutions can access system and cross-domain resources, but the users are prompted to allow it.

Manually Creating a Trusted Form

Depending on the needs of your application, you may find it easier to manually register the form as a trusted solution than to manually change the attributes. Although not always the preferred way, manually creating a trusted form provides developers with the most control and flexibility in how they register their solutions.

Let's, for example, take the Sales Follow Up example from Chapter 6 and manually register this form as a trusted form (see \Code\Chapter 6\Sales Follow Up\ ebr.xsn on the companion CD-ROM). To do so, follow these steps:

1. Make a backup copy of the form template file. This simple precaution should be done in case you need to revert to a previous version for any reason.
2. Open the form template using InfoPath. Then, using the Extract Form Files from the File menu, extract the contents of the solution into a directory.
3. Using Notepad, open the manifest.xsf and add the following attributes to the XDocument element: name="urn:myForm:myCompany" requireFull-Trust="yes". When you're done, the new element will look like Listing 9.2 (the modified section is in bold).

LISTING 9.2   Modified manifest.xsd for a Fully Trusted Form

```
<xsf:xDocumentClass solutionVersion="1.0.0.64"
productVersion="11.0.5329" solutionFormatVersion="1.0.0.0"
publishUrl="c:\ebr\ebr.xsn" name="urn:sales:followup"
requireFullTrust="yes"
xmlns:xsf="http://schemas.microsoft.com/office/infopath/2003/solutionDe
finition" xmlns:msxsl="urn:schemas-microsoft-com:xslt"
xmlns:xd="http://schemas.microsoft.com/office/infopath/2003"
xmlns:xsi="http://www.w3.org/2001/XMLSchema-instance"
xmlns:my="http://schemas.microsoft.com/office/infopath/2003/myXSD/2003-
08-24T03:18:24"
xmlns:q="http://schemas.microsoft.com/office/infopath/2003/ado/queryFie
lds"
xmlns:d="http://schemas.microsoft.com/office/infopath/2003/ado/dataFiel
ds"
xmlns:dfs="http://schemas.microsoft.com/office/infopath/2003/dataFormSo
lution" xmlns:xhtml="http://www.w3.org/1999/xhtml">
```

The URN value can be any type of string value as long as this value is unique and contains at least two values after the "urn:" prefix. These values must be separated by a colon, and the entire string can be no longer than 255 characters.

4. Open the template.xml file and remove the `href` attribute from the `mso-infoPathSolution` processing instruction; replace it with the same URN-based attribute used earlier. When you're done, the new attribute will look like the following (with the changed sections in bold):

```
<?mso-infoPathSolution name="urn:sales:followup"
solutionVersion="1.0.0.64" productVersion="11.0.5329"
PIVersion="1.0.0.0" ?>
```

The URN attribute is a way of uniquely identifying the form and must be same the same in both the template.xml and manifest.xsf. files. Any difference may cause your form to not load or run.

5. Repackage the files into the .xsn using a .cab file format using a tool such as makecab.exe or one of the other freeware utilities available on the Internet.

Even though the InfoPath design environment does support the repackaging of form files into an .xsn, do not use this method when creating fully trusted forms. During the repackaging process, InfoPath automatically reverts the form files back to their original URL-based extensions. Before you can successfully create a fully trusted form, you must package these files with an external program such as make-cab.exe to prevent overwriting your changes.

6. Create a custom installation script using the `RegisterSolution` method of the InfoPath `ExternalApplication` object to install the fully trusted form. A sample function to register the Sales Call Follow up is shown here:

```
objInfoForm = new ActiveXObject("InfoPath.ExternalApplication");
objInfoForm.RegisterSolution("C:\\MyForms\\ebr.xsn");
objInfoForm.Quit();
objInfoForm = null;
```

If you need to uninstall the application, you can use the `UnregisterSolution` method of the `ExternalApplication` object, as shown here:

```
objInfoForm = new ActiveXObject("InfoPath.ExternalApplication");
objInfoForm.UnregisterSolution("C:\\MyForms\\ebr.xsn");
objInfoForm.Quit();
objInfoForm = null;
```

Using the SDK RegForm Utility

Although you can manually create a fully trusted form, often because of the needs of the application, this conversion may be a better solution. One of the tools available within the InfoPath SDK is a command-line utility called "regform.exe." This utility simplifies the creation of a fully trusted form by automatically completing the following tasks:

- Makes a backup copy of the form template
- Makes the necessary changes to the .xsf file and the XML template files to make the form fully trusted
- Updates the version number of the form template
- Repackages the files into an .xsn CAB file format
- Creates a custom installation program

Using the regform.exe tool from the command prompt supports a variety of parameters, as shown in Table 9.2.

TABLE 9.2 regform.exe Command-Line Parameters

Usage:<tb>Regform [/V urn] [/FT formtemplatename] [/C companyname] [/V [0-9999. 0-9999. 0-9999. 0-9999]] [/T Yes|No] [/O outputfile][/MSI] [/?|/h|/help] formtemplatefile

Parameter	Description
/U	The URN to use for the form template. Must be in the form of urn: <string>:<string>. If the URN is not specified, it is built using the form template and company name. If either of these is not specified, then a GUID is used.
/FT	The form template name.
/C	The company name.
/V	The version number [0-9, 9999. 0-9, 9999. 0-9, 9999. 0-9, 9999] of the form template. If this is not specified, the version number of the form template is used. If no version number is present in the form template file, the default number of 1.0.0.1 is used.

$\rightarrow$

Parameter	Description
/T	Specifies that the form template is fully trusted. This sets the requireFullTrust attribute in the form definition file to "yes."
/O	The path and name of the output file that is to be created. If the path and name are not specified, the name of the form template file is used.
/MSI	Specifies that the output installation file is a Microsoft System Installer (.msi) file. The default is a Microsoft JScript file.
/?|/h|/help	Displays the information about using the Regform tool.
formtemplatefile	The full path to the InfoPath form template to process.

If we wanted to create a fully trusted form using this utility, we could enter the following from the command line:

```
RegForm /U urn:FormName:CompanyName /T Yes
C:\FormDirectory\FormName.xsn
```

In this example, the /T option indicates that the form should be marked as a fully trusted form. The last parameter is the path and name of the form template that should be converted. When the regform.exe utility is completed, this utility creates a .bak file and a .js file in the same folder that contains the name of the form template that was converted. The .bak file is a backup copy of the original untrusted form, and the .js file contains the installation script that is run on machines where the form is going to be installed.

The regform.exe utility (see \Code\Chapter 6\Sales Follow Up\regform.exe) also supports creating an .msi file if you have Visual Studio.NET installed on the local machine. This is done through the /MSI switch. If we wanted to create a fully trusted form using a Resource Request form, we could enter the following from the command line:

```
RegForm /U urn:resourcerequest:verylargecompanyinc /T Yes /MSI
C:\resourcerequest.xsn
```

The /MSI switch uses Visual Studio.NET to create the installation file, as you can see in the processing message in Figure 9.4.

```
D:\INFOHOLD>regform /U urn:resourcerequest:verylargeconanyinc /T Yes /MSI resour
cerequest.xsn

Microsoft Office InfoPath RegForm tool. Version 1.0.0.2
Copyright (C) Microsoft Corporation 2003. All rights reserved.

Building MSI using devenv...
Result MSI in D:\INFOHOLD\resourcerequest.msi file.

Completed.
```

FIGURE 9.4   Building the trusted form using Visual Studio.NET.

Once the regform.exe utility is completed, the directory contains an .msi file in the same folder as the form template being converted, as shown in Figure 9.5.

FIGURE 9.5   A completed trusted form that uses the /MSI solution.

If you use the /MSI switch and do not have Visual Studio.NET installed, the regform utility will create the default .js file. The regform.exe tool also creates a Visual Studio.NET setup project in the %temp%\regform directory. This is a standard setup project, as shown in Figure 9.6, that can be modified and then recompiled based on your solutions needs.

InfoPath is only one piece of the actual security required to adequately secure an application and meet the definition of a secure solution. It is important to understand the other part of the application and security that is required within the service components.

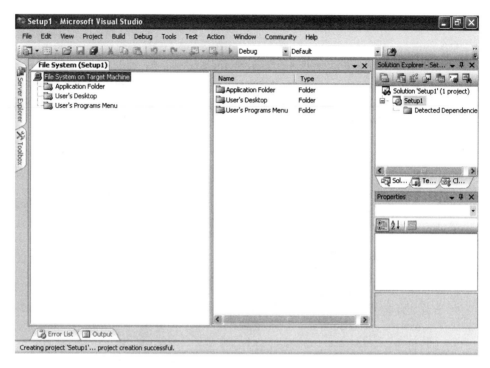

FIGURE 9.6 Viewing the installation program in Visual Studio.NET.

DEFINING SECURITY WITH THE .NET FRAMEWORK

As we have covered in many areas throughout this book, InfoPath is only one part of the solution within an SOA design pattern. The .NET Framework provides a variety of techniques and security namespaces that you can use to build and deploy secure Web- and client-based applications. Applications or assemblies written to use the .NET Framework are considered managed applications. *Assemblies* are the building blocks of .NET Framework applications. They form the fundamental unit of deployment, version control, reuse, activation, scoping, and security permissions. An assembly is actually a collection of types and resources that are built to work together. These form a logical unit of functionality. Assemblies provide the CLR with the information needed to determine the specific type implementation needed during runtime. Within the runtime environment of .NET, a type doesn't exist outside of the context of an assembly.

Defining Assemblies

You can create a single file or multifile assembly using Visual Studio.NET. The simplest type of assembly is a single file that has a simple name and is loaded into a single application. This assembly can't be referenced by other assemblies outside of the application directory and doesn't undergo any type of version checking. If this type of assembly needs to be removed, then simply delete the directory. Multifile assemblies from several code modules and resource file can be shared by multiple applications. A shared assembly must have a strong name and can be deployed in the Global Assembly Cache (GAC).

A string name consists of the assembly's identity, public key, and a digital signature. The string name is the generated from the assembly file using a private key algorithm. The assembly file actually contains the assembly manifest that names and hashes all of the files defined in the assembly.

The GAC is a machinewide code cache that is installed on any machine that has the CLR. This assembly cache stores assemblies that are designated to be shared by several applications on the computer. As a general rule, you should always try to keep assembly dependencies private, and locate assemblies in the application directory unless sharing the assembly is required.

It is not necessary to install assemblies in the GAC to make them accessible to either COM interoperability or unmanaged code.

When developing a multifile assembly and grouping code modules into assemblies, you should always keep the following design considerations in mind:

Versioning: Group modules that have the same version information.

Deployment: Group code modules and resources that support the deployment model.

Reuse: Group modules if they can be logically used together for the same purpose. For example, an assembly that consists of a specific business function should be grouped into an assembly, and that assembly should be signed with a strong name.

Security: Group modules that contain types that require the same security permissions.

Scoping: Group modules that contain the types with the same level of visibility within the same assembly.

Physically, an assembly can be a dll or an exe. When built using managed code, the result is a Microsoft Intermediate Language (MIL) instruction that is contained in a standard Windows Portable Executable (PE) file. When an assembly is loaded by a method call, the MSIL is compiled by a Just-In-Time (JIT) compiler into native machine instructions. The compiled method is executed, whereas others that are never called are not JIT compiled. The Framework's use of the intermediate language coupled with the runtime environment provided by the CLR offers assemblies the following advantages:

File Format and Metadata Validation: The CLR verifies that the PE file format is valid and that memory addresses do not point outside the PE file. This helps provide assembly isolation. The CLR also validates the integrity of the metadata that is contained in the assembly.

Code Verification: The MIL code is verified for type safety at JIT compile time. This is a major advantage from a security perspective because this verification process can prevent bad pointer manipulation, validate type conversions, and check array bounds. This virtually eliminates buffer overflow vulnerabilities in managed code, although you still need to carefully inspect any code that calls unmanaged Application Programming Interfaces (APIs) for the possibility of a buffer overflow.

Integrity Checking: The integrity of strong-named assemblies is verified using a digital signature to ensure that the assembly has not been altered in any way since it was built and signed. This means that attackers can't alter your code by manipulating the MIL instructions.

Code Access Security: The virtual execution environment provided by the CLR performs additional security checks at runtime. These allow various runtime security decisions based on the identity of the calling code.

Assemblies in Web Services

A Web Service is defined by an .asmx file that serves as the endpoint of calls. Calls made to the .asmx file are intercepted and processed by the ASP.NET runtime. The actual implementation of a Web Service is encapsulated within a class. Class definition can either appear inline within the .asmx file or can be contained in a separate

DLL. The Web Service page needs to contain the information that the runtime can use to locate the class.

Each .asmx page contains a directive at the top of the page that specifies where and in what form the implementation of the Web Service can be found. The directive is used by the ASP.NET runtime to bind the Web Service to a class that contains the actual implementation. Here is an example from the Interview Feedback Web Service that we used in Chapter 4 (this example is available on the companion CD-ROM in \Code\Chapter 9\ResourceRequest\ResourceRequest.exe):

```
<%@ WebService Language="vb" Codebehind="Feedback.asmx.vb"
Class="InterviewFeedback.Feedback" %>
```

The `Class` attribute contains the fully qualified name of the class that implements the Web Service. If the code resides within the .asmx file, you must set the `Language` attribute to specify what the code was developed in.

The first time that a Web Service is accessed, the ASP.NET runtime will use the languages attribute to compile the code. Even if the code implementing the Web Service is contained within the .asmx file, it will always be executed as compiled machine code.

By default, ASP.NET is configured to dynamically compile code using the base languages of the CLR. You can configure additional languages within the Web.config file or the machine.config file. The compiler section of the machine.config file found in the C:\WINDOWS\Microsoft.NET\Framework\v2.0.50215\CONFIG directory, shown in Figure 9.7, shows these base languages.

```
- <compilation debug="false" explicit="true" defaultLanguage="vb">
  - <compilers>
    <compiler language="c#;cs;csharp" extension=".cs"
      type="Microsoft.CSharp.CSharpCodeProvider, System, Version=1.0.5000.0,
      Culture=neutral, PublicKeyToken=b77a5c561934e089" warningLevel="1" />
    <compiler language="vb;vbs;visualbasic;vbscript" extension=".vb"
      type="Microsoft.VisualBasic.VBCodeProvider, System, Version=1.0.5000.0,
      Culture=neutral, PublicKeyToken=b77a5c561934e089" />
    <compiler language="js;jscript;javascript" extension=".js"
      type="Microsoft.JScript.JScriptCodeProvider, Microsoft.JScript,
      Version=7.0.5000.0, Culture=neutral, PublicKeyToken=b03f5f7f11d50a3a" />
    <compiler language="VJ#;VJS;VJSharp" extension=".jsl"
      type="Microsoft.VJSharp.VJSharpCodeProvider, VJSharpCodeProvider,
      Version=7.0.5000.0, Culture=neutral, PublicKeyToken=b03f5f7f11d50a3a" />
  </compilers>
```

FIGURE 9.7 Configuration file that determines .NET-available languages.

The compilation section includes a list of assemblies that are globally referenced by code within the .asmx file. Any Web Service that needs to reference entities from an assembly other than those listed earlier would add a new machine reference to the machine.config, an application reference in a web.config file, or a form-level variable reference using the following statement:

```
Imports System.Configuration
```

The last add element specifies a wildcard (*) character for the assembly name. This forces the ASP.NET runtime to search for any assembly that is not directly listed. It is also possible that the class implementing the Web Service can reside in a compiled assembly. If this is the case, then by design the assembly is placed in the Web application's bin directory because this directory is always included in the runtime search path.

User versus Code Security

The .NET Framework contains two types of security models. The first is code-based security—or more commonly called Code Access Security (CAS)—which is used to determine if the actual code has both a proper set of permissions and verifiable origins to run in the requested application domain. The second is a set of role-based permissions focused on users making the request and then determining if they have proper permissions to access the requested resources.

Code-Based Security

Code-based security involves authorizing the application's access to the required system-level resources. These can include file systems, registry services, and even database access. Within CAS, it doesn't matter what user is making the request or even which account the code is running under; rather, it does matter which permissions have been assigned to the code.

Security focused on the user is called role-based security, and security focused on the actual code called is called CAS.

NOTE

Role-Based Security

Role-based security allows a Web application to make security decisions based on the identity or role membership of the user interacting with the application. If an application uses Windows authentication, then a role directly translates to a Windows group. Other forms of authentication usually store the role details in the SQL Server or even Active Directory, as shown in Figure 9.8. The identity of the authenticated user and his associated role membership is made available to Web applications through principal objects, which are attached to the user Web requests.

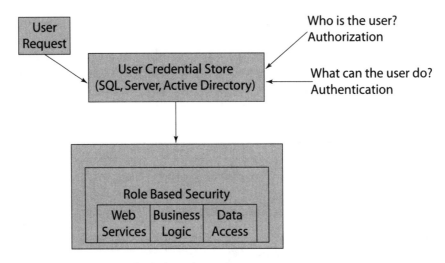

FIGURE 9.8   Basics of role-based security.

Role-based security is implemented using Principal and Identity objects. The identity and role membership of an authenticated call is exposed through a Principal object that contains a reference to an Identity object. You can retrieve the object by using the HTTPConnect.Current.User property. If the called application is not required to authenticate the Principal object, as in the case of an intranet-based application, NT-based authentication is used to represent the anonymous Internet user.

The Identity object contains information about the user or entity being validated. The IIdentity interface defines a set of properties for accessing the user name and authentication type. Within that interface, the HTTPContextUser property provides programmatic access to the properties and methods of the IPrincipal interface. By default, an ASP.NET page contains a default reference to the System.Web namespace that contains the HTTPContext class, which can be used to reference the current members of the HTTPContext within a Web page. This enables the use of the User.Identity.Name to retrieve the named user of the current request. For example, the following Web Service returns the current user identity:

```
<WebMethod()> Public Function ReturnSecurityInfo() As String
 Return User.Identity.Name
End Function
```

This then returns the name of the user on whose behalf the request is running, as shown in Figure 9.9.

```
<?xml version="1.0" encoding="utf-8" ?>
<string xmlns="http://tempuri.org/SecurityInfo/Service1">THOMSDEV\Thom Robbins</string>
```

FIGURE 9.9   The XML returned showing the current user identity.

If you wanted to use the member of the IPrincipal from an ASP.NET code behind module, you must include the reference to the System.Web namespace in the module as well as provide a fully qualified reference to the currently active request/ response context and the class in the System.Web you want to use.

There are many types of `Principal` objects; the type used depends on the authentication mechanism used by the application. However, all `Principal` objects implement the System.Security.Principal.IPrincipal interfaces and maintain a list of roles of which the user is a member.

`Principal` objects also contain an `Identity` object that includes the user's name. These are combined with parameters regarding whether the user has been authenticated and the available authentication types. This enables the Web request to distinguish between authenticated and anonymous users. There are different types of `Identity` objects (depending on the authentication type), and each implements the common System.Security.Principal.IIdentity interface. Table 9.3 shows the possible types of authentication objects that an ASP.NET Web application can use, depending on the type of authentication defined within the web.config.

The `PrincipalPermission` object defines the identity and role that the current principal must have to execute the code. These objects can be used within code either declaratively or imperatively.

TABLE 9.3 Authentication Objects an ASP.NET Application Can Use

Authentication Type	Principal and Identity Type	Additional Comments
Windows	WindowsPrincipal+ WindowIdentity	Verified credentials use the Security Account Manager (SAM) or Active Directory. Windows groups are used for roles.
Forms	GenericPrincipal+ FormsIdentity	You must add code to verify credentials and retrieve role membership from a security store.
Passport	GenericPrincipal+ PassportIdentity	Relies on the Microsoft Passport SDK.

Declarative Security

The .NET Framework enables developers to determine which users should be allowed to access a specific class or method by adding a `PrincipalPermission Attribute` to the class or method definition. This is a class-level attribute that applies to all class members unless it is overridden by the specific member-level attribute. The `PrincipalPermissionAttribute` type is defined in the System. Security.Permissions namespace.

The PrincipalPermissionAttribute can also come in handy when you are trying to restrict access to properties and delegates.

Listing 9.3 shows how to restrict access to a function in the Catalog example to a member of the Sales group. This example assumes that Windows authentication is enabled. For other types of authentication, the form of the role name becomes application specific and will depend on stored credentials.

LISTING 9.3 Web Service with Restricted Permissions

```
<PrincipalPermissionAttribute(SecurityAction.Demand, _
  Role=@"DOMAINNAME\Sales")>
<WebMethod()> Public Function InfoPathGetNewCatalog() As
System.Xml.XmlDataDocument
  Dim ds As DataSet
```

```
  ds = GetNewCatalog()
  ds.Namespace = "Http://localhost/Catalog"
  Dim Info As System.Xml.XmlDataDocument = New
System.Xml.XmlDataDocument(ds)
  Return Info

End Function
```

Listing 9.4 shows how to restrict access to the same method class to a member of the local Sales group who is identified by the "BUILTIN\Sales" identifier.

LISTING 9.4   Web Service Restricted Only to the BUILTIN\Sales Group

```
<PrincipalPermissionAttribute(SecurityAction.Demand,
Role=@"BUILTIN\Sales")>
<WebMethod()> Public Function InfoPathGetNewCatalog() As
System.Xml.XmlDataDocument
  Dim ds As DataSet

ds = GetNewCatalog()
  ds.Namespace = "Http://localhost/Catalog"
  Dim Info As System.Xml.XmlDataDocument = New
System.Xml.XmlDataDocument(ds)
  Return Info

End Function
```

Imperative Security

Imperative security checks allow developers to protect specific blocks of code by demanding the appropriate permissions. You use the `Permission` object to add imperative security checks within a code block. The `Permission` object is an instance of a specialized class that represents a particular type of permission. For example, the `FileIOPermission` class defines the right to read, append, or write files or directories. The following code creates the necessary `Permission` object:

```
Dim MyPermission as New _
  Security.Permissions.FileIOPermission(PermissionState.Unrestricted)
```

You create imperative security checks by creating an instance of the appropriate security object, and then calling the object's `Demand` function. This has the net effect of denying access to all callers except those that can supply the proper credentials. The following example shows how you can implement this within a code block:

```
Try
  MyPermission.Demand()
  ' implement the actions
Catch e as Exception
  ' Insert code to handle the exception.
End Try
```

When a user fails the Demand permissions in a code block, a SecurityException is thrown. It is always important to predetermine how to handle these types of exceptions.

Comparing Declarative and Imperative Security

When you're developing an application using role-based security, you can choose between using attributes declaratively or imperatively within code. Overall, declarative security offers the most benefits and is the easiest to use and maintain. To help you decide which one to use, consider the advantages of declarative versus imperative security.

The main advantages of declarative security are that:

- Declarative security allows the administrator to see the exact security permissions that a particular class or method needs
- Declarative security offers increased performance. Declarative demands are evaluated only once at load time. Imperative demands inside methods are evaluated each time the method that contains the demand is called
- Declarative security attributes ensure that the permission demand is executed before any other code in the method has a chance to run
- Declarative security checks occur at the class level

The main advantages of imperative security are:

- Imperative security allows dynamic security requests during runtime
- Imperative security allows a more granular authorization scheme within the conditional logic placed in code

CAS

CAS is the security system of the .NET Framework that controls access to resources by controlling the execution of code. This security feature is actually a separate layer on top of the standard operating system security. CAS is actually a resource-constraint model that allows administrators to determine if and how particular code can access specified resources and performs other privileged operations. For example, an administrator might decide that code downloaded from the Internet is by default denied access to any local resources. However, Web application code developed by one of their internal developers needs a higher degree of trust and access to the local file system, event log, and Microsoft SQL Server databases.

Traditional principal-based security like the operating system authorizes access to resources based on only user identity. For example, any program launched by a local administrator has complete control of the local machine. The problem is that if the administrator's identity is spoofed and any code is executed, it also has no restrictions. This is where CAS is important because it provides additional restrictions and security based on the code itself, rather than on user identity.

CAS works by assigning all code to a zone defined by the CLR. These zones are as follows:

My Computer: Application code is hosted directly on the user's computer.

Local Intranet: Application code runs from a file share on the user's intranet.

Internet: Application code runs from the Internet.

Trusted Sites: Applications run from a site defined as "Trusted" through IE.

Untrusted Sites: Applications run from sites defined as "Restricted" through IE.

The default assignment of the first three zones—My Computer, Local Intranet, and Internet—is based on where the actual code is located. You can override these assignments by assigning specific sites to the Trusted Sites or Untrusted Sites group in IE. This is similar to the form template-based restrictions used by InfoPath and available through the Tools Options, as shown in Figure 9.10.

On this dialog box, select the Internet Options button to access the zones setting, as shown in Figure 9.11.

With the.NET Framework version 1.1, administrators can configure specific policy settings for ASP.NET Web applications services. These may consist of multiple assemblies that are granted code access security permissions; these allow the application to access specific resource types and to perform specific privileged operations.

NOTE

Web applications and Web Services built using the .NET Framework version 1.0 always run with unrestricted code access permissions.

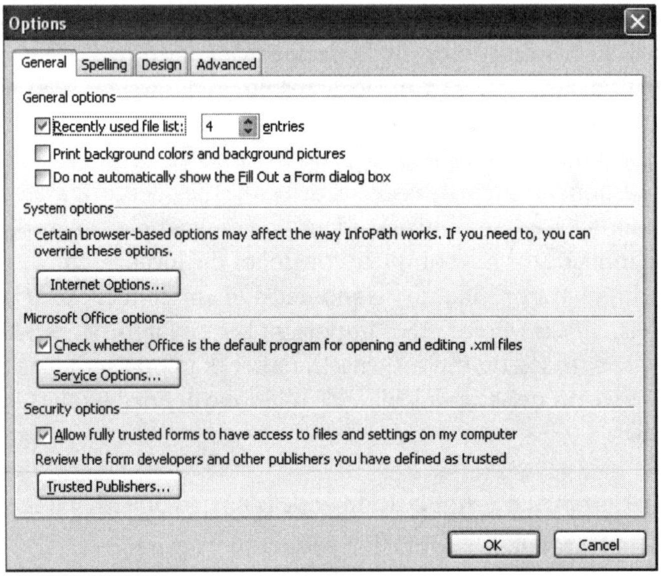

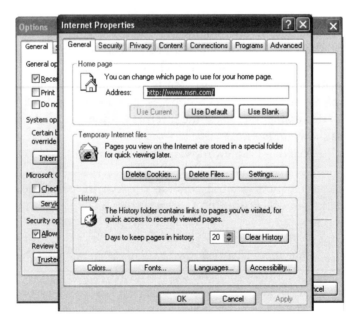

FIGURE 9.10 Selecting the Internet Options within InfoPath.

FIGURE 9.11 Accessing IE zones settings.

CAS with Web applications provides application isolation in hosted environments where multiple Web applications run on the same Web server. System administrators that run multiple applications on the same server can use CAS to do the following:

Isolate applications from each other: For example, you can use CAS to ensure that one Web application cannot write to another Web application's directories.

Isolate applications from specific system resources: For example, CAS can restrict access to the file system, registry, event logs, and network resources.

SUMMARY

Security is an extremely broad and often complex topic. This chapter has addressed two of the main components that are part of developing an SOA. You can look at application security in many different ways. Even more importantly, security may change based on the business requirements. It is important that you follow a common guideline when developing and implementing security within your enterprise. Security is an evolving process that should be continually tested and evaluated. Security is often a key consideration when you are deploying applications. In the final chapter, we will cover how you can deploy the various applications that have been built throughout this book.

10 Deployment Strategies

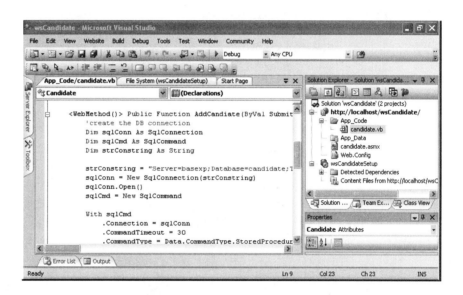

INTRODUCTION

Application deployment is a complex process that is often overlooked during the initial development cycle. For applications designed to use the service-oriented approach, this creates a significant obstacle. SOA applications are defined in tiers. A logical view of an SOA application defines a set of three separate but interdependent tiers: presentation, business logic, and data. Each component or service added enables a new set of user features, security restrictions, and complexity to the application design and eventually the deployment plans. In practice, the deployed physical application model is spread over a variety of machines and even different organizations. Each service tier used to make an application scale can make it even more complex to eventually deploy.

The reliance of an SOA application on XML and HTTP enables a loosely coupled model that reduces the binding dependencies that were part of the Windows Distributed Internet Applications Architecture (DNA). DNA-based architecture was heavily dependent on a tightly coupled model of RPC calls and COM-based components. As a loosely coupled architecture, SOA provides the additional benefit of reducing the overall complexity that was part of previous deployment models.

You can consider a variety of options when you start to deploy applications that leverage InfoPath, Web Services, and the distributed architecture discussed in the previous chapters. This chapter focuses on the fundamental application elements of InfoPath and Web Services and how they can be deployed in the enterprise. We will also cover some of the InfoPath's best practices and features that enable an easy reusable deployment structure for your applications.

DEFINING DEPLOYMENT REQUIREMENTS

During the initial application design, the focus is always on gathering business requirements and then prototyping. The end result is to determine an effective approach to solving the burning business issues. The problem is that during these initial design phases, any type of deployment requirements is often neglected. Many enterprises fail to even review these types of requirements until the application is ready for sign off. Typically, basic deployment requirements include the following:

- The application should be deployed in a secure and controlled manner
- Web Services must be consistently available
- Web Services must be scalable based on the number of users and the changing business needs
- Application upgrades must be as transparent as possible to the current business process

The result of these types of deployment requirements is what drives enterprises to create a standard data center configuration. This configuration is designed to allow an enterprise to quickly build and roll out applications that are scalable for its long-term business needs. This often provides the centralized physical architecture for server management but is not always the best practice for success.

The InfoPath Configuration

Figure 10.1 shows a typical InfoPath solution used within an SOA infrastructure. This design pattern is broken into three logical tiers. The presentation tier serves as the main interaction point for users. Within an InfoPath solution, this includes the form template and any associated resource task panes. This layer may also include other presentation technologies such as an ASP.NET Web form or even a Microsoft Word template.

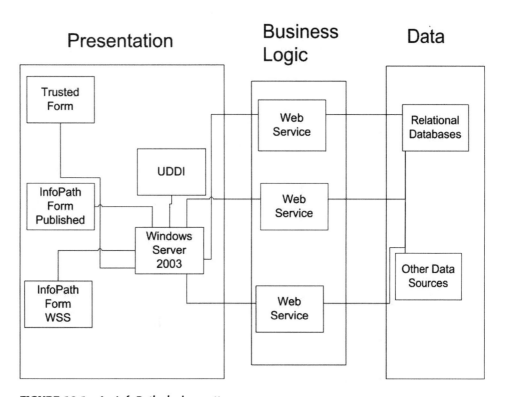

FIGURE 10.1   An InfoPath design pattern.

The middle tier houses the business logic that is presented using Web Services. This layer is responsible for providing business-based logic and the discovery-based mechanisms needed by end users to find, locate, and use their business data. At the same time, this layer is responsible for defining the business rules that are applied across the organization. This layer provides the most business value for an enterprise and is typically where application developers spend most of their time.

At the back end is the data tier. This logical layer contains the storage entity for all enterprise data. Typically, this includes SQL or Microsoft Access databases but may also include other data sources like the file system or even mainframes.

When deploying applications into this type of architecture, system administrators will deploy the logical tiers into multiple physical layers. For example, the data tier is the easiest to deploy and manage using a separate environment. Many enterprises already have in place an operation set of procedures designed to manage this type of data storage environment. These servers are often a part of a separate physical architecture, which allows you to take advantage of things like network load balancing, clustering, fail over, and backup requirements. Regardless of the actual physical implementation, it is important to understand that a service is considered a logical unit of deployment.

WEB SERVICE DEPLOYMENT

The business tier is where XML-based Web Services are deployed. Typically, the deployment of a Web Service involves copying the .asmx file and any other assemblies that the XML Web Service uses to the IIS directory. (You can see the Setup file in
\Code\Chapter 10\WebService Submit\Web Service\Setup.exe on the companion CD-ROM.)

For example, if we take the Help Desk Web Service that we created in Chapter 6 and deployed this to an IIS server, the directory structure would contain the
files shown in Figure 10.2. (You can see this in Code\Chapter 6\Help Desk\ASP 1.1 Application\setup.exe on the companion CD-ROM.)

Once the Web Service is deployed to a server, it contains the items shown in Table 10.1.

Configuring Web Services

XML Web Services use the same default configuration options as any other ASP.NET Web application. The ASP.NET configuration is based on a systemwide XML text file configuration designed to provide extensibility. These configuration files are a simple set of XML elements that represent the configuration options for a specific feature of the .NET Framework. In the case of Web Services, the configuration options are stored in the <webServices> XML element of the configuration file.

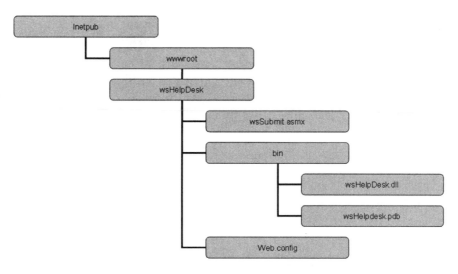

FIGURE 10.2   The files and directory structure of a deployed Web Service.

TABLE 10.1   Components of a Deployed Web Service

Item	Description
Web Application Directory	The root directory for an XML Web Service. This directory is marked as an IIS Web application.
[Web Service].asmx file	The base URL for clients calling the XML Web Service.
[Web Service].disco file	An optional component that enables Web Service discovery.
Web.config file	An XML configuration file created by Visual Studio.NET that overrides the default system configuration.
\bin directory	A default directory that contains the binary files for the XML Web Service. If the XML Web Service class is not contained in the same assembly, then the .asmx assembly class must be located in this directory.

The system root configuration file named machine.config provides the ASP.NET configuration setting for the entire Web server. Within the .NET Framework 2.0 this file has been broken into three parts to enhance application performance. The goal was to reduce the amount of XML configuration information that had to be parsed whenever an ASP.NET application was started. All systemwide default settings are contained in the Machine.config.defaults. This configuration file defines the default <webServices> element and provides the top-level configuration file. By default, this contains the information shown in Listing 10.1.

LISTING 10.1 Default Machine Configuration File

```
<webServices>
  <protocols>
    <add name="HttpSoap1.2" />
    <add name="HttpSoap" />
    <!-- <add name="HttpPost"/> -->
    <!-- <add name="HttpGet"/> -->
    <add name="HttpPostLocalhost" />
    <add name="Documentation" />
  </protocols>
  <soapExtensionTypes>
  </soapExtensionTypes>
  <soapExtensionReflectorTypes>
  </soapExtensionReflectorTypes>
  <soapExtensionImporterTypes>
  </soapExtensionImporterTypes>
  <wsdlHelpGenerator href="DefaultWsdlHelpGenerator.aspx" />
  <serviceDescriptionFormatExtensionTypes>
  </serviceDescriptionFormatExtensionTypes>
</webServices>
```

The machine.config.comments is used to document the syntax of all ASP.NET 2.0 configuration elements. Unless there is a reason to change the systemwide standard defaults all standard modification should be confined to the Machine.config file.

Each application directory in an ASP.NET Web application server can contain a file named web.config. Each individual web.config file applies configuration settings to its own application directory and any child directories below it. The child configuration file supplies other configuration information in addition to the default settings inherited from any parent directories. By default, each child directory configuration setting can override or modify the settings defined in the parent directories. The <webServices> element contains a set of XML tags, shown in Table 10.2, that configure the options.

TABLE 10.2 Configuration Options for XML Web Services

XML Tag	Description
`<protocols>`	Defines the transmission protocols used by an ASP.NET application to decrypt the data being sent from a client browser in an HTTP request. This data contains both method calls and parameters.
`<serviceDescription FormatExtensionTypes>`	Specifies the service description format that should be used within the configuration file.
`<soapExtensionTypes>`	Specifies the set of SOAP extensions used with XML Web Services.
`<soapExtensionReflectorTypes>`	Defines the SOAP extensions run when a service description is generated for an XML Web Service.
`<soapExtensionImporterTypes>`	Defines the SOAP extensions that are used when a service description is accessed to create a proxy class.
`<wsdlHelpGenerator>`	Is the default XML Web Services help page displayed when a browser navigates directly to an .asmx page.

At runtime, ASP.NET uses the configuration information contained in the machine.config and web.config files to create a hierarchical virtual directory structure that computes a collection of configuration settings for each unique URL resource. The resulting configuration settings are then cached and reused for all subsequent requests to the resource.

Inheritance is defined by the incoming URL request, not by the physical paths to the disk based resources.

NOTE

ASP.NET can detect changes to the configuration files and automatically applies new configuration settings to each Web resource affected by the changes. This edit-and-run feature of the .NET Framework doesn't require a server reboot in order for the changes to be applied. Hierarchical changes are automatically recalculated and cached whenever a configuration file anywhere in the chain is changed.

The <procesmodel> tag is an exception to this rule. It is actually read by the asp-net_isapi unmanaged.dll and not the managed code configuration system. This section is responsible for defining many of the performance tuning details. Any changes to this element may require a system reboot.

The ASP.NET configuration system is also extensible. You can define new configuration parameters and write configuration section handlers to process them. For example, you can extend the web.config file to store a connection setting to a SQL database that is then used as part of the Web Service. The web.config settings are shown here:

```
<appSettings>
<!--GLOBAL Connection string-->
<add key="constring"
value="server=localhost;database=Candidate;uid=sa;password=pass123" />
</appSettings>
```

As a security restriction, ASP.NET protects HTTP access to these configuration files by configuring IIS to prevent direct browser access. IIS will return an HTTP access error, as shown in Figure 10.3.

Server Error in '/CanidateInfo' Application.

This type of page is not served.

Description: The type of page you have requested is not served because it has been explicitly forbidden. The extension '.config' may be incorrect. Please review the URL below and make sure that it is spelled correctly.

Requested Url: /CanidateInfo/Web.config

Version Information: Microsoft .NET Framework Version:1.1.4322.573; ASP.NET Version:1.1.4322.573

FIGURE 10.3 The error returned when you're trying to browse a web.config file.

Security Recommendation

Before enabling either the HTTP Get or HTTP Post protocols for an XML Web Service, always ensure that you haven't inadvertently created any possible side effects or security vulnerabilities. For example, an unsuspecting user could receive an email with a link in it that invokes the XML Web Service on behalf of the user, using parameters supplied in the email. You should always consider whether such unintentional invocations could be harmful.

For application servers that don't need to have either the HTTP POST or GET protocols enabled, you can disable these protocols by performing the following steps:

1. Edit the machine.config file.

2. Comment out the lines in the webServices section that add the support for these protocols, as shown here:

```
<webServices>
  <protocols>
    <add name="HttpSoap"/>
      <!-- <add name="HttpPost"/> -->
      <!-- <add name="HttpGet"/>  -->
    <add name="Documentation"/>
    <add name="HttpPostLocalhost"/>
  </protocols>
</webServices>
```

3. Save and exit the machine.config file.

Once the new configuration file is saved, this automatically causes the application configuration hierarchy to be recalculated and the new changes to be implemented. The next HTTP request to the server is then rejected based on the configuration change.

The same type of edit can be done for each of the individual Web applications. The difference between editing the system configuration and individual directories is that based on the inheritance of the XML configuration system, the actual systemwide protocols are not physically contained in the local web.config files. Using the <remove> XML tag, you can disable these individual protocols. Just follow these steps:

1. Open the web.config file in the root directory of the Web application.
2. Modify the webServices section of the web.config file to explicitly remove the HTTP POST and GET protocols, as shown here:

```
<webServices>
  <protocols>
    <remove name="HttpPost" />
    <remove name="HttpGet" />
  </protocols>
</webServices>
```

3. Save and exit the web.config file.

This change causes the local configuration hierarchy to be recalculated and the next request to the application to be denied.

Service Help Page

By default, navigating to the URL of an XML Web Service application without any parameters allows clients to view the services help page. This page contains the default human-readable information about how to communicate with the XML Web Service as well as the supported methods and parameters. This page is an ASP.NET Web form that you can replace or even modify to include additional elements such as a company logo.

The file name for this page is specified in the <wsdlHelpGenerator> XML element of the machine.config file. This page is displayed only for XML Web Services that have the documentation protocol specified within the <protocol> XML element. You can disable this for an individual Web application using the following steps:

1. Edit the web.config file in the root directory of the Web application.
2. Modify the webServices section of the web.config file to remove the documentation protocol, as shown here:

```
<webServices>
  <protocols>
    <remove name="Documentation" />
  </protocols>
</webServices>
```

3. Save and exit the local web.config file.

This configuration change immediately takes effect on the next request to the XML Web Service. Removing the documentation protocol also disables the WSDL file generation for the Web application. This prevents clients from generating a proxy class unless a custom WSDL file is created. When designing an InfoPath form, you can prevent design mode access to the Web Service.

BUILDING WEB SERVICE DEPLOYMENT SOLUTIONS USING VISUAL STUDIO

Once the application development is completed, Visual Studio.NET provides a set of deployment projects that assist with the distribution of Web Services, as shown in Figure 10.4.

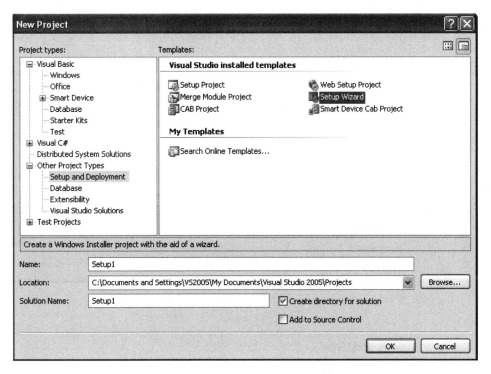

FIGURE 10.4 The setup and deployment project types available within Visual Studio.NET.

Four basic setup and deployment projects are available within Visual Studio.NET. Each project type, shown in Table 10.3, provides a wizard that helps you create a deployment project.

TABLE 10.3 Setup and Deployment Project Types

Project	Purpose
Merge Module Type	Packages shared components.
Setup Project	Is the installer project for Windows-based.
applications.	
Web Setup Project	Is the installer project for a Web-based application. This includes Web Services and ASP.NET applications.
Cab Project	Creates a cabinet file for downloading to a legacy Web Browser or Smart device.

Merge Module projects allow you to package multiple files or components into a single module to facilitate sharing. The resulting .msi file can be included in any other deployment project.

It is important to remember that the distinction between Setup and Web Setup Projects is based on the location where the installer is deployed. For Setup Projects, the installer will deploy files into a Program Files directory on a target computer. For Web Setup Projects, the installer will deploy files into a Virtual Root directory on a Web server.

Once a setup project is created, the project type cannot be changed between Web and Standard. If you decide later that you want to change the deployment mechanism, you need to create a new project.

Deploying Web Services

The Candidate Questionnaire Web Service provides a business tier component for an InfoPath form. This Web Service can be deployed using the .MSI install file created using Visual Studio.NET.

Once coding is completed on the Web Service, as shown in Figure 10.5, it is ready for packing and then deployment to a production Web server.

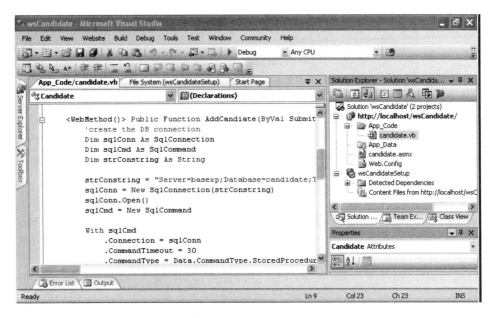

FIGURE 10.5 The completed Web Service.

To package and then deploy a Web Service to a production Web server, follow these steps:

1. Add a Web Setup Project to the existing solution, as shown in Figure 10.6.
2. Add the compiled project output to the project, as shown in Figure 10.7.
3. Rebuild the project to generate the output for the installer project, as shown in Figure 10.8.
4. When the rebuild is complete, the MSI file is stored in the application directory of the installer project, as shown in Figure 10.9.

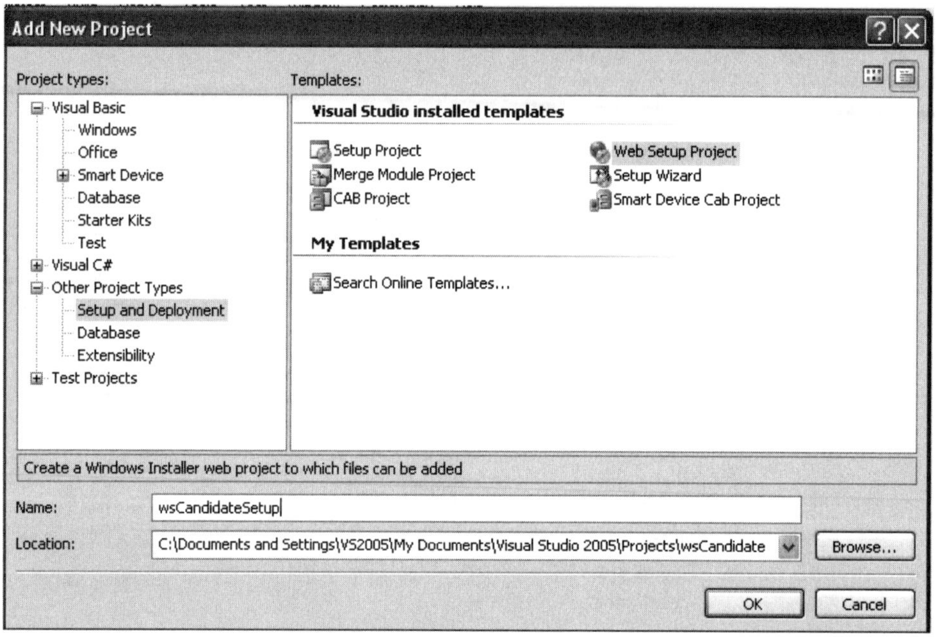

FIGURE 10.6   Adding a Web Setup Project.

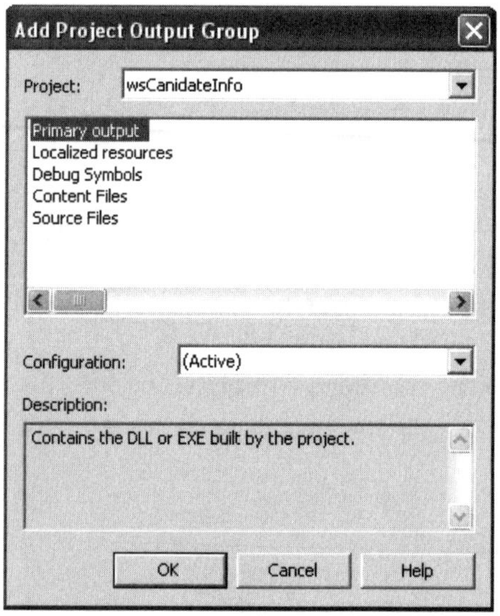

FIGURE 10.7   Adding the compiled output to the installer.

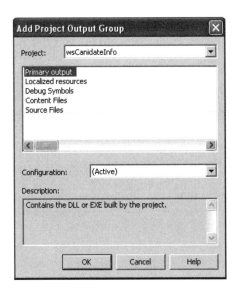

FIGURE 10.8 Rebuilding the project.

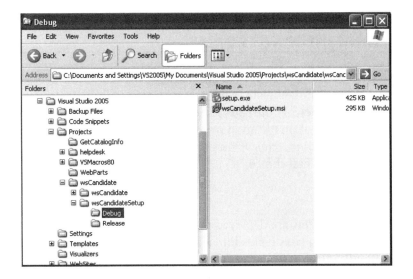

FIGURE 10.9 The newly created MSI file.

Modifying the InfoPath Form

Development and production environments always have different naming conventions. Once the Web Service has been deployed, you need to modify the associated

InfoPath forms so that they point to the right servers. Follow these steps to change the location of the InfoPath form and point it to a production server:

1. From the InfoPath File menu, select Extract Form Files.
2. Close InfoPath.
3. In the file explorer, locate the folder where you placed the extracted form files.
4. Edit the manifest.xsf file using Notepad.
5. Locate the <xsf:webServiceAdapter> tag and change the wsdlUrl attribute to point to the production server, as shown here:

```
http://productionserver/contact/contactservice.asmx?WSDL
```

6. Locate the <xsf:operation> tag and change the serviceUrl attribute to point to the production server, as shown here:

```
http://productionserver/contact/contactservice.asmx to
```

Save the changes and exit the manifest.xsf file.

PUBLISHING INFOPATH FORMS

InfoPath forms that aren't deployed as fully trusted solutions are sandboxed based on an URL. InfoPath, like IE, has no access to the local computer resources.

These types of InfoPath forms are stored in the local Internet cache, and changes are automatically downloaded to the local machine. When deploying InfoPath solutions, enterprises should always try to use the sandboxed approach to forms as their first choice.

Publishing Forms

Sandboxed forms are deployed through a publishing process. This is a feature of InfoPath that places forms into a shared location where users can access the form template. InfoPath forms are often used to collect data for review and aren't directly submitted to a Web Service until some later point of the workflow; for example, if we rebuild the New Candidate Questionnaire using the XSD shown in Listing 10.2. (You can see this example in \Code\Chapter 10\Candidate\OtherPublish\CandidatePublish.xsn on the companion CD-ROM.)

ON THE CD

LISTING 10.2 XSD for the New Candidate Questionnaire

```xml
<?xml version="1.0"?>
<xsd:schema
targetNamespace="http://schemas.mycompany.com/ns/candidate/info"
xmlns:candidate="http://schemas.mycompany.com/ns/candidate/info"
xmlns:xsd="http://www.w3.org/2001/XMLSchema">
<xsd:element name="date" type="xsd:date"/>
<xsd:element name="name" type="xsd:string"/>
<xsd:element name="ssn" type="xsd:string"/>
<xsd:element name="phone" type="xsd:string"/><xsd:element
name="positionapplyingfor" type="xsd:string"/>


<xsd:element name="highschool" type="xsd:string"/>
<xsd:element name="college" type="xsd:string"/>

<xsd:element name="employeename" type="xsd:string"/>
<xsd:element name="employeeaddress" type="xsd:string"/>
<xsd:element name="employeeposition" type="xsd:string"/>



<xsd:element name="candidateinfo">
  <xsd:complexType>
    <xsd:sequence>
      <xsd:element ref="candidate:date"/>
      <xsd:element ref="candidate:name"/>
      <xsd:element ref="candidate:ssn"/>
      <xsd:element ref="candidate:phone"/>
      <xsd:element ref="candidate:positionapplyingfor"/>


      <xsd:element ref="candidate:education"
              minOccurs="0" maxOccurs="1"/>
      <xsd:element ref="candidate:mostrecentemployer"
              minOccurs="0" maxOccurs="1"/>

    </xsd:sequence>
  </xsd:complexType>
</xsd:element>
```

```
<xsd:element name="education">
 <xsd:complexType>
 <xsd:sequence>
 <xsd:element ref="candidate:highschool"/>
 <xsd:element ref="candidate:college"/>
 </xsd:sequence>
 </xsd:complexType>
</xsd:element>


<xsd:element name="mostrecentemployer">
  <xsd:complexType>
    <xsd:sequence>
      <xsd:element ref="candidate:employeename"/>
      <xsd:element ref="candidate:employeeaddress"/>
      <xsd:element ref="candidate:employeeposition"/>
    </xsd:sequence>
  </xsd:complexType>
</xsd:element>
</xsd:schema>
```

We can design a form based on this schema, as shown in Figure 10.10.

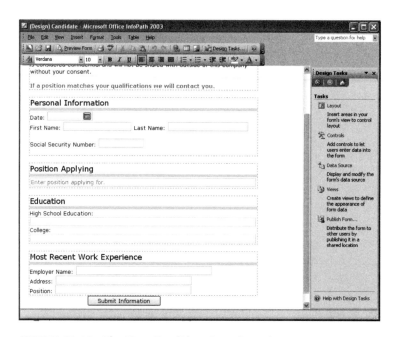

FIGURE 10.10 The New Candidate Questionnaire.

Once the form design is complete, the Publishing Wizard enables the InfoPath form to be deployed into the following shared locations:

- Shared folder
- Web server
- Sharepoint Forms Library

Publishing to a Shared Folder

When deploying an InfoPath form to a shared folder, you need to provide the common network path to the location, as shown in Figure 10.11.

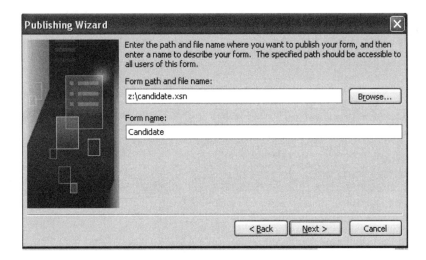

FIGURE 10.11   Entering the shared folder location.

If the network path is not a common path for network users, the Publishing Wizard provides an alternate entry point, as shown in Figure 10.12.

Defining a systemwide accessible network path is essential for this mode of deployment. For example, when you deploy forms using this method, a login script is often run to attach the correct drive letters and paths to users. This guarantees that all users will have the same path structure. As with all publishing, InfoPath provides a notification mechanism that allows user notification when a form has been deployed, as shown in Figure 10.13.

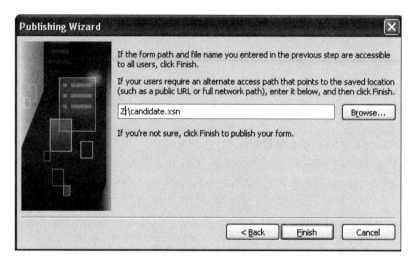

FIGURE 10.12 Defining an alternate network point.

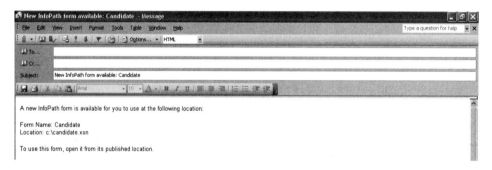

FIGURE 10.13 Email notification that a form has been deployed.

Once the form is published, users are able to open the form and save existing XML instances to the shared drive as shown in Figure 10.14.

Publishing to a Web Server

Publishing a form to a Web server involves the same deployment process used for shared folders. The major functional difference is that the form is downloaded to the local machine from an IIS virtual directory rather than being run across a net-

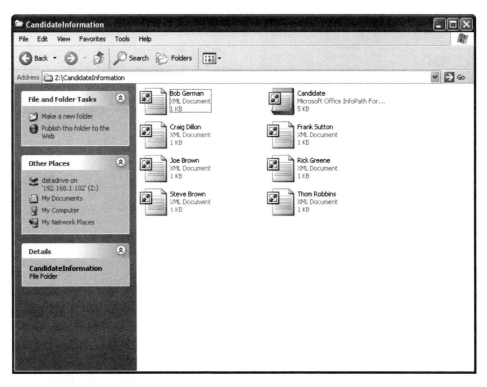

FIGURE 10.14   XML files saved on a file share.

work file system. The first step in deploying forms using this publishing method is to create an IIS Virtual Directory. You can do this by using the Microsoft Management Console (MMC) and selecting the Virtual Directory Creation Wizard, as shown in Figure 10.15.

This wizard is responsible for creating a new Virtual Directory within IIS that can be used to deploy the InfoPath form. The wizard takes you through the following steps:

1. Create the name for the new Virtual Directory, as shown in Figure 10.16.
2. Define the URL alias that is tied to the disk directory on the server, as shown in Figure 10.17.
3. Define the directory permissions for your application, as shown in Figure 10.18.

FIGURE 10.15   Starting the Virtual Directory Creation Wizard.

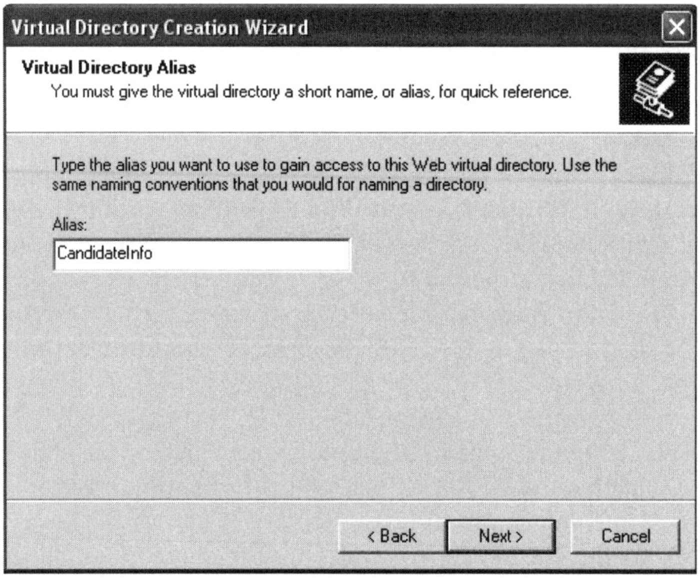

FIGURE 10.16   Defining the Virtual Directory alias.

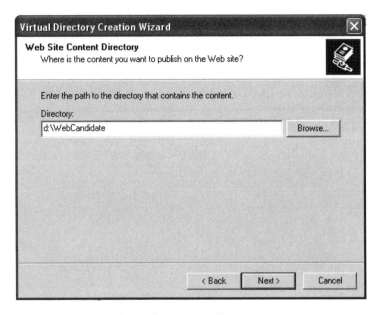

FIGURE 10.17   Defining the content directory.

FIGURE 10.18   Defining the directory security.

4. Deploy the InfoPath form by entering the URL of the IIS Virtual Directory, as shown in Figure 10.19.

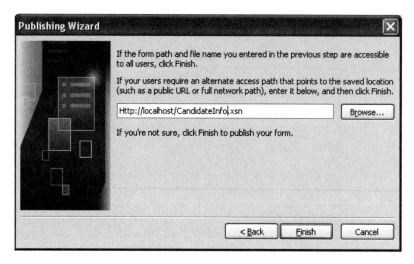

FIGURE 10.19 Defining the InfoPath HTTP path for form publishing.

Once the form is deployed, users can then download, complete, and save the forms. All instances of the form template are actually saved to their local Internet cache, as seen in Figure 10.20.

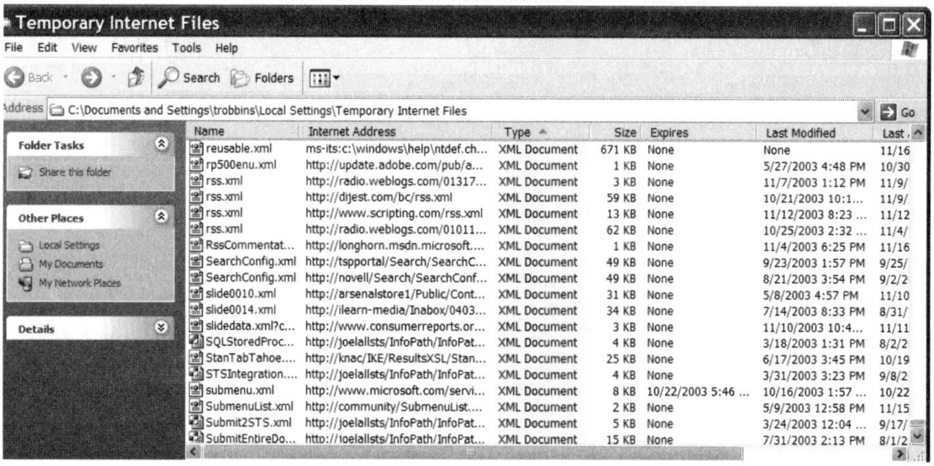

FIGURE 10.20 The local Internet cache, showing saved InfoPath forms.

Publishing to a SharePoint Forms Library

The SharePoint Forms Library is the best solution for deploying forms. The Forms Library function available within WSS allows you to both save and define reporting views of the data. Publishing a form to WSS involves the following steps:

1. Create a new SharePoint Forms Library, as shown in Figure 10.21.

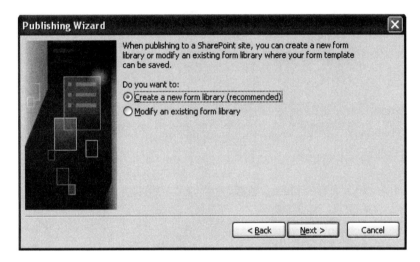

FIGURE 10.21 Creating the Sharepoint Forms Library.

2. Enter the URL to the location where the SharePoint Forms Library should be created, as shown in Figure 10.22.

The URL will change based on the WSS architecture deployed in your enterprise.

3. Define a description for the library that users will view when they add, edit, or delete forms, as shown in Figure 10.23.
4. Define the fields for promotion to columns, as shown in Figure 10.24. These are the columns that users will be able to view and sort on within the library.

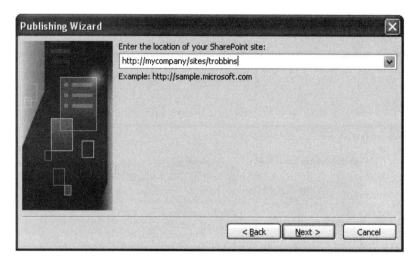

FIGURE 10.22   Entering the URL path for the new library.

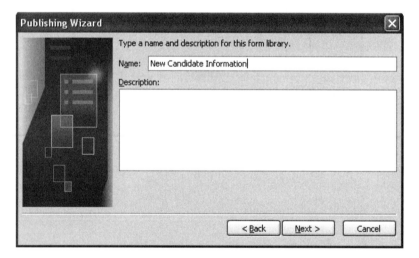

FIGURE 10.23   Providing a description for the forms library.

5. Define any filters to organize the view of your data, as shown in Figure 10.25.

FIGURE 10.24 Defining the promotion fields.

FIGURE 10.25 Defining view filters.

Upgrading Modified Forms

Applications are never really complete. They are in a constant process of modification, change, and reengineering to meet the business needs and requirements. InfoPath allows you to modify and upgrade changes in the form template both silently and automatically.

When a form template is modified in design mode, the existing form template also needs to be upgraded. This guarantees that users can continue to work with their existing forms data wherever it is published. If a form is not upgraded, this may prevent the form from opening or functioning properly, and the existing data for forms could be lost. Forms can either be upgraded automatically or using custom script functions.

Choosing to automatically upgrade existing forms when you modify the form template ensures that any changes made to a published form template don't prevent users from opening and working with an existing form. Choosing to automatically upgrade a form allows the users to open an existing form template even if the underlying XML Schema has been changed. This is because InfoPath can schematically reconstruct the .xml file so that it is compatible with the modified form template's new XML Schema. By default, InfoPath is set to automatically upgrade existing templates, as shown in Figure 10.26.

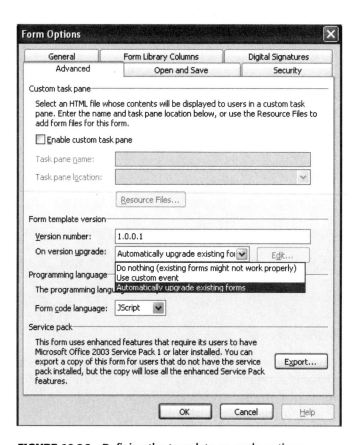

FIGURE 10.26 Defining the template upgrade options.

When the automatic upgrade option is selected, the form template maintains a copy of each version of the XSD saved in design mode.

More complicated upgrades (including element changes or XSD modification) should be handled through script. The OnVersionUpgrade event is responsible for handling form templates' upgrade events and provides access to the underlying XML schema and data. For example, the following script will alert the user that a form upgrade has taken place:

```
function XDocument::OnVersionUpgrade(eventObj)
{   XDocument.UI.Alert("An upgrade has occurred
    and the new form version is : " + eventObj.DocumentVersion +
  "\nThe form template version: " + eventObj.SolutionVersion);
   eventObj.ReturnStatus = true;
}
```

SUMMARY

It is always important to look at the various deployment options that are available when you're deciding how to distribute your application. InfoPath is only one part of the entire application architecture that you will want to review. You need to review other pieces of the solution, including Web Services and even other types of client-based applications. This chapter has covered some of the important pieces that you should be aware of when deploying your applications.

InfoPath is an incredibly powerful product that provides a variety of features. These features enable application developers to create incredibly robust data collection applications that leverage the SOA. The ability of these applications to consume Web Services, SQL databases, and XML.XSD enables them to become a powerful tool within the enterprise.

Appendix
A InfoPath Object Model Reference

SECURITY LEVELS

All properties and methods in the InfoPath object model are associated with a specific security level based on the form template. This level determines whether the property or method can be called directly from the code to a form template. The security levels are defined in Table A.1.

TABLE A.1 The security level definitions for the InfoPath object model.

Security Level	Description
1	Callable by any form template.
2	Called only from form templates that are running in the same domain and that are granted cross-domain permissions.
3	Cannot be called by any InfoPath 2003 form templates that are not fully trusted. This is the highest security restriction placed on a property or object.

APPLICATION OBJECT

The Application object is the top-level object that provides access to the lower-level properties and methods contained within the object model.

For example, this dialog box displays the current version of the application:

```
XDocument.UI.Alert("the version of this application is: " +
Application.Version)
```

The XDocument *property does not require a fully qualified path to the* Application *object. Both the* Application *and* XDocument *objects are embedded directly into the InfoPath script engine. They both do need to be declared when used as part of an expression or argument within a statement.*

ACTIVEWINDOW **PROPERTY—SECURITY LEVEL 1**

The ActiveWindow property provides access to the currently viewed window and to the properties and methods of the Window object that it returns.

The following example accesses the MailEnvelope property of the ActiveWindow to send an e-mail:

```
var objEmail;
objEmail = Application.ActiveWindow.MailEnvelope;
objEmail.Subject = "Please Review Attached";
objEmail.Visible = true;
```

WINDOWS **COLLECTION**

The Windows collection implements a set of properties that provide access to the Windows object associated with the current solution. The properties are shown in Table A.2.

TABLE A.2 Properties of the Windows collection.

Name	Security Level	Description
Count Property	1	Returns a count of the total number of Window objects contained in the collection
Item Property	1	Returns a reference to the specified Window property

InfoPath provides two types of application windows. The first is the editing window, which you use when filling out a form. The second is the design window, which form developers use. Listing A.1 loops through the entire Windows collection and displays the window type.

LISTING A.1 Looping through the Windows collection.

```
// Set the reference to the Windows collection.
  var objWindows = Application.Windows;
  var strWType;

 // show the count of windows
  XDocument.UI.Alert("There are " + objWindows.Count + " open for this
solution")

   // Look through the collection
   for (i=0; i < objWindows.Count; i++)
   {
     switch (objWindows(i).Type)
  {
    case 0:
      strWType = "Editing window";
      break;
    case 1:
      strWType = "Designer window";
      break;
  }

  XDocument.UI.Alert("Window type " + i + ": " + strWType);
}
objWindows = null;
strWType = null;
```

The Windows collection does not allow you to create, add, or remove specific Window objects.

WINDOW **OBJECT**

The Window object represents a specific InfoPath window. This object provides properties and methods that are used to interact with windows and access the underlying data associated with the window. Table A.3 shows the properties and methods of the Window object.

TABLE A.3 Properties and methods of the `Window` object.

Name	Security Level	Description
`Active` Property	1	Is a Boolean that indicates whether the current window is active
`CommandBars` Property	3	Returns an object reference to the Microsoft Office `CommandBars` object
`MailEnvelope` Property	2	Returns a reference to the `MailEnvelope` property
`Type` Property	1	Returns 0 to indicate an Editing Window and 1 to indicate a Designer Window
`TaskPanes` Property	1	Returns an object reference to the `TaskPanes` collection
`XDocument` Property	2	Returns an object reference to the associated `XDocument` object for the current window
`Activate` Method	N/A	Designates the current window as active
`Close` Method	N/A	Closes the currently active window

The following example uses the `Close` method of the `Window` object to close the currently active window and force a save if any changes in the form have occurred:

```
Application.ActiveWindow.Close(false);
```

It is important to review the security level of the properties used. For example, the `CommandBars` *object can be used only in a fully trusted form. Otherwise, it will return permission denied.*

TASKPANES **COLLECTION**

The TaskPanes collection provides properties that are used to access a collection of task pane objects and is accessed through the TaskPanes property of the Window object.

NOTE

The TaskPanes *collection is used only to get a count of the* TaskPane *objects; it cannot be used to add or remove* TaskPane *objects.*

The following example shows how to return a reference to the TaskPanes collection in the current form:

```
var objTPanes;
objTPanes = XDocument.View.Window.TaskPanes;
```

TASKPANE **OBJECT**

The TaskPane object represents the current task pane associated with the open window within an InfoPath form. The object provides properties for working with the built-in task pane, as shown in Table A.4.

TABLE A.4   Properties of the TaskPane object.

Name	Security Level	Description
Type Property	1	Returns a value of the XDTaskPane enumeration
Visible Property	1	Returns a Boolean indicating that the current task pane is visible

The task pane is the base object that the HTML Task Pane is inherited from. The available properties and methods are determined based on the type of task pane. The Type property is based on the XDTaskPane enumeration, and these values may also be used as arguments to the item property of the TaskPanes collection for returning a reference to the specific task pane type. The XDTaskPane enumeration contains the values shown in Table A.5.

TABLE A.5 Values of the XDTaskPane enumeration.

Name	Value	Note
xdTaskPaneHTML	0	InfoPath custom task pane
xdTaskPaneFillOutAForm	1	Fill Out a Form task pane used to open a form in fill-in mode
xdTaskPaneDesignerNew	2	Design a Form task pane used for form design
xdTaskPaneSearchResults	3	Search Results task pane
xdTaskPaneHelp	4	Help task pane
xdTaskPaneClipArt	5	Clip Art task pane
xdTaskPaneFind	6	Find task pane
xdTaskPaneReplace	7	Replace task pane
xdTaskPaneFormatting	8	Font task pane
xdTaskPaneBulletsNumbering	9	Bullet and Numbering task pane
xdTaskPaneSpelling	10	Spelling task pane

The following example shows how to enable the Task Pane collection and make the Spelling Task Pane active and visible:

```
objTaskPane = XDocument.View.Window.TaskPanes.Item(10);
objTaskPane.Visible = true;
```

HTMLDOCUMENT **PROPERTY—SECURITY LEVEL 2**

The HTMLDocument property is used to return a reference to an HTML document object that is running inside a custom task pane. This property is one of the inherited properties of the TaskPane object when the type is 0 (custom task pane).

The following example shows how to set a reference to a custom task pane object using the HTMLTaskPane object running inside a custom task pane:

```
var objHTMLDocument;
objHTMLDocument = XDocument.View.Window.TaskPanes(0).HTMLDocument;
```

HTMLWINDOW **PROPERTY—SECURITY LEVEL 3**

The HTMLWindow property returns a reference to the current HTMLWindow object that is running inside a custom task pane. This property is one of the inherited properties of the TaskPane object available when the type of task pane is 0 (custom task pane). Using this property form, designers can call a scripting function defined inside the HTML task pane.

This property provides the same functionality as the HTMLWindow *property but is available only for fully trusted forms.*

The following example uses the HTMLWindow property to set a reference to the custom task pane of a fully trusted form. Once the reference is retrieved, the TaskPaneSwitchView custom function is called, as shown here:

```
var objHTMLWindow;
objHTMLWindow = XDocument.View.Window.TaskPanes(0).HTMLWindow;
objHTMLWindow.parentWindow.TaskPaneSwitchView();
```

WINDOW **PROPERTY—SECURITY LEVEL 1**

The Window property returns a reference to the Window object associated with a custom task pane. This object represents the active InfoPath window associated with a custom task pane.

The following example runs from a custom task to access the active window to show a MailEnvelope object:

```
var objIWindow;
objIWindow  = window.external.Window;
objIWindow.MailEnvelope.Visible = true;
```

XDOCUMENTS **COLLECTION**

The XDocuments collection contains an object for each of the currently open InfoPath forms. Each object references an underlying XML document. The properties and methods of this collection are shown in Table A.6.

TABLE A.6 Properties and methods of the XDocuments collection.

Name	Security Level	Description
New Method	2	Creates a new form using the existing data of a form. This is *not* used to create a new form based on an existing form template.
Close Method	2	Unconditionally closes the open form and doesn't save any of the existing or changed data.
NewFromSolution Method	2	Creates a new form based on an existing form template.
Open Method	2	Opens a specified form for data entry.
Count Property	N/A	Returns the total number of XDocument objects contained in the current collection.
Item Property	N/A	Returns a reference to the specified XDocument object.

The following example uses the NewFromSolution method to pass the URI of an existing solution; a new form is created and the associated XDocument object is returned:

```
var objFormSolution;
objFormSolution =
Application.XDocuments.NewFromSolution("c:\Employee.xsn")
```

The New method is called to pass the URI of an existing form, as shown here:

```
var objFormInfo;
objFormInfo = Application.XDocuments.New("C:\Employee.xml");
```

XDOCUMENT **OBJECT**

The XDocument object represents the underlying XML document for all InfoPath forms. This is the most important object in the InfoPath object model and is the main source for access and manipulation of the underlying XML data of a form, as shown in Table A.7.

TABLE A.7 XDocument object properties and methods.

Name	Security Level	Description
GetDOM Method	2	Returns a reference to the DOM object for the specified DataObject. Once the reference is obtained, form designers can access any of the standard DOM properties and methods.
ImportFile Method	2	Imports or merges a specified form data with the currently open form.
PrintOut Method	3	Uses the currently defined printer settings and prints the form content as it is rendered in the form's window.
Query Method	2	Retrieves data from the associated data adapter object and then stores it in the underlying XML DOM.
Save Method	3	Saves the form using the default URN.
SaveAs Method	3	Saves the form to the specified URL and overrides the default URN.
GetDataVariable Method	2	Returns a string that contains a variable stored in the processing instruction of the underlying XML attribute and set using the SetDataVariable method.

TABLE A.7 XDocument object properties and methods. *(continued)*

Name	Security Level	Description
SetDataVariable Method	2	Sets a variable within the processing instructions that can be retrieved using the GetDataVariable. Currently, InfoPath supports only the InitialViews variable for the default view.
Submit Method	2	Calls the type of submit operation that is specified in the form's options during design mode.
DOM Property	2	Returns a reference to the XML DOM that contains the form's source XML data.
Errors Property	2	Is a read-only property that contains a reference to the underlying Errors collection.
DataObject Property	2	Is a read-only property that returns a reference to the DataObject collection.
IsDirty Property	2	Is a read-only property that returns a Boolean indicating if the underlying data has been changed.
IsDOMReadOnly Property	2	Returns a Boolean indicating if the underlying XML DOM is read only. This will occur if the form is digitally signed or during the OnBeforeChange event and during the OnValidate event.
IsReadOnly Property	2	Is a Boolean indicating if the form is in read-only mode.
IsSigned Property	2	Is a Boolean indicating if the current form has been digitally signed.

TABLE A.7   XDocument object properties and methods. *(continued)*

Name	Security Level	Description
Language **Property**	2	Retrieves the current defined language code for the form.
IsNew **Property**	2	Is a read-only property that indicates whether the form has been saved.
Solution **Property**	2	Returns a read-only reference to the Solution object.
UI **Property**	2	Returns a read-only reference to the UI property.
URI **Property**	2	Is a read-only string that contains the URI of the form.
View **Property**	2	Returns a read-only reference to the View object.
ViewInfos **Property**	2	Returns a read-only reference to the ViewInfos collection.
Extension **Property**	2	Returns a read only reference to the global scripting object.
QueryAdapter **Property**	2	Is a read-only reference to the data adapter object associated with the current form.

For form performance and accessibility, this object is embedded directly in the script engine. While it can be accessed through the XDocuments collection, it can also be accessed directly without going through the collection.

The XDocument object is used to access the current form's underlying XML document. The DOM property of the XDocument object returns a reference to the XML DOM that is populated with the source XML data of a form.

This object also implements the event objects shown in Table A.8.

TABLE A.8 Event objects for the XDocument object.

Name	Description
DataDomEvent Object	An event accessed during data validation.
DocEvent Object	An event fired during a merge or view switching event that allows programmatic access and interaction with the underlying XML document.
DocReturnEvent Object	An event object that fires during a form load or submission event. The event enables access to the underlying XML data.
DocActionEvent	An event object that is used during a button click event.
VersionUpgradeEvent	An event object that fires during a form version upgrade event. The event enables the interaction with the underlying XML and form template to determine version and template information.

The following example shows how to create a pop-up dialog box that contains the underlying XML information within a form:

```
XDocument.UI.Alert(XDocument.DOM.xml)
```

DATAOBJECTS COLLECTION

The DataObjects collection contains a DataObject for each of the secondary data sources used within an InfoPath form. Each object provides access to a specific data adapter that is used to connect to the external data source, as shown in Table A.9.

TABLE A.9 DataObject collection properties.

Name	Security Level	Description
Count Property	1	Returns the total number of DataObjects contained in the current collection
Item Property	2	Returns a reference to the specified data object

This object does not allow you to create, add, or delete existing data objects that are created during design time.

Listing A.2 is from the Sales Call Form. This code accesses a `DataObject` object and programmatically changes it to return a specific database search.

LISTING A.2

```
//Get the current value of the resource dropdown.
var resourceValue = eventObj.Source.text

//Construct a new command for the second dropdown listbox using a Where
clause...
XDocument.DataObjects("NextStepsUpdate").QueryAdapter.Command =
originalSQLQuery1 +" WHERE NextStepItem='" + resourceValue + "'"

//Requery the data source
XDocument.DataObjects("NextStepsUpdate").Query();

//Set the "SelectNamespaces" property so we can do selectNodes calls on
the resource's DOM
XDocument.DataObjects("NextStepsUpdate").DOM.setProperty("SelectionName
spaces",
'xmlns:dfs="http://schemas.microsoft.com/office/infopath/2003/dataFormS
olution"
xmlns:d="http://schemas.microsoft.com/office/infopath/2003/ado/dataFiel
ds" ' );

//Get a reference to the list of resources
var objTitleViewResources =
XDocument.DataObjects("NextStepsUpdate").DOM.selectNodes("/dfs:myFields
/dfs:dataFields/d:Next_Steps" );

//enumerate the TitleViewTitles, and add a AvailableTitles for each one
for (i=0; i < objTitleViewResources.length; i++){
    //update the other values
    var nextStepNote = objTitleViewResources.item(i).selectSingleNode(
"@NextStepNotes" ).text;
  }
```

```
// update the repeating section
updateSteps(nextStepNote,eventObj);

//Force the view to refresh
XDocument.View.ForceUpdate();
```

DATAOBJECTS **OBJECT**

The DataObjects object represents a link to the data adapter of a secondary data source. DataObjects serves as the intermediary between InfoPath and the data adapter object that is used to access data contained in an external data source. External data is retrieved from an XML Web Service, SQL Server, Microsoft Access, or XML file. The type of data adapter used depends on the type of data source. DataObjects provides a common set of properties and methods, as shown in Table A.10. Each specific adapter provides its own set of properties that is accessed through the QueryAdapter object.

TABLE A.10 Properties and methods of the DataObjects object.

Name	Security Level	Description
Query Method	2	Reads the data from the associated data adapter into an XML DOM associated with the DataObjects
Name Property	2	Returns a read-only string that contains the name of the current DataObjects
QueryAdapter Property	2	Is a read-only property that provides a reference to the data adapter object used in the secondary data source
DOM Property	2	Returns a reference to the XML DOM associated with the current DataObjects

The following example returns the entire DOM of a secondary data source into a string:

```
var strEmployeeXML;
strEmployeeXML = XDocument.DataObjects("EmployeeNames").DOM.XML;
```

Errors **COLLECTION**

The Errors collection contains a set of error objects for each error that occurred in the current form. Each of the Error objects contains specific information about the error that occurred and is accessed as shown in Table A.11.

TABLE A.11 Properties and methods of the Errors collection.

Name	Security Level	Description
Count Property	1	Is a read-only property that contains the total number of Error objects contained in the Errors collection.
Item Property	1	Is a read-only property that returns a reference to the specific error referenced in the index number.
Add Method	2	Adds an error to the Error object and returns a reference to the new Error object.
Delete Method	2	Deletes errors that were created using the Add method for a specific XML node and that have the same name. It cannot delete all errors because of the enforced schema validation of errors that were reported using ReportError method of the DataDOMEvent object.
DeleteAll Method	2	Deletes all errors in the Errors collection regardless of how they were created.

NOTE

The ADD method is used to create custom error messages. The following two types of errors can be created:

Modal: The user is notified of the error with an alert. After clicking on OK, the user can return to the previous value through an automatic undo operation.

Modeless: The user is notified of the error with an inline alert and can choose to return to the previous value with an undo operation.

The following example adds a custom error message to the current `Errors` collection:

```
var objErrors;
var objError;
objErrors = XDocument.Errors;
objError = objErrors.Add(anXMLNode, "A Validation Error has occurred",
"Specified data is invalid");
```

ERROR OBJECT

The `Error` object represents a specific error within the `Errors` collection and is associated to an XML DOM node located in the form's underlying XML. When data validation fails for a particular XML DOM node, an error is created in the `Error` object and then placed in the `Errors` collection.

InfoPath supports the following types of validation errors:

Schema_Validation: Data validation failure that occurs as a result of an XML schema constraint

System_Generated: Data validation failure that occurs as a result of constraints defined in the form definition file or the `ReportError` method

User_Specified: Data validation failure that occurs as a result of custom scripting errors or using the `Add` method of the `Errors` collection

The `Error` object supports the properties and methods shown in Table A.12.

TABLE A.12   Properties and methods of the `Error` object.

Name	Security Level	Description
Node Property	2	Is a read-only property that returns a reference to the XML node that is associated with the `Error` object.

TABLE A.12   Properties and methods of the Error object. *(continued)*

Name	Security Level	Description
ShortErrorMessage Property	2	Specifies or retrieves the short error message that is returned by the Error object and appears as the tool tip that is viewed by the users when data validation fails.
Type Property	2	Returns the type of the Error object.
DetailedErrorMessage Property	2	Sets or retrieves the detailed error message of the Error object. This is the error message that users can view when data validation fails in their forms.
ConditionName Property	2	Returns the name of the error condition or a null depending on the type of Error object. This property is used for custom errors only and will appear null for all other types.
ErrorCode Property	2	Is a long integer value that sets or retrieves the error codes of the Error object.

The Type *property of the* Error *object determines the type of data validation that occurred.*

The following example uses the Node property of the Error object to display the XML node of an error:

```
var objError;
objError = XDocument.Errors(0);
XDocument.UI.Alert("Name of the Error: " + objError.Node.xml);
```

SOLUTION **OBJECT**

The Solution object provides information about the properties of the form template. It contains the properties shown in Table A.13.

TABLE A.13   The properties of the Solution object.

Name	Security Level	Description
DOM Property	2	A read-only property that returns a reference to the XML DOM that is associated with a DataObject.
PackageURL Property	2	A read-only property that provides a string containing the URL of the cache folder that contains the extracted files of an InfoPath solution.
URI Property	2	A read-only property that contains a string value for the URI of a form template. Depending on where a form template is opened, it may return either a URI or URL.
Version Property	1	A read-only property that returns a string containing the current solution version number.

Listing A.3 uses the Solution object to determine if the Author node contains data.

LISTING A.3

```
var objSolution = XDocument.Solution;
  var objAuthorName =
objSolution.DOM.selectSingleNode("xsf:xDocumentClass/@author");
  var strName;

    if (objAuthorName != null){
      strName = objAuthorName.text;
      }
```

```
      else {
        strName = "Name not found";
        }

      XDocument.UI.Alert("The author of this document is: " + strName);
```

UI OBJECT

The UI (User Interface) object provides methods for displaying custom dialog boxes to users as they complete a form. The UI object supports the properties and methods shown in Table A.14.

TABLE A.14 Properties and methods of the UI object.

Name	Security Level	Description
Alert Method	2	Displays a message box with a custom text message and an OK button
ShowMailItem Method	2	Creates an e-mail message using the system default e-mail editor and attaches the current InfoPath form to the message
ShowModalDialog Method	3	Displays a custom modal dialog box that is implemented within an HTML form attached to the current solution file
ShowSignatureDialog Method	2	Displays the Digital Signature dialog box for forms that have been enabled for signatures

You can insert carriage returns into the text of the custom message by using the standard "\n" characters.

The following example shows how to use the ShowMailItem method to create a custom e-mail message:

```
XDocument.UI.ShowMailItem("jackb@mycompany.com","","","Please Approve
the following Expense Form");
```

VIEW **OBJECT**

The View object provides programmatic access to Views stored within an InfoPath solution. A form may have multiple views but there is always one default view. When using the View object, you are always accessing the currently active View. The View object supports the properties and methods shown in Table A.15.

TABLE A.15   Properties and methods of the View object.

Name	Security Level	Description
DisableAutoUpdate Method	2	Disables the automatic synchronization between the View object and the underlying XML data.
EnableAutoUpdate Method	2	Enables the automatic synchronization between the View object and the underlying XML data.
ExecuteAction Method	2	Enables the ability to programmatically perform built-in InfoPath editing commands as if the user has selected these from the menus.
Export Method	3	Exports the current file to a file.
ForceUpdate Method	2	Forces synchronization of the current View to the underlying XML data. It is often used to synchronize views based on changes to a secondary data source.

TABLE A.15 Properties and methods of the `View` object. *(continued)*

Name	Security Level	Description
`GetContextNodes` **Method**	2	Provides a reference to a collection of XML nodes populated from the DOM based on the current context. These are the sequence of XML DOM nodes mapped from the current view that correspond to the current XSLT transform that has been applied.
`GetSelectedNodes` **Method**	2	Provides a reference to a collection of XML nodes that are populated from the DOM based on the current selection of view items.
`SelectText` **Method**	2	Selects the current text contained in an editable field specified in the DOM.
`SwitchView` **Method**	2	Changes the current active view to the one specified.
`Name` **Property**	2	Is a read-only string that contains the name of the current view.
`Window` **Property**	2	Is a read-only property that contains a reference to the `Window` object associated to the current view.

The following example changes the current view to the default view specified in the solution file:

```
XDocument.View.SwitchView("");
```

VIEWINFOS **COLLECTION**

The ViewInfos collection contains a ViewInfo object for each view in the current solution. This object provides descriptive information about each view. The ViewInfos collection contains the properties shown in Table A.16.

TABLE A.16   Properties of the ViewInfos collection.

Name	Security Level	Description
Count **Property**	1	A read-only property that contains a total count of the current number of ViewInfo objects
Item **Property**	1	A read-only property that returns a reference to the specified ViewInfo object from the collection

This collection cannot be used to create, add, or remove ViewInfo objects.

Listing A.4 loops through all the current views within a solution file and displays their names.

LISTING A.4

```
// Set a reference to the ViewInfos collection.
var objViewInfos = XDocument.ViewInfos;

// Loop through the collection and display the namefor (i=0; i <
objViewInfos.Count; i++)
  {
        XDocument.UI.Alert("View name: "  +
     objViewInfos(i).Name);
  }
```

VIEWINFO **OBJECT**

The ViewInfo object contains descriptive information about the individual views that are stored in an InfoPath solution. The ViewInfo object contains the properties shown Table A.17.

TABLE A.17 Properties of the ViewInfo object.

Name	Security Level	Description
IsDefault	2	A Boolean that indicates whether the current view is the defined default view
Name	2	A read-only string that contains the name of the current view

The following example changes the third view (views are stored as a zero-based collection) into the default view:

```
XDocument.ViewInfos(1).IsDefault = true;
```

The CD-ROM included with *Programming Microsoft InfoPath: A Developers Guide* includes code and projects from the various examples found in the book.

CD-ROM FOLDERS

Code: Contains the important code from examples in the book by chapter.

Images: Contains all the images in the book, in color, by chapter.

OVERALL SYSTEM REQUIREMENTS

- Windows 2003, or Windows XP Pro
- Pentium II Processor or greater
- CD-ROM drive
- Hard drive
- 128 MB of RAM minimum. 256 MB recommended
- Microsoft InfoPath 2003
- .NET Framework SDK/Microsoft Visual Studio recommended

Compiling the examples in the book with the Framework SDK is possible, but using Visual Studio.NET will allow you to easily create the Windows application examples found in the book. Note that to use any of the Web Service examples you will need to have Internet Information Server (IIS) installed.

Glossary

Term Name	Definition
ActiveX Data Objects (ADO)	The Microsoft programming model designed to provide an application-level interface to any OLE DB data provider.
American National Standards Institute (ANSI)	An organization of American industry and business groups that develops trade and communication standards for the United States. Through membership in the International Organization for Standardization (ISO) and the International Electro Technical Commission (IEC), ANSI coordinates American standards with corresponding international standards.
Application Programming Interface (API)	A set of routines available in an application, like ADO, that developers use when designing an application interface.
Boolean	A type of variable that stores either a true or false value.
Column	In a SQL table, the area in each row that stores the data value for some attribute of the object modeled by the table.
Common Language Runtime (CLR)	The Microsoft .NET Framework engine at the core of managed code execution. The CLR supplies the managed code services, which include code access security, lifetime management, debugging, and profiling support.

$\rightarrow$

Common Language Specification (CLS)	A set of programmatic verifiable rules that govern the interoperation of types authored in different programming languages. CLS-compliant components, tools, and languages are guaranteed to interoperate with other CLS-compliant tools and languages.
Component Object Model (COM)	The Microsoft open software architecture that allows interoperation between an object broker, which is something that acts an intermediary as well as presents and controls the creation of other objects, and OLE.
Constant	A group of symbols that represent a specific data value.
Constraint	A property assigned to a table column that prevents certain types of invalid data values from being entered.
Data Definition Language (DDL)	A language that is part of a database management system used to define all attributes and properties of a database.
Data Source	A collection of information required to access a specific resource like a database. This collection includes all the source information and logon information. InfoPath stores these in the form manifest and defines the connection requirements and location of the specific data resource.
Data Transformation Services (DTS)	A set of tools available within SQL Server that can be used to import, export, and transform heterogeneous data between one or more data sources, such as Microsoft SQL Server, Microsoft Excel, or Microsoft Access. Connectivity is provided through OLE DB and ODBC.
Document Object Model (DOM)	A World Wide Web Consortium (W3C) specification that describes the structure of dynamic HTML and XML documents in a way that allows them to be manipulated through a Web browser.

$\rightarrow$

Enterprise Application Integration (EAI)	The combination of processes, software, standards, and hardware that results in the integration of two or more enterprise systems, which allows them to operate as one.
Extensible Hypertext Markup Language (XHTML)	A markup language that incorporates elements of both HTML and XML into a single specification.
Extensible Markup Language (XML)	XML is a metalanguage that provides markup as a format for describing structured data. XML is a Word Wide Web Consortium (W3C) specification and is a subset of the Standard Generalized Markup Language (SGML).
Hypertext Markup Language (HTML)	The language used in Web pages that contains a predefined set of elements.
Hypertext Transfer Protocol (HTTP)	The protocol used to carry requests from a browser to a Web server and transport pages from the Web servers to the requesting browser.
Information Worker	An individual, who creates, uses, transforms, consumes, or manages business information in the course of his work.
Many-to-Many Relationship	A relationship between two tables in which rows in each table have multiple matching rows in the related table. Many-to-many relationships are maintained by using a third table called a junction table and by adding the primary key columns from each of the other two tables to this table.
Many-to-One Relationship	A relationship between two tables in which one row in one table can relate to many rows in another table.

$\rightarrow$

Master Database	The database that controls the operation of each instance of SQL Server. Installed automatically with each instance of SQL Server, it keeps track of user accounts, remote user accounts, and remote servers that each instance can interact with. It also tracks ongoing processes, configurable environment variables, system error messages, tapes, and disks available on the system.
Method	A function that performs an action by using a COM object, as in SQL Distributed Management Object (DMO), OLE DB, and ActiveX Data Objects (ADO).
Microsoft OLE DB	A Microsoft-based specification for a set of data access interfaces designed to support interoperability of multiple data stores.
Namespace	Names or groups of names that are defined according to some naming convention.
Object-Oriented (OO)	A system or language that supports the use of objects.
Object-Oriented Programming Language (OOP)	A programming model based on the concept of modular reusable components and classes that can be combined and adapted to produce complex applications.
One-to-One Relationship	In a relational database, a relationship between two tables in which a single row in the first table can be related to only one row in the second table, and a row in the second table can be related to only one row in the first table.
Online Analytical Processing (OLAP)	A technology that uses multidimensional structures to provide rapid access to data for analysis. The source data for OLAP is commonly stored in data warehouses in a relational database.

$\rightarrow$

Open Database Connectivity (ODBC)	A data access application programming interface (API) that supports access to any data source for which an ODBC driver is available. ODBC is aligned with the American National Standards Institute (ANSI) and International Organization for Standardization (ISO) standards for a database Call Level Interface (CLI).
Primary Key (PK)	A column or set of columns that uniquely identify all the rows in a table. Primary keys do not allow null values. No two rows can have the same primary key value.
Property	A named attribute of a control, field, or database object that defines one of the object's characteristics.
Record	A group of related fields (columns) of information treated as a unit. A record is more commonly called a row in an SQL database.
Recordset	The ActiveX Database Objects (ADO) object used to contain a result set. The recordset also exhibits cursor behavior depending on the recordset properties set by an application.
Relational Database Management System (RDBMS)	A system such as SQL Server that organizes data into related rows and columns.
Relationship	A link between tables that references the primary key in one table to a foreign key in another table.
Remote Data Services (RDS)	A Web-based technology designed to support database connectivity and enable corporate publishing across the Internet and intranets.
Remote Procedure Call (RPC)	A communication mechanism that allows a client and a server application to communicate with each other through function calls sent from the client to server.

$\rightarrow$

Row	In an SQL table, the collection of elements that form a horizontal line in the table. Each row in the table represents a single occurrence of the object modeled by the table and stores the values for all the attributes of that object.
Service Oriented Architecture (SOA)	A model for application development that decouples the server business functionality from client logic. Business functionality is organized as a collection of modules that define a service. Each of these services has a clear business use and strict set of public interfaces. These interfaces allow a front-end user to map a function to a specific service without any prior knowledge of the internal design. Each service is responsible for exposing a discrete or single program flow that may involve calls to a message.
Simple Object Access Protocol (SOAP)	A simple XML-based protocol for exchanging structured data and type information on the Web.
Smart Client Applications	Software programs that consume Web Services, use local processing power, and can adapt to both online and offline scenarios.
Standard Generalized Markup Language (SGML)	An international vendor-neutral standard that describes the relationships between a document's context and its structure.
Structured Query Language (SQL)	A language used to insert, retrieve, modify, and delete data in a relational database. SQL also contains statements for defining and administering the objects in a database. SQL is the language supported by most relational databases, and is the subject of standards published by the International Standards Organization (ISO) and the American National Standards Institute (ANSI). SQL Server 2000 uses a version of the SQL language called Transact-SQL.

$\rightarrow$

System Catalog	A set of system tables that describe all the features of an instance of SQL Server. The system catalog records metadata such as the definitions of all users, all databases, all objects in each database, and system configuration information such as server and database option settings.
System Databases	A set of four databases present in all instances of SQL Server that are used to store system information.
Table	A two-dimensional object that consists of rows and columns and that is used to store data in a relational database. Each table stores information about one of the types of objects modeled by the database.
Transact-SQL (TSQL)	The language that contains the commands used to administer instances of SQL Server; create and manage all objects in an instance of SQL Server; and insert, retrieve, modify, and delete all data in SQL Server tables. Transact-SQL is an extension of the language defined in the SQL standards published by the International Standards Organization (ISO) and the American National Standards Institute (ANSI).
Transaction	Within a database, a set of operations combined into a logical unit of work that is either wholly committed or rolled back. Transactions are considered atomic, consistent, isolated, and durable.
Universal Description, Discovery, and Integration (UDDI)	A specification for publishing and locating information about Web Services. Defines a standards-based way to store and retrieve information about services, providers, and the bindings of Web Services using a set of custom and standard classification schemas.
Variable	A named, contained referenced in a code component that maintains a value.

$\rightarrow$

Web Services Description Language (WSDL)	An XML format for describing Web Services. WSDL separates the abstract description of the Web Service from the specifics of the Web Service.
Workflow	The automation of a business process. During the execution of this process, information and tasks are passed from one participant to another according to a set of predefined rules.
World Wide Web Consortium (W3C)	A vendor-neutral standards body that defines and maintains a variety of industry specifications.
XML Data Reduced (XDR)	A language subset of the XML Schema Definition (XSD) language specification on which the Microsoft XML parser is based.
XML Path Language (XPATH)	An XML language that describes a way to locate and process items in an XML document by using an addressing syntax based on a path through the document's logical structure or hierarchy.
XML Pointer Language (XPointer)	An XML language based on XPATH that supports addressing into the internal structures of XML documents. It enables you to traverse a document tree and choose the internal parts based on various properties.
XML Schema Definition (XSD)	A language that enables the definition of structure and data types for XML documents. XSD defines the elements, attributes, and data types that conform to the W3C XML Schema specification for the XML Schema Definition Language.
XSL Transformations (XSLT)	A style sheet language for transforming XML documents into other XML documents.

Index